C000092206

TRAINING FOR TRIUMPH

SECOND EDITION
published in 2001
by
WOODFIELD PUBLISHING
Woodfield House, Babsham Lane, Bognor Regis
West Sussex PO21 5EL, England.

ISBN 1-873203-71-3

Training
for
Triumph

*A history of RAF
Aircrew Training
in World War II*

TOM DOCHERTY

Woodfield Publishing
~ WEST SUSSEX · ENGLAND ~

Acknowledgements

I could not have written this book without the unstinting assistance of the many aircrew, groundcrew, civilians and historians who freely related their experiences and provided illustrations and photographs for the book. Without them there would be no book. My thanks to:

The Pilots: John Beckett, Don Caldwell-Smith, Neville Cooper, HD 'Roger' Coverley, Albert M Custers, DH Darney, Peter Frizell, WI 'Wally' Lashbrook, Hunter McGiffen, Bill Page, Fred Papple, AG Stewart, Peter Tatham and Jack Thornton.

The Navigators and Observers: Ron Allen, George Gray, John Holmes, JL MacFarland and GA Wright.

The Air Bombers: Tom Osborn and Tom Overend.

The Wireless Operator/Air Gunners: Frank Bell, Albert Carty, H Dixon, Fred Eyre, Charles Hughes and Norman Jones.

The 'straight' Air Gunners: DJ 'Jim' Davis, John T Spillane and George Stalker.

The Flight Engineer: Ralph Farmiloe

The Ground Crew: Frank Gibson, John Holmes, Charles F Scandrett and David Thomas.

The Civilian Contractor: Peter A. Weston

The Historian: Ian Foster (Ian co-ordinates the activities of a preservation group named Handley Page 57 Halifax Rescue dedicated to rebuilding a Halifax from parts recovered from all over the world.) I am grateful to Ian for allowing me to use extracts from his unpublished work on RAF Rufforth (See the stories of Ron Allen, George Stalker and Ralph Farmiloe).

Photo credits: I am most grateful for the use of photographs and illustrations to the following: D Annand, Mrs VM Campbell, Albert Carty, Neville Cooper, RD Davies, H Dixon, Fred Eyre, Ian Foster/57 Rescue, Peter Frizell, GKN Westland, George Gray, JL MacFarland, Robert W Mackenzie, Tom Osborn, Bill Page, Fred Papple and WD Park.

Finally I would like to thank my wife, Catherine, for her patience and support. She spent many lonely hours whilst I sat at the typewriter and computer or wandered the country in search of material for this book.

Contents

PART THREE: BRIEF UNIT HISTORIES

Preface

Growing up in the late 1950's and the 1960's my first memories of aviation are a wartime leather flying helmet an uncle gave me and watching the Shackletons lumbering over the Moray Firth near Kinloss during the family holidays. My interest in RAF history developed as I grew and was encouraged by the officers and civilian instructors of the Air Training Corps squadron I joined in my home town of Kirkcaldy.

The ATC led to the RAF and 22 years of postings only served to feed my passion for RAF history. Many of the airfields I served on had a long and illustrious history and usually close by were other disused airfields with equally interesting histories. Around 1980 I began to research these airfields and discovered that not all of them were fighter or bomber stations and that many of them were used mainly for aircrew training.

I decided to research this particular aspect of RAF history and discovered that a very large number of air and groundcrew lost their lives whilst training. There are many books telling the story of RAF aircrew on operations and I felt that something should be written about all those men who trained for war but died in training accidents before they could see action on operations. This book is the culmination of twenty years of research and writing and is dedicated to all those aircrew who did not survive, to those who did and to the overworked and very often overlooked groundcrew who kept them flying in all weathers and sometimes at great risk to themselves.

Tom Docherty
Antrim, January 2001

PART ONE

The Development and Expansion
of the Royal Air Force Training System

1939 – 1945

Introduction

1938 saw the beginnings of the rapid expansion of the Royal Air Force. The Munich Agreement gave a years breathing space in which to prepare and training of aircrews was to assume great importance. In 1938 the RAF first line comprised some 1,600 mainly obsolescent aircraft with 400 in reserve. This equated, at a conservative estimate, to less than one week's reserve. This force was up against a Luftwaffe strength of 3,200 aircraft with 2,400 in reserve. It was estimated that the Luftwaffe would be able to man the 4,500 first line aircraft and 3,400 reserves it would have by April 1940. The RAF by the same date would have an estimated 2,400 first line and 3,400 reserve aircraft of which only Fighter Command would be able to man its reserves.

Plans were in hand in 1938 to produce 12,000 aircraft, which would require an increase in RAF strength of 40,000 men by April 1940. It was assessed that the RAF would be short by 500 pilots alone by March 1940 and the opening of new flying training schools was accelerated to meet the demand. To meet the shortfall and supply 200 additional fighter pilots two Service Flying Training Schools (SFTS) and two civil Elementary Flying Training Schools (EFTS) were to be formed. The pilots from these units would not go directly to the squadrons but be held in Group Pools which were to be set up in each Command. Six in Bomber Command, three in Fighter Command and one for Coastal Command.

The training of pilots was unsatisfactory at this time but the training of non-pilot aircrew was in an even worse state. Observers were given a ten-week training course at civil schools, Air Observer

Aircrew Training Strengths

	Pilots	Observers	W/Ops & AGs	Total
Jan 1939	7400	950	1100	9450
Sep 1939	9721	1040	1496	12257

Schools (AOS) and Armament Training camps (ATC) under varied and different conditions. Wireless Operators (Air Gunners) (WOp/ AG) and "straight" Air Gunners were recruited from ground trades and were part time aircrew. This caused the dilemma of aircrew being required to fly full time in war conditions to the detriment of their ground trades where they were just as important. In October 1938 this problem was resolved by making all Wireless Operators and "straight" Gunners full time, recruits being drawn from Boy Entrant Wireless Operators.

By the end of 1938 pilots were still below the numbers required even though there were now fifteen FTS training pilots in courses lasting six months. Like gunners and wireless operators, Observers were now full time, but there were still not enough of them. By 1939 there were only 622 trained Air Gunners with a further 691 under training. This was still 250 below the required number.

In the year leading up to the outbreak of war the training of aircrew was structured as follows; Four weeks at an Initial Training School (ITS) for all aircrew. Here discipline and elementary ground subjects were taught. After this training each aircrew member went their own way. Pilots went to EFTS for eight weeks followed by SFTS for four weeks intermediate and four weeks advanced training. EFTS flying consisted of some 50 hours and SFTS provided a further 100. The Air Gunners and observers went on to AOS flying 12 and 45 hours respectively.

With the expansion of the training system accidents were on the increase due to several factors. More modern aircraft types, poor navigation and lack of modern radio and wireless at FTS which caused pilots to keep visual contact with the ground all contributed to accidents. In spite of the accidents and the problems of training so many aircrews the RAF aircrew strength at the beginning of 1939 was 7,400 pilots, 950 Observers and 1,100 Wireless Operators and Air Gunners. By the end of 1939 this figure would almost double.

By September 1939 the RAF had 9,721 pilots, 1,496 Air Gunners and Wireless Operators and 1,040 observers. A total of 12,257 trained aircrew. To train these aircrew and their replacements the RAF now had nineteen EFTS, sixteen SFTS, seven Bombing and Gunnery Schools (BGS), ten Air Observer Navigation Schools (AONS), two

Operational Training Units (OTU) and three Wireless Schools. A total of fifty-seven training schools, one of which was based in the Middle East. The RAF went to war with these units and that number of trained aircrew in 1939. Over the next six years the strength of the RAF training units would increase out of all recognition. It would support the greatest air force Great Britain has ever seen.

SELECTION, RECEPTION AND INITIAL TRAINING

From 1939 till 1942 the selection of aircrew was by interview and depended largely on the experience and qualities of the selecting officers. In early 1942 the procedure was modified introducing a flight test prior to entering flying training. Recruits were chosen who fitted a broad category of Pilot/Navigator/Air Bomber (PNB). (By this time the Observers role of navigation and bomb aiming had been split into two distinct aircrew groups – Navigator and Air Bomber). Those showing the most aptitude in the air were graded at the top of the list and proceeded to pilot training. The middle grades became navigators and the lower grades were destined for Air Bomber training. Wireless Operators, Air Gunners and Flight Engineers were still selected by interview.

By early 1944, all aircrew categories were scientifically tested for aptitude. Flight-testing continued as the main method for pilot selection. In early 1945 an Aviation Candidate Selection Centre

UK-based Flying Training Schools in operation on 3 Sept 1939

Elementary Flying Training Schools	19
Service Flying Training Schools	15
Bombing And Gunnery Schools	7
Air Observer Navigation Schools	10
Operational Training Units	2
Wireless Schools	3
Total	56

(ACSC) was formed to centralise the selection and categorisation of all aircrew candidates.

In 1941 an Aircrew reception centre (ARC) was introduced between Selection and Initial Training Wing (ITW). This took up the potential aircrew awaiting training and provided a reception centre for those who failed pilot or observer courses. It also allowed the ITW to specialise in only one aircrew category.

ELEMENTARY FLYING TRAINING SCHOOLS (EFTS)

At the outbreak of war the RAF had nineteen EFTS. One year later there were seventeen in the UK and twenty-one overseas. The number of EFTS peaked at sixty-seven in 1941 of which only eighteen were still based in the UK. The others were spread over Australia, Canada, India, New Zealand, Rhodesia and South Africa. The number of EFTS declined thereafter until at the war's end there were only twenty-nine. Fifteen of these were overseas.

Initially the plan was to run eight-week courses but the original ten-week pre-war course was retained. In the early stages there were so many reserve pilots at an early stage of training that a number were returned to civilian life to await training places.

In 1939 the EFTS received instructions to increase the time spent on instrument and general flying practice. This policy increased the standard of training which had come under criticism. By April 1940 the EFTS course was reduced to the previously planned eight weeks and course strengths were increased to 144 pupils. This helped to ease a bottleneck at the ITW stage.

In September 1939 the Empire Air Training Scheme (EATS) was introduced and many future aircrew found themselves despatched overseas to be trained at EFTS in the Commonwealth countries. Many were also trained in the USA at schools set up there.

By the end of 1940 nineteen EFTS were producing pupils for twelve SFTS. The winter of 1940 saw extensions of the, by then, five week course due to bad weather and aircraft unserviceability. The five week course gave 35 hours flying, ten of which was solo. This was increased to 42 hours in the same length of time. The course was increased to six weeks in December 1940 but it was clear that more schools were urgently required. The situation was aggravated by an increase in the accident rate, which in turn caused a shortage of aircraft.

By March 1941 pilots were receiving up to 50 hours at EFTS. Another change in 1941 was the increase in the number of EFTS in Canada which released some of the EFTS capacity in the UK for initial grading and weeding out of unsatisfactory pupils prior to being sent overseas, thus cutting down the number of failures in later stages. The grading was introduced in November 1941 and consisted of a three-week course with up to 15 hours of dual instruction. Those with pilot potential were taken off the course after a minimum of five hours flying and posted to overseas training units. Less able pupils went to the UK schools and those not considered good enough were transferred to other training. By July 1941 night flying training was introduced for pupils at some EFTS, priority going to twin engine pilots. Another change at the end of 1941 was the increase of the course length to eight weeks. This now gave the pilots about 80 hours flying before going on to SFTS. This situation remained at EFTS until the gradual run down of training facilities towards the end of the war. By the end of the war 15,000 pilots had passed through UK based EFTS and a total of 117,000 world-wide.

SERVICE FLYING TRAINING SCHOOLS (SFTS) AND
PILOTS ADVANCED FLYING UNITS ((P) AFU

The next phase for the pilots after EFTS was a posting to the SFTS where the training became more specialised. The SFTS concentrated on either single engine or twin engine training. At the outbreak of war there were fifteen SFTS in the UK and one in the Middle East. By September 1941 there were fifty, twelve of which were in the UK. By September 1943 only two of the fifty were in the UK, most SFTS being transferred to Africa, Rhodesia and Canada. By 1944 the number of SFTS had reduced to around forty, many of these units having been re-designated (Pilot) Advanced Flying Units ((P)AFU). In 1943 there were ten UK based (P) AFU and these would survive to the end of the war.

Shortly after the outbreak of war the proportion of pilots required to be trained on twin engine aircraft compared to single engine was six to one. Attempts to specialise the SFTS initially broke down due to the shortage of suitable twin engine trainers. During this period the course length at SFTS was reduced from 24 weeks to sixteen weeks although flying hours remained at 100. Each course was increased from 96 to 152 pupils per school as facilities and accommodation improved. Until the beginning of 1940 some schools trained Observers but these were now being sent to the new Air Observer Navigation Schools (AONS).

By late 1939 the SFTS course had been increased to twenty weeks and in the winter of 1939-40 courses were extended by up to ten weeks due to the poor weather. The situation improved, however, and by April 1940 courses were back to sixteen weeks.

In January 1940 it was decided to split the SFTS into two groups. Group 1 – Single Engine and Group 2 – Twin Engine training. Armament training was stopped for Group 2. Group 1 still received armament training at Armament Training Stations (ATS). The Group 2 pupils carried out bombing practice in the Advanced Squadron stage but did not carry out any high level bombing until posting to OTU. This allowed more training time for night and instrument flying. Problems with the specialised training were encountered, however, since at that time there was a severe shortage of spares, skilled maintenance personnel and aircraft. A lack of Relief Landing Grounds (RLG), shortage of bombing ranges and radio aids restricted night flying training.

In May 1940 the plans the plans for pilot training were revised and it was decided to reduce the single engine course to twelve weeks by cutting bombing, recce, air firing and photography out of the syllabus. By June 1940 plans were in hand for four Group 1 schools and eight Group 2 schools. The Group 2 schools would have a fourteen-week course. The two SFTS training pilots for the Fleet Air Arm would continue with a sixteen-week course. Each pupil would now fly a minimum of 50 hours. These plans went ahead but were hampered by shortages of airfields, groundcrews and aircraft. While all this was happening a transfer of training to Canada, Rhodesia, Africa and the USA was in progress.

In August 1940 the course length for SFTS was reduced to twelve weeks and then in September 1940 reduced again to ten weeks. Against this reduction OTU course lengths were increased. By December 1940 the changes in training began to cause problems. Unserviceability of Miles Masters was running at 21% and Airspeed Oxfords at 13% due to lack of spares. The grass runways at SFTS were rapidly becoming unserviceable due to the heavy traffic. Night flying training at this point was only two hours per pupil but this improved a little with the introduction of gooseneck flares to illuminate runways. In spite of all the problems the output to OTUs from August to October 1940 was 2,007 compared with an expected 1,428. The training in Canada and the USA along with the absorption of allied personnel from Occupied Europe into the RAF also helped to ease the burden of the UK training units at this time.

By December 1940 twenty of the planned thirty-eight SFTS were operating and in that month they trained 792 pupils. Of these, 150 were to be trained as instructors and staff pilots. It was estimated that 178 training schools would be needed for which over 5,000 instructors would be required. Hence the "creaming off" of pilots for these duties.

In March 1941 there was still a shortage of training aircraft but overseas production was helping and by May 1941 the situation was improving. The transfer of basic training overseas and the introduction of shift systems for groundcrews at SFTS increased the flying hours from 4,200 per month in 1940 to 7,000 in 1941. One school achieved 9,000 hours per month.

By the winter of 1940-41 the SFTS were training at a rate of 4,000 pupils a year and it was hoped that by April 1941 that this would have increased to 8,000 per year. By now most SFTS pupils were averaging about 70 hours on the course. In early 1941 it was decided to base all but two SFTS overseas. And 25 SFTS were established in Canada, Australia and New Zealand. A further fourteen were transferred from the UK to Canada with four in Rhodesia and another seven in South Africa. With two in the UK and another five to be formed this would give a total of fifty-six schools.

With the closing down of the UK based SFTS and transfer to the clearer skies of the overseas locations it was found that pilots were not adapting easily to European climate on their return. It was therefore decided to open up AFUs to acclimatise pilots to flying in bad weather, in "black-out" conditions and map reading and navigation over the densely populated UK. The first three AFU opened on 1 November 1940 and by the end of March 1942 there were ten. Courses lasted three weeks, later increased to eight weeks, for those destined for Bomber Command and four weeks for other commands. It had originally been planned that crews should train with their pilots but this was not possible due to lack of W/T equipment in the trainers and the differing training requirements of the pilots and crews. Separate AFUs were set up for Observers ((O)AFU).

During the winter of 1940-41 most SFTS pupils averaged two hours night flying and it was found in January 1941 that the Link Trainer syllabus being used was obsolescent. In addition instrument flying training needed to be standardised. Of the instructors 95% examined were no better at instrument flying than their pupils and a fair number of them held the belief that it was unnecessary for the instructor to be competent in instrument flying in order to teach it! This misapprehension was swiftly corrected and by July 1941 instrument flying was standardised with the instructors required to practice instrument flying for half an hour per week. The Link Trainer syllabus and Instrument Flying syllabus were also revised.

By November 1941 pilots were graduating from SFTS after sixteen weeks with an average of 120 hours. They were then posted to an AFU in the UK for four weeks and 30 hours for single engine pilots and eight weeks and 60 hours for twins before posting to OTU.

In July 1942 pilots for twin engine aircraft completing AFU courses were being given a shortened course due to the lack of capacity at AFU which had curtailed the planned AFU course length. Another problem encountered in the first eighteen months of the war was that almost all the instructors for the SFTS had to be taken from SFTS courses as no ex-operational pilots were available. This caused a serious dilution of operational experience being passed on to the pupils until such time as the flying training organisation expansion was complete and the number of ex-operational pilots posted to instructional duties increased. The fact that only 15% of SFTS pupil output were suitable for training as instructors compounded the situation.

From mid 1943 training was gradually reduced and in 1944 the release of up to 75 pilots per month from operational units helped to cut the number of pilots "creamed off" as instructors from SFTS courses. Although there was a reduction in training in some areas by September 1943 there were still five AFU planned for opening under the current expansion scheme. In December 1943 it was decided to proceed with an expansion programme to bring all units up to full establishment until the autumn of 1945 and concurrently reduce aircrew being trained to the number required for the war against the Japanese.

By January 1944 there was a large reserve of aircrew available and it was decided to close some of the schools in Canada. By late 1944 other overseas schools were being closed and intakes into AFU were reduced from April 1945. By May 1945 there were only nineteen SFTS – only two of these in the UK and nine (P)AFU.

Non-Pilot Training

The training of aircrew other than pilots was carried out at a variety of other schools which included Bombing & Gunnery Schools (BGS), Air Observer navigation Schools (AONS), Air Observer Schools (AOS), Air Gunners Schools (AGS), (Observer) Advanced Flying Units ((O)AFU), Wireless Schools (WS) and Signals Schools (SS).

At the outbreak of war there were seven BGS, ten AONS and three Wireless Schools. By September 1941 there were ten BGS (nine of them overseas), one AONS and twenty-one AOS and ANS (of which fifteen were overseas), five AGS and ten WS and SS (seven overseas). By September 1943 the number of BGS had increased to fourteen, all overseas, there were now no AONS and the sixteen AGS and ANS were all based in Australia, Canada and India. The number of AGS had doubled to ten and the WS and SS increased to thirteen, seven of them based in the UK. Also by September 1943 nine (O)AFU had been formed in the UK. The end of the war saw a marked reduction of these training units and by May 1945 there were only four BGS, two AOS and ANS, eight AGS, seven (O)AFU and nine Wireless and Signals Schools.

Uk Based Flying Training Schools in operation on 3 Sept 1940	
Initial Training Wings	5
Elementary Flying Training Schools	17
Service Flying Training Schools	12
Bombing & Gunnery Schools	7
Observer Navigation Schools	5
Operational Training Units	17
Wireless Schools	3
General Reconnaissance Schools	1
Total	67

In 1938 the training of non-pilot aircrew was in a very unsatisfactory state. The Observer, who was responsible for navigation, received ten weeks training at AOS and various Armament Training Camps (ATC). Over 2,000 Observers were required at this time but recruiting was slow. Wireless Operator/Air Gunners (WOp/AG) and "straight" Air Gunners were taken from ground trades but were part time only. By October 1938 the Observer was to become full time aircrew and all WOp/AGs and Air Gunners would be drawn from the Wireless trade. The gunners were also to become full time aircrew.

In early 1939 there were only 622 trained Air Gunners and 1,576 were required. The increase in demand for gunners was causing training problems as it clashed with Observer training. Of the 10½ ATC 4½ were training Observers and there was a shortage of training and target towing aircraft. In April 1939 it was decided that Air Gunners and Observers would go to an AOS for training. At AOS they would receive twelve and forty five hours flying respectively. In addition specialist courses for armament and navigation instructors would be established.

In 1939 the standard of training for Air Gunners was giving cause for concern. The gunners were low on the list of training priorities and there was no standardisation in their instruction. The squadrons themselves were responsible for gunnery training at ATC and by now six of the ATC were training Observers. Compounding the situation

UK-based Flying Training Schools in operation on 3 Sept 1941

Initial Training Wings	15
Elementary Flying Training Schools	18
Service Flying Training Schools	12
Bombing & Gunnery Schools	1
Air Observer Navigation Schools	1
Air Observer Schools & Air Navigation Schools	6
Air Gunners Schools	5
Wireless Schools & Signals Schools	3
Operational Training Units	39
Total	100

was the shortage of equipment, aircraft, ranges and instructors. In early 1940 navigation training was separated from pilot training and Observers were now trained at AONS. As far as the WOp/AG were concerned there was very little wireless experience and virtually no experience operating the modern turrets coming into service. The standard of navigation was so heavily criticised at this time that in April 1940 the AONS syllabus was increased to 67 hours flying. Night flying was stopped due to a shortage of wireless aids. This plan was also hampered by the lack of aircraft and equipment.

There were several changes in armament training during 1939. The ATC were to become AOS training Observers in bombing, gunnery and navigation and Air Gunners in gunnery. Due to the impracticality of combined gunnery and navigation training the navigation training was dropped from the syllabus and the schools renamed BGS in November 1939.

Only eight stations became BGS and due to a shortage of aircraft, equipment and accommodation and lengthening courses caused by the sever winter of 1939-40 the planned output of aircrew was halved. There was still a shortage of trained gunnery instructors but this problem was partly solved by the establishment of the Central Gunnery School (CGS) on 5 November 1939. CGS began training

UK-Based Flying Training Schools in operation on 3 September 1942

Initial Training Wings	15
Elementary Flying Training Schools	17
Service Flying Training Schools	2
Air Gunners Schools	8
(Pilot) Advanced Flying Schools	8
(Observer) Advanced Flying Schools	8
Wireless And Signals Schools	3
Operational Training Units	49
Heavy Conversion Units	4
Technical Training Schools	1
Total	**115**

Gunnery Leaders at a rate of twenty-four every four weeks. By January 1940 all the operational units had Gunnery leaders.

By April 1940 armament training was still in difficulties. One of the problems was that the available ranges were not close enough to the schools. Observers were given an eight-week armament course at BGS after their navigation course. The gunners had a six-week course after completing the wireless course. By the summer of 1940 it was planned to move much of the training overseas and it was decided that two AONS would go to South Africa and the School of Air Navigation (SAN) to Canada.

In early 1941 it was thought that by the end of 1941 there would be a need for 7,200 Observers and 19,000 WOp/AG and Air Gunners. It was assessed that by the end of 1942 this figure would double. It was hoped that the overseas training units would supply them. This would entail a doubling of the number of observer schools by the end of 1941 and the air gunners schools would have to treble in number. The doubling of the Observer requirement was complicated by the need to train them in navigation, bombing and gunnery. This was achieved at navigation school and then BGS and there was some criticism that the Observer grew out of practice in navigation whilst at BGS. It was decided to combine both types of training at one unit and in February 1941 an experimental combined course started at

UK Based Flying Training Schools in operation on 3 September 1943

Initial Training Wings	23
Elementary Flying Training Schools	17
Service Flying Training Schools	2
Air Gunners Schools	10
Wireless And Signals Schools	7
(Pilot) Advanced Flying Units	10
(Observer) Advanced Flying Units	9
Operational Training Units	57
Heavy Conversion Units	17
Technical Training Schools	1
Total	**153**

Millom (No 2 BGS). By mid April the experiment had proved successful. Combined courses lasting eighteen weeks were introduced at six of the AOS. Until 1942, when the duties of the Observer were split between the Air Bomber and Navigator, this scheme produced 3,500 Observers a year.

The splitting of the Observers duties was due to the increasing complexity of the aircraft then coming into service and in March 1941 the need for another crew member, the Flight Engineer, became apparent for the same reason. In August 1941 it was proposed that new schools for Observers should be formed in Canada and the USA due to the difficulties of training in the UK. In November 1941 another proposal was made to grade Observers and Wireless Operators at the AFU stage. At this time seven of the AOS were tasked with training up to 650 Observers per month on courses lasting six week with a minimum of twenty-five hours flying. Two other AOS were training Observers and Wireless Operator prior to their training at another AOS in navigation and bombing and gunnery.

The demand for Air Gunners at the end of 1941 was such that 4 ½ AGS were required. Two training WOp/AG, one and a half training "straight" Air Gunners and one training Flight Engineers (Air Gunner). These schools were training 1,080 pupils per month. It was expected that by mid-1942 a further 2 ½ more AGS training 600

UK-based Flying Training Schools in operation on 3rd September, 1944

Initial Training Wings	6
Elementary Flying Training Schools	16
Service Flying Training Schools	2
Air Gunners Schools	7
(Observer) Advanced Flying Units	9
(Pilot) Advanced Flying Units	11
Wireless Schools & Signals Schools	7
Technical Training Schools	1
Operational Training Units	49
Heavy Conversion Units	19
Total	**127**

gunners per month would be required. Navigation training for Observers had greatly improved by the end of 1941 and they were now being given training in astro-navigation at the (O)AFU stage. At the end of 1941 plans were laid to give five times the amount of night flying and to double the capacity at AFU. In addition it was decided to open a further twelve half strength AFUs equipped with Airspeed Oxford. These would be brought up to full strength when more Oxfords became available.

During 1942 the operational commands began to put pressure on the AFUs. The defence of a lack of night flying aids and radio equipment countered complaints that little night flying was being done. It was planned, though, that once the AFUs were capable, 50% of the flying would be at night. Another problem at this time was that approximately 15% of each SFTS course was being "creamed off" as instructors for overseas schools and newly opened AFUs. This caused a shortage of instructors in the existing AFUs.

In January 1942 dissatisfaction was again being expressed at the standard of navigation and bomb aiming. In response an Elementary Air Observer School was set up at Eastbourne. Observers were now required to complete a twelve-week ITW, six weeks at Elementary AOS and eighteen weeks of navigation, bombing and gunnery at AOS. The Elementary AOS allowed the AOS to concentrate on the flying

UK-based Flying Training Units in operation on 3rd September, 1945.	
Initial Training Wings	5
Elementary Flying Training Schools	14
Service Flying Training Schools	2
Air Gunners Schools	6
(Observer) Advanced Flying Units	7
(Pilot) Advanced Flying Units	9
Wireless Schools & Signals Schools	7
Technical Training Schools	1
Operational Training Units	43
Heavy Conversion Units	15
Total	109

aspects of the training. By January 1942 the flying hours at AOS had increased to 130 and it was planned to send the AOS overseas and introduce (O)AFUs to replace them. By March 1942 the splitting of the Observers duties between the Navigator and Bomb Aimer was underway. Navigators would complete eighty hours flying (Fifty as first navigator) and the Bomb Aimer (officially designated Air Bomber) fifty hours, thirty of which were armament training and twenty map reading. By April 1942 the new roles had been officially adopted.

During 1941 the demand for "straight" Air Gunners increased considerably but the training system was not able to produce sufficient numbers. An experiment was started in September 1941 at the AOS at Penrhos. The training was a nine-week course in gunnery for Wireless Operators and the results were found to be successful. It did, however, severely tax the accommodation at the AOS. Penrhos continued to train WOp/AG and several other AOS followed suit producing WOp/AG for their own staff only. Although the experiment succeeded no permanent increase in output was obtained. No less than 5,000 Air Gunners were awaiting training during 1941 and it was decided to give these men training in the maintenance as well as the use of their weapons. As there was little room for them in the Technical Training Schools maintenance instruction was to be provided at the ITW.

In April 1942 several aircraft types were flying with two Wireless Operators on board. There was a tendency for the more skilled operator to do all the wireless duties whilst the other was used as a gunner thereby losing some wireless skills. For this reason it was decided to reduce the number of Wireless operators and replace one of them with a "straight" Air Gunner to man the turret. With the four-engined "heavies" then coming into service in larger numbers it was found that a pilot's assistant was required. This brought about the introduction of the Flight Engineer. The Flight Engineer would be trained in duties previously performed by the second pilot such as manipulation of the undercarriage, flaps, engine and pitch levers. He would also be trained as an Air Gunner. No pre-OTU training was required for a Flight Engineer and later they would join their crews at the HCU stage. By mid-1942 heavy bombers had only one pilot, the Observer duties had been split between the Bomb Aimer and

Navigator and there was only one Wireless operator per aircraft with the addition of a "straight" Air Gunner and a Flight Engineer to assist the pilot.

Until mid-1942 there was a shortage of Bomb Aimers but this was partly overcome by reducing the (O)AFU course by taking the pupils off courses at an earlier stage. Conversely Wireless Operator training time doubled due to the reduction to a single operator per aircraft. The output of "straight" Air Gunners increased, due in part to volunteers from other specialisation's completing shorter Air Gunners courses.

By mid-1943 the training system was being affected by a reduction in manpower available to the RAF. Flying Training Command continued to produce aircrew steadily and under the current expansion scheme planned to establish five more AFU, expand one Flying Instructors School (FIS) and the Elementary AOS. Also in 1943 a new commitment appeared in the form of glider pilot training. This involved the formation of several new units. The Allied air superiority achieved in 1944 coupled with the output from the training system changed the picture completely. By this time the RAF had more pilots, Navigators and Bomb Aimers than it could use. It was also becoming difficult to find employment for "tour expired" aircrew and with a surplus the training demand reduced and many prospective aircrew found themselves re-mustered to ground duties. The reduction in aircrew training continued till the end of the war by

Total Aircrew Output From UK-based Training Units 1939-1945

Specialisation	Royal Air Force	Royal Indian Air Force
Pilots	15,287	15
Observer/Navigator	9,869	4
Air Bomber	728	1
Wireless Operator/Air Gunner	27,190	6
Air Gunners	28,243	2
Flight Engineers	17,885	–
Air Force Totals	99,202	28
GRAND TOTAL		99,230

This total includes over 6,000 foreign nationals trained for Allied Air Forces within the RAF

which time, world-wide, a total of 62,713 Observers and Navigators, 19,021 Air Bombers, 55,606 WOp/AG, 51,283 Air Gunners and 20,260 Flight Engineers – a grand total of 326,552 aircrew – had been trained.

OPERATIONAL TRAINING UNITS, CONVERSION UNITS & FINISHING SCHOOLS

At the beginning of the war there were few units operating as Operational Training Units (OTU). Fighter Command had a Fighter Group Pool and formed another on 25 September 1939. This was formed despite much resistance from the CinC Fighter Command who wished to use the available aircraft to form additional operational fighter squadrons. He was over-ruled and in April 1940 two more OTUs were formed and all four OTUs had their establishment increased.

Coastal Command was carrying out operational training on the squadrons at the beginning of the war and only formed the first Coastal Group Pool in November 1939. In February 1940 this group pool was re-designated No 1 OTU. Coastal Command had another two units at that time working effectively as OTUs. These were the Seaplane Training Squadron, training flying boat crews and the Torpedo Training Unit (TTU), training strike crews. Army Co-operation Command had the School of Army Co-operation again acting as an OTU.

The biggest problem in operational training was the lack of OTUs within Bomber Command. Two thousand aircraft would be required to produce the 1,200 pilots per month to make up losses on operations and allow the command to expand. A major factor in complicating the bomber OTU training was the policy of having two pilots per aircraft. Eventually this would be changed with one pilot per aircraft and this considerably improved the training.

The OTU was the stage in training where the pilot, navigator, bomb aimer and gunners came together for the first time. Flight Engineers would join their crews later at the heavy conversion stage. From this point on the crew would complete training together and be posted as a crew to an operational squadron.

In the early stages of the war bomber OTUs had to cope with pilot and Navigator training due to a lack of instructors at other units. Fighter Command was no better off. Many pilots were inadequately trained in the use of wireless aids and often became lost. The solution was to post a navigation officer to each fighter squadron. Most Coastal Command pilots passed through the School of General Reconnaissance (S of GR) but the school was unable to cope with the demand and a second school was formed at Squires gate in my 1940.

On the outbreak of war Fighter Command had one Group Pool, but by June 1940 it had established three OTUs, under the control of No 10 group, through which all fighter pilots would pass en-route to the operational squadrons. During the Battle of Britain demand for replacements was such that the OTU course for some pilots was drastically cut to maintain the flow of pilots to the desperately short front line squadrons. In May 1940 Bomber Command had twenty-three operational squadrons with six more about to form. These units required 600 crews but only 342 were available. With a monthly output of seventy-eight crews from the OTUs this was clearly inadequate, but things were about to improve and by September 1940 there were seventeen OTUs of all types supplying crews to front line squadrons. This was the start of a major expansion of operational training and by September 1941 this figure had increased to thirty-nine OTUs. By September 1942 there were sixty-two, thirteen of them based overseas. The number continued to expand and in September 1943 the OTU strength stood at seventy-five, eighteen overseas. This was the peak of OTU expansion and by the end of 1944 there had been a slight reduction to sixty-nine and by the end of the war a further reduction to sixty-two of which nineteen were overseas.

In March 1942 with the change in crewing policy, which had seen the reduction to a single pilot per aircraft on the four-engined heavy bombers, a new crewmember, the Flight Engineer was introduced. He joined his crew after the OTU stage and from October 1942 this was normally at the Heavy Conversion Unit (HCU). The HCUs were formed from the existing Conversion Flights, which had been tasked with converting existing squadrons to the heavy bombers coming into service. These flights were normally attached to the squadrons and in order to relieve them of this training burden it was decided that all new crews would pass through HCU. This measure also produced a reduction in the number of training accidents in the operational squadrons. Courses at HCU were only a few weeks in length and most crews arriving from OTUs had little difficulty in passing.

Many crews were destined for Lancaster equipped squadrons; however, the HCUs were mainly equipped with Stirlings and Halifaxes. Nos 1, 3 and 5 Groups (and later No 6 Group) introduced Lancaster Finishing Schools (LFS) to give crews a very short introduction to the Lancaster prior to posting to a squadron. The courses lasted seven to fourteen days. The first LFS formed in November 1943 and conversion to the Lancaster continued at these units until shortly after the end of the war.

Similar units to the HCUs were training crews for Transport and Coastal Commands. These included Heavy Transport Conversion Units (HTCU), Transport Support Conversion Units (TSCU), Heavy Glider Conversion Units (HGCU) and Glider Training Schools (GTS). HGCU were training tug and glider crews whilst GTS trained glider pilots for Transport Command. Coastal Command had several training units including Torpedo Training Units (TTU), Schools of General Reconnaissance (S of GR), and Coastal OTUs training strike and flying boat crews. Several OTUs in Fighter Command specialised in the training of night fighter crews whilst others trained for ground attack, these latter OTUs were re-designated Tactical Exercise Units (TEU) at the end of 1943.

No matter how these units were named, from the first day of the war to the last, these units trained crews to fly a myriad of aircraft types under all weather conditions, day and night, all over the world. By the end of the war there were 110,024 trained aircrew and 66,906 still in the training system. Each and every one of these men was trained for triumph.

The second part of this book is their story in their own words.

PART TWO

The Aircrew Experience

*The flying training system produced aircrew to
man aircraft such as this Halifax Mk I NP-P of
No 158 Sqn. (Ian Foster/57 Rescue)*

"Where's Pat?"

FRANK BELL – WOp/AG – 1942/44

Volunteering for aircrew duties during World War two was not an easy business. Many men were turned down; some were too old, some too young. Others were told to join a ground trade and apply later. Frank Bell was one of these.

> "I volunteered for the RAF in June 1942 when I was seventeen and a half years old. Naturally, I wanted to join as aircrew but was politely informed that at that particular time they were not after aircrew. I was given an intelligence test and a trade test qualifying interview. I was recommended to join as a ground wireless operator and, when aircrews were required, to volunteer then for WOp/AG duties. This I did. I had to wait until my 18th birthday in November 1942."

After being accepted the next step was to successfully negotiate the initial training course at an ITW. Many of these units were based in pre-war seaside resorts using the hotels and holiday guesthouses for accommodation.

> "I did the initial course at Blackpool which included drill and discipline routines plus having to qualify in receiving and sending Morse Code at twelve words per minute. I successfully passed and after seven days leave was posted to No 4 Radio School, at Madley near Hereford, for the ground wireless operator course."

Frank Bell started the ground wireless operators course and was about half way through his training when his fortunes too another turn.

> "They were looking for volunteers for aircrew duties again. I applied and, after a stiff aircrew medical and another education test, I was accepted for aircrew training as a WOp/AG. Naturally, I had to finish the ground wireless operators course first. After qualifying as a ground wireless operator I was sent on seven days leave. On returning to Madley I started on the Air Wireless Operators Course. There was an airfield at Madley and the aircraft we flew in were, initially, Dragon Rapide twin engined jobs and then on to Percival Proctors where there was just you, the WOp instructor and the pilot. I qualified as a WOp/

Air and was promoted to sergeant. Once again I was sent on seven days leave after which I was posted to an AGS."

The journey around the country and through the training system continued and Frank Bell next found himself at No 10 Air Gunnery School, near Barrow.

"Actually, the airfield was on Walney Island, connected to Barrow by a bridge. The course for an Air Gunner was only about six weeks and I passed it OK, receiving my Air Gunners brevet. Of course I already had the 'Sparks' badge for WOp on my right sleeve."

From Barrow, Frank was posted back to Madley to hold awaiting his next course. After a few weeks he was posted to RAF Llandwrog in North Wales to commence a course at No 6 (O)AFU. Frank flew with trainee Navigators in Avro Ansons. The navigators were accompanied by instructors, the WOp/AGs were not. On completing the course another move was made, this time to No 16 OTU at Upper Heyford near Oxford.

"After the AFU I was posted to No 16 OTU arriving there on 16th May 1944. We were only received there and after a couple of days we were sent to the satellite airfield at RAF Barford St John, near Banbury. This was where we would be crewed up and do our flying. It was here that a batch of all the trades – pilots, navigators, bomb aimers, WOps, WOp/AGs and "straight" Air Gunners, who had all arrived on approximately the same date were assembled in a large hall or empty hangar and addressed by the Chief Flying Instructor and the Station Commander. After this we were told to socialise, mix with each other and form ourselves into crews. We had all day to do this and I know it seems a strange, hit and miss way of going on, but it seemed to work out. Any who were not "crewed up" by the end of the afternoon were made up into crews by the CFI."

Upper Heyford was a pre-war permanent base with brick buildings and well laid out roads. Officers were accommodated in the Officers mess and the permanent staff SNCOs in the Sergeants Mess. The NCOs on courses ate in the Sergeants Mess but were accommodated in brick barrack blocks. Whilst Frank Bell was there the airfield was closed to flying to have runways laid and the day after crewing up they were transported by coach to Barford St John. This was a typical wartime camp – very dispersed, with temporary buildings. The living site was about 1-½ miles from the airfield where the mess was situated. The living quarters were tin Nissen huts, as were the Officers and Sergeants messes.

"Small transport took you from the living site to the airfield every morning and brought you back in the evening after the evening meal. Of course, you could walk it; sometimes you had to, but never if you had been flying – day or night.

The reason you were here was to crew up, fly together and become efficient. On top form in your own job in the aircraft and also to have faith and confidence in the rest of the crew. This would take time. Hours and hours of flying together in all conditions and all kinds of weather. The weather would have to be really bad to cancel flying.

The Wellington was new to everyone, so for the first few flights, for familiarisation, there was a staff pilot at the controls. He would fly it for a couple of two to three hour sessions then he would sit next to our pilot and let him do take-offs and landings. After a couple of times we were on our own. It was quite a testing time for everyone, especially the 'Skipper'.

In 'B' Flight you did circuits and landings to familiarise the pilot in the handling of the Wellington. Then you progressed to Cine Gun Camera exercises and instrument flying. These trips usually lasted one to two hours. Sometimes you flew two or three times a day. Now and again you missed flying for a day to go into the classroom for lectures and examinations. You usually finished from lunchtime Saturday till Monday morning unless anything special came up.

The badge of No 16 OTU.
The motto translates as "Nothing without learning".

After about four weeks in 'B' Flight, if everything had gone OK, you went into 'C' Flight which was the navigational, cross-country exercise side of it. These usually lasted from three to five and a half hours and you flew various legs all over the UK. My special duty was to contact as many WT HF/DF stations as I could. The further distance the better. I got QDMs (bearings), some of which the Nav requested for his work. I also got position fixes from MF/DF stations, which also helped the Nav. I also had to send position reports, which included height, true course, present position and time. These had to be sent to Group Control every hour and I had to listen out for Group Broadcasts every half-hour in case of recalls, diversions or important messages. I was fully occupied all of the time. I loved flying though the 'Wimpey' where I was, immediately behind the pilot behind a bulkhead door, you could not see outside at all as there were no windows. I enjoyed my job though. Contacting an HF/DF station a couple of hundred miles away was thrilling. Especially if he could give you a first class bearing as well. Mostly you worked the large number of stations there were in the Midlands and East Anglia.

If the weather was unfit for flying some crews would go into the classroom for extra tuition or lectures and others would go for Wellington Crew Drill exercises. There was Parachute Normal, Parachute Emergency, Dinghy Drill, oxygen, Aircraft layout and undercart, Fire, Intercom and R/T, Petrol and Oil Systems, and Forced Landings (Home and Away). These were practised time and time again.

You did not have much time for entertainment during the week; you were very busy day and night. There was no camp cinema at Barford, so if you did want to go out on an evening you could walk a couple of miles to Bloxham village, to the local pub there. On a weekend you either went into Banbury or to Oxford. A meal, a drink, a trip to the cinema, another drink and catch the bus back. If you were fortunate enough you got off with a 'Popsie'."

Some crews were fortunate enough to pass through OTU with few problems and no mishaps. Frank Bell's crew was not so lucky. Fate was about to take a hand.

"Nearing the end of the course we were on a cross-country daylight navigational exercise in Wellington JA461 'H for How'. We were approaching our home base at Barford St John and our ETA was nearly up. We were still far too high, at about 12,000 feet. I was on the wireless set inside with the bulkhead door shut. Knowing we were nearly home I stood up to go to the rear of the aircraft, where the long trailing aerial for the MF/DF was situated. This had to be wound in before landing. It was about 350 feet long and weighted with ten or twelve lead balls on the end. You can imagine what damage it would do going in to land with it still swinging about. It could cut a chap in two. Just as I stood up to pass the Navigator, who sat sideways behind me, the aircraft went straight down in a spin. I was just stuck there, hanging on to some geodetic frames, not knowing what the heck was going on. After a couple of minute, which seemed like a lifetime, she came out of it.

I looked at the navigator and he looked at me and then I continued to do what I had set out to do. I went to the rear along the catwalk and wound the trailing aerial in. I had already closed my W/T watch with Group and with our own HF/DF station, so when I retraced my steps I switched off my W/T equipment as we seemed to be entering the circuit. I opened the bulkhead door and nearly had a fit at what I saw. The main escape hatch was wide open, a great gap with all the earth and fields below in full view. We were at about 1,500 feet and there was no Bomb Aimer. The 'Skipper' was as white as death and shivering like hell. I stood on the bulkhead step with my hands above me gripping the sides of the door. I plugged in on the intercom and asked Hendy, the 'Skipper', "Where's Pat?" He just looked at me and waved his hand. He was concentrating on going in to land so I just shut up and stood there. I wish I hadn't. We were about sixty to seventy feet up on the way in to touch down when she went straight into the deck just past the start of the runway. I went flying forward. How I did not go through the gaping hole I don't know. I went straight over it into the nose, under the front gun turret and that is the last I remember.

The badge of No 10 AGS. The 'Bee and Arrow' are taken from the Arms of Barrow in Furness, which was adjacent to the airfield on Walney Island. The motto translates as "We prepare for flight".

The others were all right, as they had been sitting down at their positions. The aircraft was a complete write off and the 'Skipper' was put under close arrest straight away, no messing. They got everybody out as quickly as possible because of the high risk of fire. There was fuel all over the place. My face was a bit of a mess but I was soon attended to and although my eyes and nose were 'black and blue' I was let out of hospital after a few days.

Naturally there was a Court of inquiry. The Bomb Aimer had baled out. He had been down in the Bomb Aimers position when she had suddenly gone into a spin. The 'Skipper' had waved to him, meaning for him to get up and give him a hand with the stick. He was not on intercom and thought the 'Skipper' meant something else, which he promptly did. He was in the nose and he could see the ground getting nearer and nearer and being in a spin he thought we had all had it. He 'upped' the front hatch and baled out. He lost one of his flying boots on the way down and when he finally got back to camp, four hours later, he was in his stocking feet with the other flying boot under his arm.

A Royal Observer Corps unit nearby had seen us coming down and, as we vanished behind a distant hill, reported us as having crashed. However, the 'Skipper' had managed to pull her out and to gain a little height to get us home and into the circuit. The Bomb Aimer was severely reprimanded and at the end of the week we were all called into the COs office. The Co, the CFI and our 'Skipper' were there. They asked us whether we wanted to continue flying with our 'Skipper'. Having discussed this beforehand we all said we wanted him as our 'Skipper'. He was given a severe reprimand and a Red Endorsement in his Log Book. He was a good pilot and we were right to put our faith in him. Later on he was to save us a few times with his quick thinking and expertise. We completed our flying at Barford on August 8th 1944 and went back to Upper Heyford. We got our clearance 'chits' signed and were sent, once again, on seven days leave."

After OTU the next move was to Heavy Conversion Unit where the crew would meet one of the four-engined 'heavies' for the first time. It was here also that the Flight Engineer joined the crew. Frank Bell's crew was posted to No 1653 HCU at Stradishall in Suffolk.

"We arrived on August 19th 1944 and booked in. Then, after hanging around for a week, we were transferred by lorry to the satellite airfield at Chedburgh. This was similar to Barford St John, Nissen living quarters and messes. They were comfortable inside for the type of structure. Here we were introduced to the Stirling and she seemed a monster. What a size she was – and that undercarriage! She looked so ungainly on the deck but looked beautiful in flight. She was lovely to fly in; even the' Skipper' said so. The main snag with her was her inability to gain height. About 15,000 feet if you were lucky. The syllabus here was practically the same as at OTU. Getting to know all about the aircraft and so on. It was more difficult for the 'Skipper' though, handling a four-engined aircraft, especially one this size. There were a couple of weeks of lectures and classroom work and then we commenced flying on 15th September 1944. The first three lessons of three hours each were dual control 'circuits and bumps', then we went solo doing the same, then, without a dual check, we went straight into night flying – 'circuits and bumps'. We did three sessions at night and then moved into 'C' Flight."

The syllabus at No 1653 HCU included cross-country flights, high level bombing, and 'Flashlight' and 'Bullseye' exercises. Frank Bell's crew was kept busy flying these exercises until early October 1944.

"We did one cross-country and 'Flashlight' exercise which was a washout as we were recalled after two hours because the weather was clamping in. One night we did a 'Bullseye' and a 'Flashlight' plus high level bombing. The former two were done over the city of Bristol and were done in conjunction with the Army and Fighter Command. 'Flashlight' was done with the searchlight batteries and 'Bullseye' involved the anti-aircraft batteries and night fighters after us. Quite exciting but a bit heart stopping at times. Afterwards we popped off down to Chesil Beach near Portland to do high level bombing. The whole exercise lasted five and quarter hours. Of course, we were given exact times for the 'Do' at Bristol, as we were only allowed a certain time for the barrage balloons to be lowered. 'Jerry' visited Bristol fairly often."

Once again, almost at the end of the course, fate almost denied Frank Bell and the crew their chance of reaching a squadron and flying on 'Ops'.

"On 2nd October 1944 we were due to go on a Night Flying Test followed by high level bombing in the afternoon, flying in 'O for Oboe'. We were gathering speed and nearly reached the 'point of no return' when there was a hell of a bang and we slewed off the runway onto the grass, turning all the time, finally coming to a halt facing the way we had set off. The port tyre had burst giving us the fright of our lives. The aircraft undercarriage looked out of sorts, terribly mutilated, but still holding the aircraft up. A wagon came trundling up in company with the 'Blood Wagon' and, as no one was hurt, we were transferred to another Stirling, 'U for Uncle' and just carried on with the detail. We did our last cross-country and high level bombing on 6th October 1944, a four and a half-hour flight and that ended our course.

We picked up the seventh member of our crew at HCU. The Flight Engineer, Flight Sergeant Ernie Wall. Up to this time most of his training had been done in the classroom and on the ground. He had not got many flying hours in prior to HCU, about thirty I think. The rest of us had about 160 hours at that time. Still, he soon fitted in and by the end of the course we were all one big happy family. We got cleared from all the sections as quickly as we could on 7th October and as we were nearing 'OPS' I think they felt sorry for us and gave us another seven days leave."

The crew was destined for operations on the Lancaster. Because of this there was one more hurdle to be surmounted. At this time Lancaster crews were required to complete a course of conversion at a Lancaster Finishing School (LFS). Frank and his crew went to No 3 LFS at Feltwell.

"LFS was only a three week course after which crews were allocated straight away to squadrons. We reported to No 3 LFS at Feltwell in Norfolk on 14th October 1944. I was amazed to see there were no runways, it was all grass. It was a permanent camp though, well laid out with permanent brick buildings and messes. It was the usual formula – dual familiarisation with the Lanc – but just one dual session and then solo the same day. The 'circuits and bumps' were done at nearby Methwold on their runways and also at Foulsham. We did tow or three day flights and night flights of 'circuit and bumps' followed by high level bombing and fighter affiliation, finishing off with one cross-country and high level bombing at night.

The Stirling was a nice aircraft to fly but the Lanc was better. She was the 'Lady of the Sky'. The loads she used to carry were amazing. When you landed in a Lancaster she would float down the runway. She did not want to land and had to be forced down. She would bring you back on two engines even. The course only lasted eighteen days and on 31st October 1944 each crew was told which squadron they had been allotted to."

Frank Bell and his crew were to commence operations with No 514 Squadron based at Waterbeach in No 3 Group.

Fighter Pilot

JOHN BECKETT – PILOT – 1940/41

John Beckett joined the RAF on 1st July 1940 at the age of eighteen and a half; the earliest permitted age for pilot training. After two weeks at the Receiving Wing at Babbacombe in Devon he moved to Paignton, also in Devon for ITW. The ITW was accommodated in a hotel and the course consisted of five weeks of drill, physical training, airmanship, theory of flight and navigation. All of the instruction was in the classroom.

On completion of ITW John was posted to No 11 EFTS at Perth in Scotland. Perth was a grass airfield, originally opened as a civil airport pre-war. The accommodation for the four hundred or so students and staff was wartime temporary buildings. The EFTS also used Whitefield and Findo Gask as Relief Landing Grounds (RLG). John completed fifty hours here flying Tiger Moths.

John Beckett was destined for fighter training and his next posting was to No 8 SFTS at Montrose. Montrose had opened before World War One in 1912 and by the next war had been developed into a three-runway training airfield. Montrose was a much larger station than Perth, accommodating some 1,800 personnel, again in temporary wartime huts. The

SFTS used RLG at Ballhall, Balmain, Cairnbeg and Edzell. John Beckett remembers Montrose mainly for two reasons.

"I went to No 8 SFTS at Montrose and between 6th October 1940 and 6th January 1941 I flew sixty-six hours on Miles Master Mk Is, gaining my wings and being promoted from Leading Aircraftsman to

The badge of No 8 SFTS. The SFTS received its badge in September 1937, having been based at Montrose since January 1936. The motto translates as "We train in the best traditions".

Montrose pictured in February 1994. The remaining hangars are centre left and the gorse covered runways are in the left foreground. (Authors collection)

The remains of the airfield at Findo Gask in October 1987. (Authors collection)

Sergeant. Whilst I cannot be sure I think my pay went up from seven shillings and sixpence (37.5p) to twelve shillings and sixpence (63p) per day!"

The next move for the fledgling fighter pilot was to OTU and John Beckett went to Sutton Bridge and No 55 OTU. Sutton Bridge had opened in 1926 and as a permanent RAF station had some better accommodation. Due to the expansion of the unit however, some was of temporary construction. Beckett completed twelve hours flying Hurricane Mk Is at Sutton Bridge and on completion of the OTU he was posted to No 605 Sqn. He was later commissioned and after serving in Malta he returned to the UK for instructor duties.

On his return to the UK John Beckett received a three-week course on basic instruction and became an instructor at No 59 OTU. The OTU was based at Crosby on Eden and Milfield, equipped with Hawker Hurricanes and Miles Masters. After a spell instructing here John was on the move again.

"I went to Cranwell to instruct Turks on Spitfires and then I went back to Montrose and in three months learnt to be a proper 'Qualified Flying Instructor'. I was posted to No 9 (P)AFU at Errol on 1st April

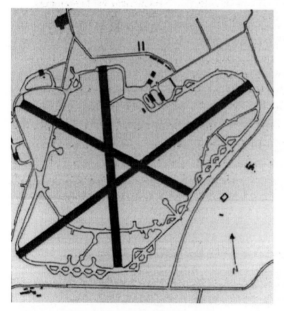

Crosby on Eden. Home to No 55 OTU.

1944. The unit was just changing over from Master Mk Is to Master Mk IIs and a change from the in-line Rolls Royce Kestrel to the rotary Bristol Mercury engine which was not the most reliable piece of kit. We had numerous engine failures at Errol but to the best of my knowledge no fatalities. Either the forced landing training was very good or the fields were plentiful and large!"

Errol was a wartime airfield situated on the banks of the Firth of Tay. It had opened in 1942 with three tarmac runways and held up to 2,300 staff and pupils. The role of No 9 (P)AFU was to acclimatise pilots who had trained in Canada and the USA to flying by day and night over the UK.

"The accent was very much on navigation and the visual 'look' of the countryside. We were organised with two flights per squadron and had two squadrons when I arrived. Although still a Flight Lieutenant I had two flights – Flight Lieutenant Bill page being one of my flight commanders. The syllabus ensured that students were safe on 'circuits and bumps', aerobatics, spinning, precautionary landings, forced landings, instrument flying and night flying. There was night cross-country flying too. The week before Christmas 1944 I flew four one-hour flights in the back seat of a Harvard, carrying out night cross-country checks on four different Fleet Air Arm Sub Lieutenants.

We appear to have stopped flying Master Mk IIs on September 24th 1944 and on October 5th and 6th I flew a total of 3.5 hours on 'General Flying Practice' which was my own conversion, solo, onto the new aeroplane – the Harvard. On 8th June 1945 we moved from Errol to Ternhill in Shropshire and pursued a similar succession of courses. My last trip was on 6th February 1946 and shortly afterwards I 'took a bowler hat' and left the service for nearly three years."

John Beckett returned to the RAF in 1949 with a permanent commission finally leaving the service in 1960 having flown Vampires, Meteors and Victors. In the period from 1946 to 1949 he continued flying on Tiger moths at No 22 Reserve Flying School at Cambridge.

Bomber Pilot – 1

H.D. 'ROGER' COVERLEY – PILOT – 1942/44

Roger Coverley trained on Tiger Moths and Magisters at EFTS followed by Oxfords at SFTS. Destined for bombers he was posted to Wellington equipped No 27 OTU at Lichfield in Staffordshire. From there he was posted to No 78 Sqn. The squadron was in the process of converting to the Halifax and like the other early heavy bomber squadrons the conversion training was carried out on the squadron rather than the later HCUs. Roger was posted initially to No 78 Sqn Conversion Flight.

> "On 13th August 1942 I flew down to Riccall with the redoubtable 'Bunny' Bunclarke, who as a Squadron leader was later killed over Duisburg, to complete my Halifax conversion at the newly opened airfield. We all arrived in a gaggle having had a monumental party at Middleton St George, No 78 Sqns home base, the night before. Among the objects of comfort 'acquired' for the mess from various pubs and hotels in the Darlington area, I recall, was a large potted palm tree! I was in 'B' Flight commanded by Flt Lt Harry Drummond (later Wing Commander). Others who formed the nucleus of the unit included Sqn Ldr Dobson and Fg Off Woodhatch (later Sqn Ldr), whom incidentally I met up with again in 1944 at Stalag Luft 1 in Germany. I completed my Halifax conversion on 17th October 1942 and was posted to No 78 Sqn again, this time at Linton on Ouse under 'Willy' Tait who later sank the Tirpitz."

On completion of his tour with No 78 Sqn, Roger was posted for instructional duties. His first port of call was No 3 Flying Instructors School (FIS) flying Oxfords and learning the instructional techniques he would use on posting to No 1658 HCU based at Riccall. No 1658 HCU was an amalgamation of the earlier Conversion Flights of Nos 76, 78, 10, 102 and 158 Sqns. The unit flew a mixture of Halifax Mks I, II and III and they had been converting crews to the Halifax since October 1942. Riccall had opened in 1942, constructed to the heavy bomber base pattern, with three concrete runways, two T2 type hangars and sufficient hardstandings for up to fifty aircraft.

Accommodation was wartime temporary for the staff and pupils who numbered 2,900 on average.

"After Linton, a pre war base with nothing but the best in comfort and messing – room to myself (with batwoman) and grapefruit for breakfast (how the hell did they manage to get hold of them!) – Riccall was primitive. Nissen hut accommodation and mud everywhere. Being keen on shooting I obtained permission to shoot within the perimeter of the airfield. Cartridges were hard to come by but a friend in the War Agricultural Committee managed to let me have sufficient for my requirements and I supplemented the Mess fare with hares, pheasants, partridges, snipe, pigeon and rabbits.

Of the training syllabus we were expected to put in forty hours flying a month. We were each allotted three or four pupil pilots who one took right through the course. Familiarisation flights would be followed by general handling, circuits and landings, overshoots, three engine and cross wind landings, all the emergencies, solo and then night flying. Cross-countries were carried out solo, as were bombing practices, but fighter affiliation flights with Spitfires were carried out with the instructors in the left hand seat."

Hullavington was used as a satellite by No 3 FIS in 1942.
(Authors collection)

Instructing at HCU was not all work though and occasionally the hard worked instructors, supposedly on rest from operations would relax in the local towns and cities.

"Off duty we let our hair down in 'Betty's Dive' in York, but when that city became over-congested with Canadians I switched my affections to 'Powolny's' in Leeds – not to mention the 'Yorkshire Hussar' and the 'Robin Hood'!"

Considering that the duty at HCU as an instructor was supposed to be a rest, the dangers appeared to be only slightly less than 'Ops' and the instructors sometimes took many risks in the course of their duties.

"We instructors never carried parachutes – useless in the circuit anyway, but nevertheless a rather foolish show of bravado. We sat on a jump seat from which we had little control of the aircraft.

On the night of 8th September 1943 I was giving Fg Off Baldwin circuits and landings in Halifax V9989. The runway in use was the main one running East/West. The perimeter track leading to the threshold ran nearly parallel to the runway. I was at the head of a queue of three or four aircraft awaiting permission to turn on for take off. Permission was delayed as a pupil returning from a cross-country was on three engines and had priority for landing. I was sitting on the jump seat talking to Baldwin as we watched the aircraft turn onto finals, and it was soon apparent that he was having difficulty lining up on the runway and was making straight for us. I ducked, there was a crash, and I switched off. The props of both inner engines had gone, but otherwise we were undamaged. The other aircraft overshot (on three engines) and landed without incident, while I taxied back to dispersal on my outers. A few inches to either side and one of those massive wheels would have gone through the cockpit, a few feet lower and the aircraft would have ploughed through us and have most surely taken the aircraft behind us as well. The strangest of all – why did he not burst at least one of his tyres as they hit our props?

Instructing at HCU between tours was supposed to be a form of rest, but I for one was glad to get back on operational duties – even if I did eventually get the 'chop' en route to Nuremberg on the night of 30/31st March 1944."

Freedom Fighter

ALBERT M. CUSTERS – PILOT – 1940/44

The RAF during World War 2 relied not only on the men of Britain and the Commonwealth for its pilots and aircrews but also on those men who had escaped from the occupied countries of Europe. One of these was Albert Custers of the Belgian Air Force who escaped to fight again.

"I set out as part of a group of fifty-three Belgian Air Force personnel of all ranks from Captain to enlisted man, plus a few young student escapees, from Gibraltar on the evening of 21st July 1940. We sailed on board the British cargo ship 'David Livingstone' and ploughed our way in a twenty-five ship convoy to the middle of the Atlantic before turning north round Ireland and down the Irish Sea. I set foot on British soil at Pembroke Dock in the early hours of 5th August 1940. It is a historical debt to them and a testimony to their indomitable courage and determination to mention the more than 200 Polish Air Force and 100 Czech Air Force personnel who crowded our and other ships in the convoy. Many of them in French Air Force uniform and a good number wearing the Croix de Guerre and some the Legion d'Honnuer.

We the Belgians were gathered for ten days rest at Tenby then sent to St Athan under direct RAF analysis and scrutiny. Only one of our crowd was a fully-fledged pilot and he had already left for No 235 Sqn, Coastal Command. The rest of us had to remain medically fit, work on the English 'aerial lingo' get accustomed to tea, porridge and foamless beer and wait for training facilities."

Albert had a wait of almost two months before he was eventually posted to a flying training unit, No 13 EFTS at White Waltham, a small grass airfield just outside London. No 13 EFTS had formerly been the 'De Havilland School of Flying'.

"I was in the first small batch of ten (7 officers and 3 SNCO's) to leave St Athan for training. We were posted to No 13 EFTS. We were there from 13th October to 22nd November 1940 and I completed over forty-two hours on Tiger Moths. Squadron leader GM Cox was the CFI and my instructor was an excellently patient Flight Lieutenant Hordern, a 'boat man' living on an impressive barge on the Thames. Another instructor was Ralph Munday, later a famed Typhoon test pilot. On 8th November we (the already officers) were re-vamped, re-tailored and commissioned in the RAFVR as acting Pilot Officers on probation. The NCO's became LAC's – Hurrah!? We were already half way to winning the war!"

Destined for twin engined aircraft Custers was posted to the Oxford equipped No 11 SFTS at Shawbury near Shrewsbury.

"Five of us were posted on 23rd November to No 11 SFTS. This was at 'SHawbury, SHrewsbury, SHropshire'. It took me two weeks to master the pronunciation of this most un-Latin suit. We were there as No 29 Course, 'F' Flight, No 2 ITS. The CFI was Sqn Ldr AR Leggate. Our stay was from 25th November 1940 until 26th April 1941 and I totalled over seventy-nine hours flying. Our course was forty-six strong and it was blessed with the presence of a batch of thirteen fellows from what was then the shiniest Jewel in the Crown – India. All were commissioned and they were very friendly to everyone. I became very close with two of them, Pilot Officers Shiv Dev Singh and Chauduri, both magnificent individuals and highly motivated fighters. In 1942 I learned that Chauduri had been killed in action. As for Shiv Dev, he became Indian Air Attaché in London in the 1950's."

Like his acquaintance on the 'David Livingstone' who ended up on No 235 Sqn, Custers was also destined for Coastal Command but fate was to take a hand.

"We, the five Belgians, were directed to Coastal Command. Posting from Shawbury was to No 2 (Coastal) OTU at Catfoss in Yorkshire where we stayed from 10th may to 5th July 1941. We flew Blenheim Mk I and Mk IV. The CFI was Sqn Ldr E Hyde DFC. However, with the projected forming of the first Belgian fighter squadron, No 350 Sqn, I was re-directed to No 59 OTU at Crosby on Eden in Cumbria where I remained from 11th August to 21st October 1941 flying Miles Masters and Hurricanes."

After completing the OTU Albert Custers was posted to No 350 Sqn and after an operational tour with the squadron came back to the training system, this time as an instructor. He was posted to Cranwell in Lincolnshire which at that time was home to an SFTS operating over 150 Airspeed Oxfords and with such a congested airfield circuit that it had to utilise RLG's at Barkston Heath, Caistor, Coleby Grange, Fulbeck, Spitalgate and Wellingore.

"I took my instructors grade at No 2 FIS, Montrose from 26th August to 22nd October 1942 in No 14 Course. Qualified for day instructing on Oxford after 118 hours there. The CFI was Wg Cdr Scott AFC. The night flying instructing test was delivered by Sqn Ldr Toyne DFC. A nice fellow-student instructor and a good friend during that period was Fg Off Czarnecki, a Pole.

My first appointment as an instructor was at RAF College Cranwell SFTS. I took my post within 'D' Flight, No 1 Sqn (Twins) and worked there for three months, from October 1942 to February 1943. There were two flying fields at Cranwell, North Drome and, of course, South Drome. The twins operated from the latter. Flt Lt RB Gibsen was OC 'D' Flight and Sqn Ldr EH Irving was OC No 1 Sqn. I flew over 123 hours there of which 113 was as Instructor/Day. Twenty four pupils were trained as follows - Eleven British, four Belgian, one Free French, two Polish, three Czech, two Ceylonese (Sri Lankan) and on US Volunteer. The American volunteer was Fg Off Westinghouse. I often wondered whether he was from the famous family, but never found the correct answer. In the course of activities with 'D' Flight I had the great pleasure and the inspiring advantage to know and appreciate Warrant Officer Wheeler, a very active instructor. The unusual thing about him was that he was holder of the DFC, from sustained and successful operations on Catalina, one particular mission having lasted for more than twenty-seven hours. Despite a number of enquiries I could never find an answer to the query – how many of these rare birds did the RAF ever possess?

On the 5th of February 1943 I had a re-categorisation test flight with the CFI, Gp Capt McPherson AFC. OK, successfully re-categorised to 'B' – that was Day/Night Instructor. However, the 'Groupie' did not even have time to write his report, because the very next day I was posted in a hurry to No 3 (P)AFU at South Cerney, flown down there, 'taken in' into 'E' Flight, No 2 Sqn, given a locker in the instructors dispersal and allocated my first three pupils – two middle aged Belgians and one Frenchman straight out of 'liberated' Morocco. None of them could speak English! I started flying with them the next day, instructing them 'en francais'. There stood, of course, the reason for my 'emergency posting' to South Cerney. No 3 (P) AFU was taking in a flow of French chaps from North Africa. A more or less steady flow of them kept coming in for many months after this February 'invasion'. It also became the port of call for smaller and more sporadic batches of Belgian Air Force escapees who had spent more or less lengthy terms in French jails or Spanish camps. Few of all these could utter more than a few words of Shakespeare's tongue and none would have been able to swallow any tuition in English.

The Air Ministry's 'gift' to No 3 (P) AFU would have been a poisonous apple without the lucky availability of ONE French speaking instructor within the whole of Training Command. My hands were soon filled up to overflowing. The first week I saw five 'friendly alien' pupils come my way, three Belgians and two French. While trudging along with them I was sent away to Cranage for five days with a Belgian pupil to No 1531 Beam Approach Training (BAT) Flight, flying sixteen hours there, half of that to receive the beam approach instruction in English, the other half to repeat it in French to my pupil and thus have one more arrow for my instructing bow. All very well. As a mark of appreciation, the day after our return from Cranage, I was allotted four more 'friendly aliens', two of each sort. So, at the end of the first month I was teaching nine 'grown up pups'. At the end of the second month, March, I was taking care of fifteen of them. I call these men 'grown up pups' for want of better terminology, because all of them had some previous flying experience, mostly pre-war. The job was to pass them through a fast turning mill, with 'adaptations' to their particular past and to their projected future. A bit more of this, a bit less of that, a bit less by day, a bit more by night and so forth.

For the night job I was again re-categorised by the AFU CFI, Wg Cdr D Radford DFC on 27th February. I had already ten hours Night Instruction. In March after re-cat I furnished thirty-seven hours Night – as much as my thirty-nine hours day. The 'pups' had to have their teeth lengthened and their hopes uplifted. All that 'en francais'. The instructing tempo was kept at the highest possible level throughout my seven month stay at South Cerney, so much so that towards the end of July I collapsed from exhaustion and had to take ten days compulsory rest – no complaint whatsoever, just a fact. 'C'est la guerre!', the chaps in the operational commands were also exhausting themselves.

I was immensely glad and relieved when a second French-speaking instructor arrived in mid-March 1943. He was a pre-war Belgian Air Force pilot and a very good one at that, whom I knew slightly. He set to work in the same feverish manner so that the two of us significantly increased our output of 'puppies'. I quite think (but this is only a personal opinion) that the British and RAF powers, on the one hand, and the De Gaulle aviation wizards, on the other hand, were quite pleased with our work. The first because the problem was being solved without too many headaches, the second because of the free and inexpensive profit, in terms of purely Free- French effort to achieve it. To us, my comrade instructor and I, it was just a job neatly done. 'C'Est la guerre' and 'Vive la France'...

My comrade instructor was Fg off (later Flt Lt) Walter Henri. We became very close friends and when he departed I lost a greatly endeared brother. Eluding captivity after the collapse, he immediately entered the Resistance. In 1942 he was high on the wanted list of the Gestapo and actually escaped through his hide out back door as the sinister bastards were forcing the front door open. He made his way alone across France and Spain without being caught and locked up anywhere. As instructors we worked with the same urgent fever and purposeful intent. Although I do not have access to his logbook and can only make a logical projection, I am sure to be close to the truth when saying that his achievements at South Cerney have been in every aspect comparable to what I may venture to put forward. In seven months instructing at No 3 (P) AFU I took care of ninety-four young student pilots and not so young 'foreign puppies' as follows – forty-five British, nine Belgian, twenty-seven French, one Dutch, one Norwegian, one Canadian, two Australian and eight New Zealanders. As Walter Henri functioned there for a nine-month period he must also have taken care of about thirty-five French and a dozen Belgians, apart from all the others.

I think it is fair to say that the two of us have probably furnished roughly sixty pilots for the Free French Air Force and enabled about twenty-five Belgian men to pursue a decent flying activity in wartime UK. This without mentioning the odd 150 British, Commonwealth and alien chaps we also looked after during the same period. My monthly average for this period was eighty-two hours of which seventy-nine were instructional flying. The job had to be done. I am terribly glad and a bit proud that it was. In particular, my instructional total of 111 hours for May 1943 might very well stand as an all-time record for the whole of Training Command. In August, when it became known that I had applied for posting to operations, I heard a verbal hint that the AFC might come my way, should I stay 'a bit longer'? My decision remained firm and I quit at the end of that month. Walter Henri was still there, so I could go."

To return to operations Albert Custers had first to become a student again. His first posting was to No 12 (P) AFU at Grantham. No 12 (P) AFU was equipped with Bristol Blenheim Mks I and IV and the MK V, known as the Bisley. He remained there until November 1943 then moved to No 51 OTU at Cranfield to learn the night fighter business on Beauforts, and Beaufighter Mks I and VI.

   After Grantham and Cranfield I joined No 219 (Night Fighter) Sqn, just re-equipped with Mosquito's and stayed with it until September 1945. Walter Henri, after his nine months of instructional duty, followed exactly the same path and joined No 219 early in September 1944, with a Belgian Radar/Navigator (Nav/Rad). My Nav/Rad was a Southern Irish volunteer. His name was MacNamara, born in Tipperary. Walter and his Nav/Rad were shot down near Cologne on the night of 20/21st March 1945 and killed in action. I had lost my dear brother.... Amen."

Albert Custers survived the war and returned to the Belgian Air Force from which he retired having reached the rank of Colonel.

The control tower at Coleby Grange which was used as a relief landing ground by Cranwell photographed in 1986. (Authors collection)

Guns & Radios – 1

ALBERT CARTY – WOp/AG – 1939

In June 1939 Albert Carty enlisted as a Wireless Operator. He was too young for aircrew and at that time there were no direct entry Air Gunners. After completing his Wireless Operator training he was accepted for WOp/AG training by an Aircrew Selection Board. Shortly after his eighteenth birthday in March 1940 he was posted to No 7 AGS at Stormy Down near Porthcawl, South Wales.

"Training was on Wallace biplanes, Fairey Battles and Whitley's with Lewis, Vickers gas operated (VGO) and Browning machine guns with, briefly, 20mm Hispano. One of the volunteers on my course was Charlie Farnes who had come all the way from Manila in the Philippines. At Stormy Down we were in the usual wooden huts and in the dining room we ate at separate tables – Fitters at one, trainee AG's at another. The day started at 7am with physical education followed by breakfast. The school began at 9am for theory and stripping of Lewis, VGO's and Brownings.

I flew only once in a Wallace and found it very enjoyable. We flew at 1,000 feet and had a Lewis gun on a Scarfe mounting. The Battle was the main aircraft used and nobody came up with us. Two trainees at a time with a VGO and a pan of 100 rounds each. If a designated number of rounds had not been fired a belt to the amount unused was taken up and dropped in the sea and the figures adjusted! When we reached Port Talbot the pilot would bank the aircraft and begin a run along the beaches where there were targets. The first time I went up the pilot banked the aircraft and I fell half way out, holding onto the Scarfe mounting, with my partner hanging onto my legs. When we reported this it turned out we should have been told about the 'Monkey Chain' which was a harness attached to a column in the cockpit. In any case the one we should have used was unserviceable.

Conditions at Stormy Down were quite good and when we passed out we felt capable of anything. Even with hindsight I think the Battle, with fighter escort, could have been reasonable. The Whitley training was using Brownings, stripping them blindfold and the use of the mid-under 'dustbin' turret. This turret slowed the aircraft and because of poor visibility was useless. Although the Whitley had a longer range and a heavier bomb load than the Wellington it did not seem as fast or manoeuvrable and the Wellington for my money was the 'Queen of the Air'."

After completing the AGS course Albert was posted to No 11 OTU at Bassingbourn and was introduced to the Wellington for the first time.

"After Easter 1940 we were posted to OTU. Most of us to Bassingbourn near Cambridge where we met the Wellington Mk I and Ic nicknamed the 'Wimpey' after the cartoon character 'J Wellington Wimpey'. We spent some time on theory in the use of the 1082/1083 R/T sets, loop bearings and Aldis signalling lamps. Sighting training was done using scale models of Luftwaffe aircraft held on posts at marked distances up to 1,000 yards. We sat in a turret on the ground using the sights. Some nights we went onto a range where lights would be beamed and we had to fire short bursts. There was also clay pigeon shooting with a shotgun fitted in a Frazer Nash turret.

Several nights a week we were on 'circuits and bumps' with trainee pilots and an instructor. For a short spell pilots were coming through after six weeks on Tiger Moths and 'pile ups' were common. I had two when they forgot to put the undercarriage down! There was also daylight cross-country flying which provided experience for all of the crew and was very good.

Whilst at Bassingbourn, hoping for promotion to AC1 (Aircraftsman First Class), we were the first batch jumped up to sergeant and although we were in the same 'erk' huts we dined in the Sergeants Mess – 'civvie' waiters in white jackets and a choice of menu! By and large we were resented though. While we were there Battle trained gunners were wanted for France and we all put in for it, but the collapse came before we got there."

During the early part of the war, weapons and equipment for the defence of airfields was at a premium and many weird and wonderful methods were employed as Albert Carty recalls.

"The defence of the base against possible airborne attack was supposed to be the NCO's with a Lewis gun and a pan of ammo each, plus a squad of eight airmen with pick axe handles. The CO had a Magister with a gun fixed for use as a fighter. A sergeant armourer, nicknamed 'Rocky', decided to make a mobile pillbox from an old lorry, steel plate and concrete. Come demonstration time the chassis had broken under the weight! Just after Dunkirk we had one Canadian Ross Rifle with six rounds and a plan with a machine gun post marked on it! In the event of an attack we were to round up the eight 'erks', see that we were issued with the rifle and clip of six and a bayonet and man the machine gun post. However, there were no rifles, pickaxe handles instead and no bayonets, the only four being on the main gate guard. There was also no machine gun post as there were no machine guns to spare. We did have instructions to charge any enemy left when we ran out of ammo!

During his time at Bassingbourn, Albert Carty's course had a four-week spell at No 5 BGS at Jurby on the Isle of Man. Jurby had opened as a grass airfield in 1939 and trained Observers at the BGS. By 1940 work had started on a tarmac runway utilising the 'deads' from the Laxey mines nearby for hardcore.

Part of Albert Carty's course at No 11 OTU Bassingbourn in 1940. Centre row, far left is Charlie Farnes from Manila. (A Carty)

"In between times we were attached to Jurby. A non-event and waste of time for us, only once firing from a Frazer Nash turret in a Wellington at a sea marker. Nobody was very interested. The one radar exercise with Aldergrove was a flop. After all the sweat and effort it transpired that the section we were supposed to be working with had been closed."

Albert's war almost ended at Jurby and was to cause something of a stir for one of his roommates at Bassingbourn.

"I had two 'pile ups' at Bassingbourn, both caused by failure to lower the undercarriage. On another occasion, on returning from Jurby, I saw a burnt out 'Wimpey' on the runway. When I went to our hut there was only one fellow there, reading on his bed. He turned white and was obviously shaken when I greeted him. I was said to have been in the wreck and he thought I was a ghost! I had been switched to another aircraft at the last minute."

Albert Carty almost fell out of a Wallace like this one. K3562 was the first of a batch of Mk I's delivered between January and March 1933 and served with AAEE, No 2 ATC, No 3 BGS, No 5 BGS and No 1 Ground Defence Gunnery School before being struck off charge on 3 June 1942. (GKN Westland)

Like many other aircrew he was later to be shot down on operations and meet his contemporaries 'in the bag' at a POW Camp.

> "At Bassingbourn the NCO in charge of ground gunnery training was Sgt 'Jock' Mathieson, who had a part-metal leg. I later met him in POW camp and despite calling me a 'little Sassenach B……..!' gave me a few pounds of camp money. When I was an 'erk' I must admit I overstepped the mark and had no complaints when put on a charge by him. We were jumped up to sergeant shortly afterwards and when I saw him in the Mess I was able to offer him a drink. A week or so later I called a group of 'erks' to attention whilst I saluted an approaching officer. The officer returned the salute with a smile – it was 'Jock', whose commission had come through."

In July 1940 the course was complete and the postings to squadrons came in. Albert Carty was posted to No 214 Sqn at Stradishall. He was told that 214 Sqn was there to replace No 218 Sqn, which had been completely wiped out.

Staff Pilot

NEVILLE COOPER – PILOT – 1939/45

Neville Cooper was one of that band of young men who decided to join the Royal Air Force Volunteer Reserve (RAFVR) before the outbreak of World War Two. This gave him a good grounding for what was about to transpire.

> " I joined up as a Sergeant Pilot RAFVR pre-war and did a two month ab-initio course on Tiger Moths at No 13 ERFTS, White Waltham in July and August 1937. After this I was attached to No 19 ERFTS at Gatwick with Hart variants until July 1939, then as I had moved from London to Dover to No 23 ERFTS at Rochester."

On the outbreak of war Neville was called up for full time service along with thousands of others. Conditions were initially somewhat chaotic, mainly due to shortages of accommodation, but also because the demands for fully trained pilots were outstripping the capability of the training organisation to provide them. Pilots were posted to operational units with little training and literally thrown in at the deep end.

> "On the outbreak of war I was called up to full time service and posted to No 3 AOS at Aldergrove as a Staff Pilot. I had the impression that this unit had just been moved from North Cotes near Grimsby. Aldergrove had so little accommodation that we all slept in a hangar. About three hundred all in neat rows of beds, until it rained, then you moved to catch the least drips. After a week or two we were moved into new huts.
>
> Most of the Staff Pilots were VR like myself and had not qualified for 'Wings' as we had done part time ground training but not taken the exams. We had also not completed the normal flying training; I had done 125 hours, well short of the normal 200. So we did a bit of conversion onto the units aircraft, Battles and Westland Wallaces, but then came to a halt as we could not take passengers, while the CO and OC Flying got stroppy with No 25 Group. For a time I was put in charge of a section amending Air Publications (AP)."

Shortly after this another group of VR pilots joined Neville's group having arrived by a rather circuitous route. They were destined not to stay for long and not many were to survive the war.

"Before Christmas we were joined by another group of about fifteen Sergeant Pilots who were also VR, but with 'Wings', which relieved the situation. They had seen a notice early in 1939 offering a fortnight's experience on a carrier (the RAF had a similar scheme for VR pilots to be attached to a regular squadron during the summer). They had put their names down but heard nothing until the outbreak of war. Then they were posted to the carrier HMS Argus, a bit of an old hulk, which took them from Portsmouth to the Mediterranean doing deck landings and so on. At the end of the course they were invited to transfer to the Fleet Air Arm and all said "NO – we have lived like pigs cooped up in the rating pilots quarters and don't fancy anymore." So three were offered commissions and two accepted and remained on board. The rest were dumped ashore at Marseilles with their fares to report back to the Air Ministry in London, whence they were posted to Aldergrove."

At long last there had been some activity at Aldergrove and Neville and his group became fully-fledged pilots.

"The name of the unit changed to No 3 BGS in February 1940 and in early April our 'Wings' were gazetted. I do not recall taking any exams but I think the CO was instructed to make his own assessment and recommendation. I always felt I had missed out on part of the training."

In May 1940 the fifteen previously 'Wing-ed' VR pilots departed. Only two were to survive from the group. Jim Pickering, one of the two, related their experiences to Neville in 1985.

"The 'carrier' group were posted to No 7 (Fighter) OTU at Hawarden. All except two survived the Battle of Britain in various squadrons, then in September 1940 they were collected together again back on the Argus. Equipped with Hurricanes they sailed for Gibraltar. Then they were taken for a couple of days steaming in the Mediterranean and flew off to Malta. They were the first reinforcements by this route. They had been told they were only to ferry the Hurricanes and a Sunderland would follow to pick up any that might ditch and would bring them all back to Gibraltar. The OC RAF Malta, Air Commodore Maynard who told them they were to be retained to reform No 261

Sqn, greeted them. So they remained and their numbers diminished until only two were left."

Shortly after this group departed Neville was posted too, but not to an operational unit. Neville was to remain in the training organisation for quite some time yet.

"I was posted in July 1940 to No 8 BGS at Evanton, near Invergordon, where I was put, to my disgust, in the Target Towing Flight. Then to add insult we were told the CO had an instruction from No 25 group that no application for posting to an operational squadron could be considered. We had Battles and Henley's and in twelve month I logged almost 500 hours towing. The other aircraft on the unit were Handley Page Harrows; I remember seeing one in the air with a spare engine fastened under the belly. This was a replacement for one that had force landed at Sumburgh. From the autumn of 1940 we had Polish pilots as staff pilots. They wore their own 'Wings'; an eagle made of a dull metal, possibly pewter. I was commissioned in December 1940 and in June 1941 the unit was re-designated No 8 AGS. At this time the Harrows were being replaced by Blackburn Bothas."

After a year at Evanton Neville was posted again, but yet again, he was denied a posting to an operational unit.

"In July 1941 I was posted to No 10 AGS at Castle Kennedy, which was just being formed. Another unit also being formed there was the Central Gunnery School (CGS). Castle Kennedy was a grass airfield and the whole unit lived under canvas. I had the luxury of a bed and a shared bell tent with another officer until the middle of December. We had an open slatted floor with grass growing through; the 'other ranks' had close boarded floors to sleep on (no bed) and eight or ten to a tent. The Mess marquee had a ditch around it to drain off the wet. SHQ moved into huts in September. Here I was a flight commander in charge of the Towing Flight with Lysanders, while the Gunnery Flights had ex-night fighter Defiants, all painted matt black. In November most of the AGS pilots wore gumboots rather than flying boots."

By December 1941 Neville was on the move again. No 10 AGS went to Barrow on Walney Island and Neville remained with them.

"I became flight commander of the two Defiant flights run together, because there was no one else with any experience. Such is the urgency of war. Most of the OC Flying and flight commanders in these

The pilots of No 10 AGS at RAF Castle Kennedy, November 1941.

Rear row, from left: ?, Sgt D Elliot RAAF; Sgt Walker RAAF; Sgt Burgess RAAF; Flt Sgt J Dasent RNZAF; Sgt Goulter RAAF; Sgt Austin RAAF; Next eight all Polish sergeants, Sgt Earuaker RNZAF; ?, Sgt Bilborough, Sgt Stark; ? ground staff sergeant.

Front row, from left: ?, Flt Sgt Ravenhill, Flt Sgt Wood, Fg Off ? ground staff, Flt Lt CP Thompson, Sqn Ldr PH Campbell, Plt Off Dean, Fg Off Trilsbach, Flt Sgt Robinson, Flt Sgt ? ground staff, Flt Sgt ground staff.
Most Poles wore their own 'Wings' but a few wore RAF 'Wings'. (NT Cooper)

units were too old for operational flying. I had four Defiants taking off every fifteen minutes all day, for a trip lasting thirty minutes for one gunner under training in the turret. It was not a very efficient set up as using the Defiant as attack aircraft meant that only one gunner could be taken up at a time, so we had a lot of pilots and aircraft. The engines were pretty 'clapped out' and one or two ditched on take off with fatal results. The pilots were mostly Polish, Australian and New Zealanders."

In October 1942 Neville found himself being sent back into the training system as a student. This training was to lead to a change of role and eventually to an operational unit, though not in a flying post.

"The CO, Wg Cdr Giles asked me if I would like to go on a Specialist Armament Course. I agreed and joined No 48 Course at No 1 Air

Castle Kennedy in October 1987. The hangars and technical site aligned along the wood. (Authors collection)

The pilots of No 10 AGS in 1941. (NT Cooper)

Armament School (AAS) at Manby in Lincolnshire. The course lasted five months, instead of the usual peacetime two years. The Armament Branch was a separate branch until sometime after the war and the Station Armament Officer reported direct to the Station Commander. The SAO was responsible for all bombs, guns, ammunition, turrets, bomb racks and other equipment such as gunsights, ranges etc. My course lasted from November 1942 to March 1943 and in April 1943 I was posted to yet another training unit- No 5 (O) AFU at Jurby, as Station Armament Officer (SAO). The nearest I got to bomb disposal was at Jurby. I was called out to the south end of the Isle of Man where the sea, at high tide, washed against some low cliffs and there was a sandy beach at low tide. The Coastguard said they were being cautious because a few weeks before a mine had washed ashore and people sat on it having their photos taken. Then, when the next tide came in and bumped it on the rocks, it blew up. All he had to offer me was a small red and yellow float down on the sand, which I happily assured him was harmless."

Five months later Neville was posted again and the possibility of an operational job drew nearer, but once again fate decreed that this was not to be. He had been posted to Blackpool to an Overseas Embarkation Unit but after three days was re-posted to HQ Bomber Command where he worked in the Armament Branch dealing with defect report on guns and turrets. Together with Fg Off Denham, who dealt with bombs and bombing equipment, he would fly to operational units and OTU's from time to time in the HQ Bomber Command Communications Flight Proctor. In March 1944 he was again posted, this time to Skellingthorpe in Lincolnshire, as the SAO. No 50 Sqn equipped with Lancasters was based there and shortly afterwards No 61 Sqn arrived. The station sent off forty-five Lancasters a night, four nights a week until D-Day when they started operating by day as well as night. Neville was frequently on duty for forty-eight hours at a stretch. After the excitement of an operational station during the heady period surrounding the D-Day landings and the aftermath, Neville was posted to No 20 OTU at Lossiemouth almost at the end of the war.

"I was posted to No 20 OTU in March 1945 as Chief Armament Instructor. No 20 OTU was controlled by No 6 Group in Bomber Command and supplied aircrew for the bomber offensive. There were two satellite airfields at Milltown and Bogs o' Mayne (Elgin). No 19

OTU was close by at Kinloss doing the same job. The aircraft were Wellingtons and Martinets were used for fighter attacks. There was a practice bombing range inland on some moorland about nine miles south of Nairn.

The set up of the school was that the Navigation leader and the Chief Armament Instructor reported direct to the OC Training Wing, a Wg Cdr. The CAI was responsible for all aspects of bombing and gunnery training, the station armoury, bomb dump and ranges, his deputies were the Bombing Leader, Gunnery Leader and Station Armament Officer, all Flt Lts.

The Bombing and Gunnery leaders prepared reports on the pupil's work at the end of each course and I submitted this to OC Training. The main job was to train pilots and navigators in night cross-country flying and there were some ground navigation trainers. The accommodation was in huts built in the expansion period pre-

No 20 OTU, Lossiemouth, showing the wartime layout of the airfield.

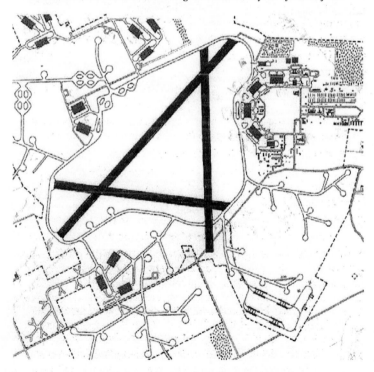

war, with central heating pipes running between the huts (it looked a bit like an oil refinery) and really quite comfortable. Three houses had been taken over in Lossiemouth village to provide accommodation for pupils and WAAF officers occupied another. The unit continued to operate until after VJ Day and then the last course was completed and the unit disbanded in August 1945."

With the closure of No 20 OTU, Neville found himself posted again. This would be his last unit.

"I was posted to No 17 OTU at Silverstone, also a bomber training unit, where I did the same job. Courses had been discontinued and there was, in fact, nothing to do. The instructors were busy making domestic furniture from the benches and tables. The said, 'The war is over and this equipment will be virtually given away in surplus sales. We are badly off for furniture as a result of the war, so why not be doing something useful?'"

Neville Cooper was demobbed from the release centre at Uxbridge in December 1945.

Guns & Radios – 2

H. DIXON – WOp/AG – 1943

After the surrender of Poland many Poles made their way via France and other European countries to Britain to carry on the fight against the Germans. Polish aircrews were trained mainly at No 18 (Polish) OTU at Bramcote. Dixon was one of these, but before arriving at OTU there was ITW, Signals School and AGS courses to get through.

> "I began in Blackpool as a wireless operator. Six or seven months of radio theory and Morse. There was theory and message procedures, sending and receiving in 'Q' codes, which one had to memorise. One important part of any message sent was the time, which was always included. In case one forgot the 'Q' code the WOp carried a codebook. This was the 'Bible'. There were also highly secret codes lasting only for a limited time, about 24 hours, after which they had to be destroyed. In an extreme case they were to be consumed! Practical Morse had to be passed so many words and figures at a certain speed. After a satisfactory ground test I was posted to Signals School.
>
> The Signals School aircraft were Dominies into which four pupils scrambled and performed communications exercises with a ground station on different frequencies. We passed messages for fifteen hours in the air and sixteen hours in the 'Harwell Box', a ground trainer. At the end of the course the instructor gave an estimated percentage pass and if you passed the next step was posting to a gunnery unit."

Dixon proceeded to No 8 AGS at Evanton, north east of Dingwall on the Cromarty Firth. The AGS operated the Blackburn Botha, which was universally loathed by the crews who flew them. The Botha was underpowered and had a reputation for crashes.

> "I was posted to the Air Gunners School at Evanton for practical gunnery training and weapons theory. The aircraft were Botha's and the targets were towed behind an aircraft. We flew camera gun sorties and did some air to ground firing – about 100 rounds. There were several other air to air exercises, firing about 1200 rounds in all. After three weeks the course finished and I was promoted to Sergeant and posted to OTU."

As with almost all the Poles destined for Bomber Command, Dixon was posted to No 18 (Polish) OTU based at Bramcote, situated north east of Coventry. No 18 OTU had been formed at Hucknall and moved to Bramcote equipped with Wellington Mks Ic and III, on 15th June 1940.

> "I was posted to 18 OTU at Bramcote flying Wellingtons. The WOp had the TR1034/1035 transmitter/receiver to operate. Most of the aircrew were strangers to each other and crewing up was like being in a poker game where each crewmember wished to be included in the winning hand. Once a crew was found they had a feeling of being a family and, above all, very dependant on each other. Bound to each other in their duties and for their survival.
>
> The OTU syllabus was wide ranging and was carried out to the letter. The pilot and the WOp would fly several circuits and landings to get familiar with the aircraft and the airfield then the rest of the crew would join for the rest of the exercises. Instrument flying, low level flying, overshooting, SBA, fighter affiliation and bombing by day and night. Dinghy drill, cross-country flying day and night and so on. When all the exercises were completed satisfactorily the crew were posted to an operational squadron. After the OTU training the crews were keen to join the 'Game of War'."

Dixon and his crew were posted to No 305 (Polish) Sqn at Ingham in Lincolnshire and carried out their first operation, to Hamburg, on the night of 29/30 July 1943. This was the third operational raid on the city in what became known as the 'Battle of Hamburg'. 777 aircraft

The cannon and machine gun range at Ingham on 1995. (Authors collection)

took part in the raid and twenty-eight were lost. Dixon was not to remain with this crew, however, or to share their fate.

"After this trip I caught a nasty cold and lost my voice. The camp doctor gave me some medicine for the cold but could not bring my voice back so I was grounded for a few days. On the night of 3/4th August 1943 the target was Hamburg again. I was still grounded so another WOp flew with my crew. They were posted missing. I was terribly upset and felt like an orphan.

After a few days I was called in to see the CO. He asked me to remain in the squadron as a spare WOp. I refused and suggested that I go back to OTU to join a new crew. The CO was surprised but at the same time I could see that he was relieved of the anguish of losing one of his crews and partly solving my personal grief for my crew. The

Bramcote. No 18 (Polish) OTU moved here
from Hucknall in June 1940.

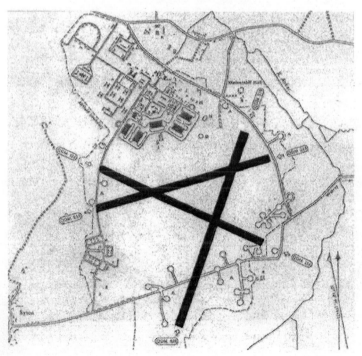

same day I packed my belongings and the CO personally flew me back to Bramcote and 18 OTU."

Dixon joined his new crew at Bramcote and they all received a surprise near the end of their course.

"The new crew I joined had two more night cross-country exercises to finish the course. We did one flying from England to Wales to Scotland and back. The second, to our surprise, was an operation to Boulogne. The Boulogne operation was more or less the same as a cross-country but this time over the Channel, plus flak, searchlights and night fighters. We found the target with no problem, without markers either. Three days later we were with No 305 Sqn."

After five operations on Wellingtons with No 305 Sqn Dixon's second crew were split up. The crew was posted to Italy and Dixon and the rest of the squadron went to Blyton to convert to Halifaxes then Lancasters. Eventually Dixon joined the newly formed No 300 (Polish) Sqn.

Dixon (4th from left) and crew prepare for the raid on Kiel on 23/24 July 1944. The aircraft is Lancaster BH-B of No 300 (Masovian) Sqn which converted to Lancasters in March 1944. (H Dixon)

Guns & Radios – 3

CHARLES HUGHES – WOp/AG – 1942/43

Charles Hughes joined the RAF as a WOp/AG and after completing the wireless operators course at No 1 Signals School at Cranwell was posted to Calshot as a ground operator whilst waiting for a gunnery course.

> "I did a little flying at Cranwell in Percival Proctors and Vickers Valentias, known to us as the 'Flying Pig'. I did no flying at all at Calshot, as the station was only a flying boat maintenance unit. I moved from Calshot to No 2 Signals School at Yatesbury for a refresher course and did a little flying on De Havilland DH86B's, Ansons and Dragon Rapides."

After passing the refresher course Hughes was posted to Evanton situated in Alness Bay for a gunnery course.

> "My gunnery course took in pyrotechnics and so on and I did quite a bit of flying in Whitley's and Blackburn Botha's. The Botha's were real killers and everyone hated flying in the things. However, having become a fully blown Sergeant WOp/AG, I went off via some home leave to my next posting at Harwell."

Harwell, with its three concrete runways, was the home of No 15 OTU, equipped with Wellingtons. When Charles Hughes arrived it was operating two satellite airfields at Hampstead Norris and Mount Farm. Both of these airfields had concrete runways in the familiar triangular pattern.

> "I never went near Mount Farm. In fact I only ever saw the place from the air. After some checks and the changing of some items of flying gear at Harwell my course went off to Hampstead Norris where we completed our OTU. This was made up of 'circuits and bumps', cross-country flights, dummy bomb runs and gunnery practice out to sea. We were using mostly well run in Wellington Mk Ia's with the long window down the fuselage and two single .303 Browning gun positions half way along the fuselage. The Vickers Gas Operated (VGO) gun had just about been phased out of the OTU and we were 100% Brownings."

Charles Hughes and his crew were just finishing the course at the time that 'Bomber' Harris began the series of '1000 Bomber raids' against Germany.

"When the third one, to Bremen, came up my crew were briefed for the raid. I will always remember building a scaffold to stand on for the crew to help the ground staff spread a dark khaki coloured de-icing paste all over the leading edges of the wings and tailplane. I don't really know why we bothered. We were briefed to fly at 16,000 feet but our old 'Wimpey' hung on its props a 7,500 feet and we had to bomb at that height. We were bombed up with six cans of incendiaries and when looking through the inspection window one can only see the

Hampstead Norris was used by No 15 OTU from 1940 till 1944.

end of the canister and it is not possible to tell if the bombs had dropped or not.

We lost an engine on the return trip and had to force land at Coltishall – or so we thought. In fact, when we landed, we found we were at Horsham St Faith. When the bomb doors were opened it was discovered that the three canisters of bombs on the port side had hung up and we had been to Bremen to drop only half a load of bombs. We had expected to go on more raids from Hampstead Norris, but no, we were shipped back to Harwell, given tropical kit and sent off on seven days leave."

On returning from leave Charles Hughes and his crew had a surprise in store for them.

"When we returned from leave we were given a brand new Wellington Mk X to take to Portreath in Cornwall where it was filled up with spares and we were off to Gibraltar. The aircraft was the first to be fitted with torpedo dropping equipment. The Wellington was 'P for Peter' and our callsign for the trip was 'Tablet'. We overshot at Gibraltar and had to go round again to avoid going into the sea. The short runway had not by then been extended into the sea. We stayed for twenty-four hours at Gibraltar while they put overload tanks on board for a direct run to LG224, twenty-six kilometres from Cairo. We never saw 'P for Peter' again. We went by road to Almaza near Cairo then off to Kabrit on the edge of the Great Bitter Lake and 148 Sqn."

Charles Hughes survived a crash landing on his first operation with 148 Sqn and went on to complete thirty-eight operations with the squadron. He later returned to England to become an instructor at No 16 OTU.

Torpedoes at Turnberry

FRED EYRE – WOp – 1940/43

Fred Eyre began his wartime service by being conscripted into the Army but after a time he saw an opportunity to transfer to the RAF and began a long journey through the training system which would eventually take him to operations in the Middle East.

"I was conscripted into the Army in June 1940 for a new battalion, the 7th Buffs (Royal East Kents) formed at Maidenhead. In early September we were put on a troop train bound for Cornwall. We were stuck all night in Newton Abbot marshalling yard while an air raid went on. We eventually arrived at St Germans, where we were taken by lorry to an old fort. We weren't allowed out of the place, mind you I don't think there was anywhere to go. After a few days there, around the 14th or 16th of September, waves of German bombers were flying over. We realised they were on their way to Bristol Docks.

That night there was panic, we were issued with a rifle (mine was a 1914 lee Enfield) and a bandoleer of fifty rounds of .303. When it got dark I was taken by the Sergeant Major out of the fort, down a sharp incline and put into a trench, which had a Bren gun in it. I was told to stay there. I hadn't a clue where I was, it was too dark. The road up to the fort must have been a little below because a couple of times what looked like a 15cwt army truck came along it. I was cold and miserable and the night never ending.

The sight I saw when dawn came I have never forgotten. I was looking out over Plymouth Sound. Early in 1941 in Battalion Orders was an order asking for RAF pilots. I think there were eighty of us put our names down. We all went to Exeter to face RAF officers, who asked us questions. I can remember one asking me what my father did for a living. I couldn't see then or now, what the point of the question was. I told him – packer. One asked me what that was and I said – packing parcels. I think I really stumped them there.

After that we were told that thirty of us would be going up to Oxford for physical, mental and health checks. It was great. I had some decent food and a night sleeping on a proper bed. I had only slept on the floor on a straw palliase since going into the Army. On battalion orders for 26th May 1941 it had – Transfer to the RAF, Stratford on Avon, No 9 Receiving Wing. There were five of us listed.

We were brought before the CO a week before we went. He told us if we weren't interested in the Army he didn't want us, he didn't even wish us luck. I was a week at Stratford, getting kitted out and was issued a RAF number. After a week of luxury, with sheets on the bed and eating off china plates, I was off to ITW at Aberystwyth, where we were billeted in the Queens Hotel. We did navigation, maths, Air Force Law, health and Hygiene and meteorology at the university. We were there about a month and were given leave at the end of the course and I got married before going on to EFTS."

Fred was posted to No 6 EFTS at Desford. Desford had a satellite airfield at Braunstone, a grass airfield operating Tiger Moths. This was a small unit with only 126 officers and men occupying the former flying club airfield.

"Arrival at Desford saw me posted off to its satellite at Braunstone. We were told that five hours instruction should be enough to go solo. This

Fred Eyre's Logbook for Sep/Oct 1942 at No 2 Signals School. (Fred Eyre)

was on Tiger Moths. I had a Polish sergeant for an instructor and I always had difficulty understanding him speaking over the voice tube. The first flight of Air Experience, I remember well. Right and left hand spins, loops and stalling the aircraft, which was a slow as 40kts. Anyhow, the instructor wasn't very pleased with me and I then found myself with an Indian Pilot Officer, turban and all. My first trip with him was a disaster. Climbing into the Moth with my helmet on, the speaking tube end connection hung down and as I stepped onto the wing I trod on the end. I got into the cockpit and the tube would not fit into the hole, it was more oval than round. I spent the next few minutes biting it, squeezing it, and trying to get it to fit.

In the front cockpit the Indian was going mad. I could see his arms going up in the air. He beckoned the groundcrew over, who came to my rescue and got it to fit. I think that incident numbered my day as a trainee pilot. I lost my confidence and I lived in awe of that Indian. As a twenty-one year old I never had the strength of character to stick two fingers up to him. At five hours instruction I went up with the CFI. He was a nice chap and told me to take him on a 'circuit and bump'. It all went so well and the landing was a dream. Actually, I thought he had taken over control a few times.

When we landed he climbed out, took off his helmet and said, "Nice landing, but I don't think you knew much about it." He took me to his office and said he couldn't recommend me to go on. Did I want to go back to the Army, or try for another part of aircrew? A couple of days later he told me I would be going to Blackpool for training as a WOp/AG. Two of our five came with me to Braunstone. One stalled his Tiger moth on his solo at sixty feet. It all fell apart around him. He came out of it with minor injuries. The other chap was sick on his first few flights and used to land looking like death. He went solo in four hours and was posted to single engine advanced training. Probably became a fighter pilot."

Having failed to make the grade as a pilot Fred was destined for training as a Wireless operator and took a sideways step in the aircrew world which led him to Initial Wireless Training at an ITW in Blackpool.

"Blackpool was the intake for WOp's to be. The course lasted three months and was mainly to sort out if the individual was capable of reading and sending Morse code at high speeds. The training took place in the tram sheds towards the South Shore. Friday we were marched to Burtons where there was a Test Room. The tests took plain language and code, which was a mixture of letters and numerals. Each

RESULTS OF AB INITIO COURSES AND REMARKS

RESULTS OF AB INITIO GUNNERY COURSE.

STATION HELD...... No.10 A.G.S.....BARROW......
PERIOD OF COURSE 25.10.42.......TO 31.10.42.

EXERCISE.	Rounds Fired.	% Hits.	Type of Aircraft.
25 Yds.Range.	100.	N/A	N/A
200 Yds. Range.	200.	N/A	TURRET.
400 Yds.Range.	200.	N/A	– do –
BEAM.R.S	200	NIL	
Cine Footage.	37½ Ft	N/A	DEFIANT
TRACER DEM.	200	N/A	"
BE.M.	200	17.0	"
BEAM R.S.T.	200	6.0	"
Q.X.U.T.	200	5.0	"
Air to Sea		N/A	"

EXAM MARKS. 81.50 %.

FLYING TIME. ....Hrs. 4...30.Mins.

REMARKS: PASS/FAIL.

Carriage

O.C. TRAINING WING.

The final result certificate pasted into Fred Eyre's logbook at No 10 AGS.
(F Eyre)

week the speed was stepped up and by the end of the course twelve words a minute, sending and receiving, was the pass rate. I remember doing some Semaphore training and a little with the Aldis lamp. Otherwise, we were mainly on drill and marching up and down the seafront and Stanley Park. On bad weather days PT was in the Tower Ballroom and 'pep talks' were given in the Winter gardens. We were all billeted out with the landladies of Blackpool, mostly in Hemby Road, a long road full of young AC's. The famous footballer, Stanley Matthews, was a PT Instructor there and Max Wall, the comedian, was a 'Discip' sergeant."

Basic wireless training over it was time for Fred to move on to a specialist Signals School for further training. He was posted to No 2 Signals School at Yatesbury in Wiltshire. Yatesbury was a pre-war training depot and at this stage of the war was a major training unit with almost 8,000 staff, instructor and pupils on strength and a grass airfield operating De Havilland Dominies and Percival Proctors.

"We now got down to the serious stuff regarding wireless. We had theory, history and practical lessons. I found the three months here very absorbing. Very little time wasting, the occasional PT session being the only interlude. The instructors seemed to be very good and managed to make some boring lecture quite interesting. We had very little leisure time, though there was a cinema on the camp. No leave was granted, but some of us sneaked away on Saturday evenings, hitched a lift into London, came back by train to Calne on Sunday evening, dodging the Military Police at the stations. One of the instructors was Flt Sgt John Hannah, who was awarded the VC in 1940. At the end of the course we were awarded our Wireless Badge and made up to LAC. We now had to get six months experience on a ground station before we went on to flying."

Having mastered the intricacies of Wireless training Fred was now ready to commence flying training. The RAF, however, had other ideas and sent trainees at this stage to other units to gain wireless operating experience.

"Early 1942 at the finish of my Wireless Course at Yatesbury I was posted to Cottesmore near Oakham for ground experience before going on a flying wireless course. Cottesmore was an OTU operating with Whitley's and Hampdens. My arrival at the main gate coincided with the funeral of a crew killed a few days previous. During my stay there this seemed a regular feature, with a Flt Sgt whose slow march in front of the funeral was a regular sight. The Hampdens seemed to take a heavy toll. The first 1,000 Bomber Raid (on Cologne) took place – every serviceable aircraft on the station was to take part in the operation. Much consternation was seen when the instructors were informed they would be crewing the aircraft with OTU trainees filling the vacant places. Many had to beg, borrow or steal flying equipment, having lost or mislaid theirs. Many never made the target for various reasons but the propaganda effect of putting up 1,000 aircraft for a raid had been achieved."

This was followed by periods at Boscombe Down and Clyffe Pypard, a glider pilot training unit, where the glider pilots flew Tiger Moths prior to going on to an AFU. Fred then returned to Yatesbury and finally flying training.

"I was posted back to Yatesbury for my flying course and flew fourteen trips in the Dominie on various exercises including tuning, DF bearing and homing and air experience flights. The Dominie carried several students at a time each taking a turn at the key. The Proctors took one operator working for the whole sortie. From here it was off to Gunnery School."

The next step for the now proficient WOp was to become a proficient gunner and Fred was posted to the north west of England, to Walney Island near Barrow. This was home to No 10 AGS and a grim place.

"My first thoughts when posted to 10 AGS at Walney Island in November 1942, on a cold grey day, was what a depressing place it was. The Vickers submarine yards on view crossing the bridge seemed to add to the greyness. The cold is something I do remember, of trying to keep warm in the Nissen huts. The first sight of the airfield was equally depressing, with a huge slagheap at the end of the runway. The training aircraft were Defiants, which hadn't inspired much confidence in the RAF. To me they seemed cumbersome and landings used to be so heavy. Most of the gunnery course was taken up with theory and using turrets positioned around the place. The ground training was quite good with working models of electrical, hydraulic and air systems of gun turrets.

Arrival at dispersal for my first air firing was greeted with the fact a Defiant could not lower its wheels and was flying around to use up fuel before coming in for a belly landing. Eventually it came in and made a perfect crash landing. The noise was alarming; it sounded like scrap metal being tipped from a great height. When the two occupants climbed out and 'legged it' 'way from the aircraft a little cheer went up from the onlookers. The dent in my confidence soon faded after my initial trip and I enjoyed the flights over the Lake District. The air time of four hours and thirty minutes was inadequate. It is an entirely different situation operating a turret when the aircraft is banking and diving, than a stationary one. The course consisted of eight flights of various flying exercises, four of them being made on the same day. The longest flight being forty minutes. The living conditions consisted of Nissen huts with a wood burning stove in the middle of the hut. I can remember sleeping in my greatcoat there because of the cold. Course finished we were then wore the AG brevet."

On completion of the gunnery course the WOp's on Fred's course were required to complete more ground training on radar. This was very much to Fred's liking as the course was in London.

Barrow airfield situated on Walney Island was home to No 10 AGS.

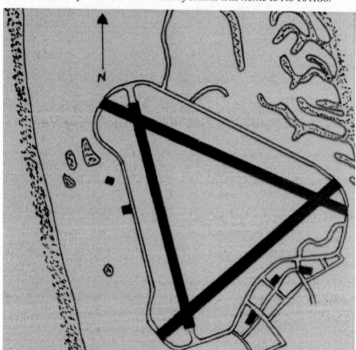

"It was now on to a Radar course at the Victoria and Albert Museum in South Kensington. This involved theory of radar and getting familiar with the equipment before operation ASV sets at the next stage. The two weeks at the Victoria and Albert Museum were a nice diversion for me. Although billeted in some flats near South Kensington station I went home to my wife every evening in Enfield. We had only been married eighteen months but had seen little of each other. It was like having a city job. The museum had been cleared of all the exhibits and one of the galleries had all the radar equipment init. It was known as SE (Special Equipment) but later known as ASV (Air to Surface Vessel). We were given a good grounding in radar with a written exam at the conclusion. We were now promoted to the rank of Sergeant and it was off to Hooton Park."

Hooton Park was the base of No 11 Radio School, equipped with Blackburn Botha's. The airfield had been established in 1917 as an RFC station and between the wars was used for civil aviation until the 1930's when a unit of the Auxiliary Air Force was formed there. This was the first of several RAF units to use the airfield until the arrival of No 3 Radio School from Prestwick at the end of 1942. Shortly afterward the school was renumbered No 11 and was well established by the time Fred Eyre arrived for ASV radar training in January 1943.

"At Hooton Park we operated the set on Botha's. There were about half a dozen pupils to each aircraft, taking turns working the sets. This was mainly over the Mersey and Liverpool Bay area. I found myself quite proficient with the sets and could identify the 'blips', whether port or starboard quite readily. I found it very interesting, so that helped, others found it boring. The airfield was grass and we were billeted in a large house, which we used a coach to get to and from. I was assessed a scoring 67%/66%/66% which I was told was highest on my course. We now would be going to Coastal Command. I think we were all happier knowing that."

Following ASV training it was on to yet another Radio School, No 10 RS, at Carew Cheriton. The school operated Oxford's and Anson's and supplied WOp's for OTU's. Whilst there Fred flew in both types and completed over thirty two hours as WOp, practising homings and fixes.

"This small airfield just outside Tenby, Pembrokeshire, beside Carew Castle and its lake was unlike any RAF camp I had ever been on. There was a relaxed atmosphere. We did more flying here and all the daylight hours seemed to be filled. I can only remember leaving the camp once to go to Tenby. We had quite a lot of air operating experience and I think we left there a much more confident bunch of WOp's."

With the course at No 10 RS completed Fred was now ready for operational training. To complete this he moved to No 7 OTU at Limavady in Ulster. He was placed in No 2 Sqn of the OTU and completed over seventeen hours of operational training with his crew. Limavady had housed operational Coastal Command squadrons previously and was well equipped with three concrete runways, several large hangars and accommodation, dispersed to the south and south east of the airfield, housing up to 2,500 staff and pupils.

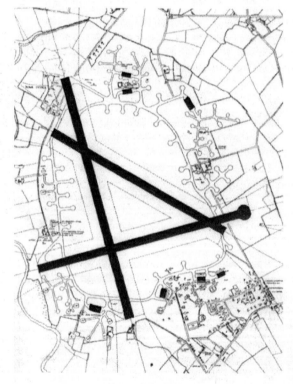

No 7 OTU utilised Limavady for it's Wellingtons.

"Limavady, situated not very far from Lough Foyle with a backdrop of the Donegal Mountains, was a Wellington OTU. Within a couple of days there was a gathering of pilots, navigators and WOps. We were all collected in a large room, going around chatting, trying to spot a pilot who inspired confidence or a long life. I spotted a tall, thin pilot with handlebar moustache, a good deal older than I. It turned out he was twenty-nine and had done a part tour on Leigh Light 'Wimpey's' at Chivenor. We seemed to take to each other and he asked me if I would be his WOp. We then went around and found a second pilot, navigator and two more WOp/AG's. It was a good choice because I spent the next eighteen months to two years with him. We did one navigational trip out to Rockall on a very nasty day and night with gales and very heavy rain. I recall one nasty crash when a Wellington took off and went straight up before stalling and going down with a huge explosion which killed the pilot and the instructor. The

The technical site and hangars at Limavady in October 1993.
(Authors collection)

Wellingtons were early types, which needed a lot of maintenance. As a crew we were sent to Belfast harbour to go aboard a Dutch merchant ship to talk tactics on attacking shipping with the captain and crew. I remember a lot of Dutch gin being drunk aboard."

The operational training course over, Fred and his crew moved to No 1 Torpedo Training Unit for specialist training in over water operations and torpedo and low level bombing. No 1 TTU was based at Turnberry on the West Coast of Scotland, just south of Ayr. Turnberry had been a First World War training base and then fell into disuse. Used as an AA landing ground in the 1930's it returned to RAF service in February 1942. No 1 TTU was formed there in January 1943 and five months later Fred and his crew commenced training there.

"We now knew what operational aircraft we were going on. We were surprised to find the aircraft were Wellingtons and never knew they operated as night torpedo bombers. There were concrete runways laid along the old golf course at Turnberry and Nissen huts for

No 1 TTU operated from Turnberry on the Clyde Coast south of Ayr

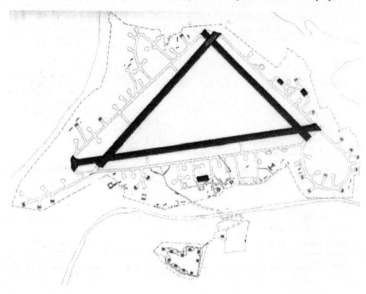

accommodation. The Clubhouse being Officers and aircrew messes. We were an all NCO crew, which made socialising much easier. The pilot had to gain experience of calculating the height of the aircraft above the sea, which meant flying at 60 feet to release the torpedo at 600 yards from the target. The airspeed had to be kept between 140 – 160 kts. At sixty feet the waves could be picked out but the trouble began on a calm glassy sea and on a moonlit night even more dicey. Two crews on our course went straight into the sea on such nights. They just disappeared. All this took place over the Clyde area near Ailsa Craig We also now knew that we would not be operating in the UK. It was the Middle East or Far East for us. Rumours were going galore. We were a pretty efficient crew, the captain and navigator were seven or eight years older that the rest of us and we did have a bit of respect for those older than ourselves. We finished the course and were told we would be sent on embarkation leave and informed where to report to whilst at home."

Fred Eyre's logbook for the course at Talbenny. (F Eyre)

Date	Hour	Aircraft Type and No.	Pilot	Duty	Remarks (including results of bombing, gunnery, exercises, etc.)
		WELLINGTON			
30-7-43	15.30	HZ 142	F/Lt DONATI	GUNNER	AIR TEST.
30-7-43	16.15	HZ 142	F/Sgt. KEYMER	GUNNER	LOCAL FLYING
3-8-43	10.20	HZ 142	F/Lt DONATI	WoP	HEAVY LOAD TAKE OFF
3-8-43	1050	HZ 142	F/Sgt. KEYMER	WoP	H.L.T.O., CONSUMPTION TRIALS, AIRSWING
6-8-43	1100	HZ 142	"	"	S.E. OPERATOR	AIR TEST
6-8-43	2030	HZ 142	"	"	"	NAVIGATIONAL EXERCISE "
9-8-43	1755	HZ 142	"	"	WoP	ANTI SUB PATROL
11-8-43	1035	HZ 142	"	"	WoP	CONSUMPTION TRIALS
13-8-46	1100	HZ 142	"	"	GUNNER	" "
15-8-43	15.50	HZ 142	"	"	S.E. OPERATOR	" "

SUMMARY FLYING FOR JULY 1943
SUMMARY FLYING FOR AUGUST 1943
SIGNED .... F/L
TOTAL FLYING HOURS AT 303 F.T.U.

SIGNED ....

In preparation for a move to the Middle or Far East it was necessary for crews to be trained in long range navigation over water and the techniques for maximising fuel consumption on long flights. This training was carried out by Fred and his crew at Talbenny in Wales. Talbenny was the airfield occupied by No 303 Ferry Training Unit, which flew its Wellingtons down from Stornoway in March 1943 to take over the station. Fred and his crew arrived there in mid-July 1943 to complete the last stage of training prior to flying out to an overseas operational squadron.

"I was informed by telegram to report to 303 FTU at Talbenny, near Haverfordwest, Talbenny had only recently become a ferry training unit having previously been a Coastal Command Czech squadron operating base. The runway practically finished at the cliff edge with St Davids Cathedral not far off the flight path. I have pleasant memories of the place because my wife came and stayed in Haverfordwest for a couple of weeks. These were our last days together for three years.

We all arrived within twenty-four hours to be introduced to a new Wellington, which we had to knock into shape, before taking it through to the Middle East. This involved fuel consumption trials, compass swinging, testing everything aboard the aircraft. We even did an anti-submarine patrol to the Bay of Biscay during trials. On the 17th of August 1943 we loaded our kit on the aircraft then took off for Hurn, near Bournemouth. After loading with stores and overload tanks on 19th August we took off for North Africa. It was a ten hour ten minute flight with headwinds all the way and fuel running very low. My radio training paid off, using the DF beam to Ras el Ina, near Fez, flying straight in without a circuit."

After a tour of ops with 38 Sqn Fred Eyre went to a ferry unit based in Morocco followed by a posting as Signals Briefing Officer as Bishra and Catania.

The 'Paddy' Train

D.J. 'JIM' DAVIS – AG – 1944

Jim Davis completed his air gunnery training at the windswept and desolate Castle Kennedy airfield in the south west of Scotland in 1944. His story of the kindness of the locals and the perils of crossing the path of the Discip Staff is brief but interesting.

"I was at No 3 AGS at Castle Kennedy in 1944. It was a desolate place, not surprisingly, with the fleshpots of Stranraer being some eight miles away. We stayed on camp most evenings, though we did have on diversion to break the boredom. The campsite bordered the Stranraer to Glasgow railway line. We made quite a few contacts on the trains when the Boat Train, which we called the 'Paddy Train' was held up by the local signal. People would throw us sandwiches, cigarettes and so on. The engine drivers were best. They would push off coal from the tender and supply us with a fire bucket of hot water (then a luxury).

On completion of the course the newly promoted sergeant Air Gunners would be entrained for leave. The train would be sprayed by stirrup pump whenever they, or anyone else, appeared at the windows. We even caught 'Groupie' once! However, our fun was brought to an end by the appearance of Cpl (Discip) Bater. It was a bad thing to cross his path at any time. Came the day when we too were seated on that train. Our departure was quiet but we noted with satisfaction, Cpl Bater with a black eye and cap perched on top of a bandaged head, having fallen from his cycle two nights previously. The train drew away, we closed the window, a more deadly game yet to come."

"Which Way To The Target"

D.H. DARNEY – PILOT – 1941/1945

In the first few years of the war many men in training had their courses shortened or completely missed out courses in order that the losses in aircrew on the operational squadrons could be quickly replaced. Other men found themselves destined to become trapped in the training system for long periods, either because of the move of flying training units en masse to Canada, or because they were retained in Flying Training Command as instructors after their training. DH Darney was one of these men, destined not to see an operational squadron until the war was over. He commenced his training in 1941 at Lords cricket ground.

> "I joined the RAF at Lords on 7th July 1941. We stayed in requisitioned luxury flats around Regents Park; however, we were not living well. We slept on hair mattresses on the floor for three weeks. The food we ate in the Zoo canteen was disgusting. More people watched us queuing for the food than those who watched the animals! After this ITW at Babbacombe in Devon was heaven for six weeks, in spite of the spartan conditions."

On completion of ITW, Darney was posted to No 22 EFTS at Cambridge, which was run by Marshalls of Cambridge using civilian instructors in RAF uniform.

> "We lived in requisitioned new houses just outside the airfield with nothing on the floor and very few amenities. Food was fair apart from carrots twice daily – I was due to go to night fighters. We did our day flying training at Bottisham, five miles east of Cambridge airfield. We shared the field with and Army Co-operation squadron of Tomahawks and Lysanders. We were only there a few days when we watched a Tomahawk do a flat spin. He went in nose first. We were told the pilot lived but lost both legs. On my second solo I saw the 'Blood Wagon' pull out near the landing area. I thought I must have undercarriage trouble, like the day previous when an instructor returned, but it was only because of the high winds.
>   We were training in Tiger Moths and flew in weather which would make people nowadays shudder. No vis, very low cloud base and high

winds. Owing to the SFTS's falling behind on courses our time at EFTS was extended from the planned seven weeks until 13th January 1942. During that time I did 135 hours including over fourteen hours at night. I actually had more night flying hours than some of the new instructors. Night flying was carried out at Caxton Gibbet. While at 22 EFTS there was still the threat of invasion and through this I did six low-level bombing trips. We, on the senior course, plus the instructors would have been used to carry six small bombs, three under each wing. On the training trips we flew below the level of the Fens and only found the target three times. That included an instructor landing at an anti-aircraft site and 'asking the way'!"

After two weeks leave Darney was posted to the Pool Flight of No 17 EFTS at Peterborough to hold. No 17 EFTS was equipped with Tiger Moths and had moved to Peterborough from North Luffenham on 15th July 1941.

"On Pool we were only able to fly at lunchtimes. I only did five hours. It was at the time that the Scharnhorst and Gneisenau made their dash up the Channel and on going to the airfield in the morning we saw a Hampden which had broken the back of a steamroller. The nose did the damage. On the airfield itself was a 'Wimpey', bombs on board, with one wheel bent. After a few weeks it was off on leave, then on the boat to Canada."

On arrival in Canada Darney proceeded to No 42 SFTS at Weyburn, Saskatchewan, where he survived a mid-air collision whilst effecting a formation change with another student. From there he moved to No 3 FIS at Armprior, Ontario where he trained as an instructor prior to an instructional posting to No 32 EFTS, Bowden, Alberta, following this with a further posting to yet another training unit, No 37 SFTS at Calgary as an instructor. He finally managed to escape from his round of instructional postings in September 1944 when he was posted back to the UK for yet more training at No 29 EFTS, Clyffe Pypard.

"I arrived at Clyffe Pypard on 7th September 1944 to 'learn how to fly in English weather' – on Tigers! I was there when Arnhem was on. A 'Dak' diverted from Lyneham full of wounded. I went to the aircraft and asked if the boys would like tea from the NAAFI wagon, which was nearby. The NAAFI girl refused to supply it and I was just about to pay for it myself (only about five shillings (25p) for the whole aircraft load at 1 ½ d (less than 1p) a cup). Just then 'WingCo' Flying arrived and the tea was provided."

Just over a month later Darney was posted to No 12 (P) AFU at Grantham. He did his flying from Harlaxton, Grantham's satellite, and was also accommodated there. Whilst he was there one incident occurred from which the student was lucky to escape.

"We flew Oxfords and Blenheims at the AFU and we flew with the top canopies of the Blenheim removed. One day one of the course, whilst flying in the circuit, found himself in mid-air with no aircraft, so he pulled his ripcord and landed safely near the mess. A crew from 2 ATA was ferrying up another aircraft and collided with him. They were killed."

A Tiger Moth at a training unit in Canada. Canadian Tigers were fitted with a cockpit canopy due to the adverse weather conditions encountered there, though the shape will be instantly recognisable to all who trained on this ubiquitous aircraft. (WD Park)

The mood at Harlaxton was not all 'doom and disaster' though and as with all service units there was humour to be found, both on and off duty.

"One evening the staff took on our course in a beer drinking competition. One person beat everyone – SHE just opened her mouth and a pint of beer disappeared. In January 1945 the AFU moved over to Hixon in Staffordshire and my last job was flying a Blenheim over there. I was then posted to OTU."

Darney was posted to No 51 OTU at Cranfield in Bedfordshire. It seemed that the long road to an operational night fighter squadron, which he had started out on at EFTS, was almost at an end, but this was not to be.

"I was posted to No 51 OTU and a Mosquito night fighter course. In the last few weeks of the war the course was posted to squadrons – but not me. My navigator went sick. Instead I went out on a bicycle each afternoon and slept in a haystack."

Whilst on a night trip at 51 OTU Darney almost became the victim of the 'friendly' defence of London.

"I was directed by radar, solo and unarmed, at 5,000 feet over London. I could see our own aircraft flying with nav lights on and above me the Germans dropping their last few bombs near the Thames. Every searchlight, it seemed, was shining on me!

My nav returned to duty and shortly after the war in Europe ended. I was away from camp for this but the boys who lived too far away to go home told me it was impossible to cross the sports field from our quarters as everyone was celebrating the end of the war. After a week or two the navigators on the course were interviewed and eight were selected for a special squadron in Burma. The rest of us went to 54 OTU."

No 54 OTU was based at Charterhall near Duns and was another night fighter training unit. Just as he arrived Darney was given a classic example of the 'Don't do as I do, do as I tell you' attitude found in some quarters of the RAF.

"On arrival at Charterhall we read Station Routine Orders and saw that the CO was speaking to the airmen in the cinema and the 'Queen Bee' (OC WAAF) was talking to the WAAF about their 'sleeping' out in the fields. A day or two later the 'Queen Bee' came into the mess. She had her tunic over her arm and her skirt was green from top to bottom!

One day a friend and I went up in separate aircraft for a height climb sortie. He lost his port engine at 14,000 feet, feathered the prop, and let down. I got to 17,000 feet and lost my starboard. On final approach I intended landing to the right of the runway but the crosswind pushed me to port and I did a perfect landing on the runway. It was not allowed to feather the prop and 'WingCo' Tech was in a temper with us. He never apologised when it was discovered that the aircraft involved were limited to 10,000 feet."

The war in Asia ended before Darney completed the course and he finally reached an operational squadron at Church Fenton after the war, having spent five years either training or instructing.

Invergordon 'Boats'

PETER FRIZELL – PILOT – 1940/1945

Peter Frizell joined the RAAF in August 1940 and after 'square bashing' was posted to Southern Rhodesia to learn to fly. His was the first course from Australia to do so. After learning to fly on Tiger Moths and Harvards he was posted to a general reconnaissance course at George in South Africa. A posting followed this to Invergordon in Scotland and training on flying boats. He converted by way of Saro Londons to Sunderlands between November 1941 and January 1942. He was posted to No 210 Sqn at Castle Archdale on Lough Erne in Northern Ireland. After serving as a second pilot for some time he was posted in June 1942 to Wig bay, near Stranraer in Scotland, a detachment of No 4 (Coastal) OTU, for the first part of Captain training. The course then took him back to Invergordon until training was completed in August 1942. At this point he was posted back to Lough Erne and No 423 Sqn RCAF. The squadron was just forming with a mixed composition of RAF, RAAF and RCAF crews. He completed a tour of operations with 423 Sqn and was then posted back to Invergordon as an instructor in October 1943.

"No 4 (Coastal) OTU was probably one of the lesser known OTUs, being devoted to flying boats. I was there on three occasions – Initial Conversion, Captain Training and as an instructor. Situated as it was in a rather remote part of Scotland it was a little out of the usual. The station itself was rather primitive and accommodation of poor quality. I remember Invergordon was a small, rather quaint place, with few signs of Service activity. The mess was situated in the town and the quarters, Nissen huts, were somewhat outside the town.

There were no amenities and no heating to speak of. Many of us decided that this was not acceptable, so we obtained living quarters in the town, as did those who were married. We slept there and had our meals in the mess, but had to cheat a little by asking our mates who lived on the unit to answer our names at the roll call (when it was held) at the camp. This worked out well (and I'm sure the authorities were aware of it) until such time as we had a Gale warning in the middle of the night and our presence was required on board the aircraft as boat guards. On these occasions our friends in the camp managed to get a phone message to us in time."

Frizell recall that the local community was a friendly, welcoming community, but they did have one or two traits that he, as an Australian, found peculiar:

"The local townspeople, of course, welcomed us as boarders, as we were busy, mostly quiet and very grateful for the comfortable house atmosphere they provided. The Scottish people had but one foible – 'twin' rooms always contained only a double bed, which was rather disconcerting to young men who had, in all probability, never slept with anyone else in their lives, let alone with one of the same sex! However, Scotland in winter is a very different proposition to Australia in the summer and none of us dared call into question the accepted normal behaviour in Scotland and found no fault with the arrangements.

Invergordon was a misty, cold place and frequently 'socked in' with rain and low cloud. The friendliness of the people was a delight. The town itself was small, many of the houses were old fashioned but

A Short Sunderland, similar to those used at No 4 (C)OTU at Invergordon. (P Frizell)

comfortable and there were only one or two shops. The rather bleak harbour was enlivened by the hulls of the 'Boats', which were our whole lives. To reach them we had to be taken out in dinghies, which often meant that we were wet and cold before we even started our days work. The locals were amazed at our proclivity for frequent (daily) baths, and I fear, were none too happy about the heating bills!"

The business of learning to fly the enormous Sunderland flying boat could be fraught with danger. Pupil pilots, who had not long before been flying Tiger Moths sometimes found the art of landing a flying boat difficult to master.

"In late November 1943 I was on Flare Path Officer duties. It was a flat, glassy calm night, and there were several OTU 'Boats' returning from training trips. One of them was in the charge of one of my pupils, and whilst approaching to land, he flew straight into the water quite a long way short of the first flare. This was not uncommon with inexperienced crews, since in wartime we had only three flares, quite long way apart and no other lights of any sort, being in blackout conditions. It was impossible to judge height in a flat calm and any attempt to do so was fraught with danger. The only answer was to set up a constant rate of descent and airspeed and disobey all other instincts until the aircraft 'arrived', which it would do safely if set up properly. Somewhat like the early lessons in instrument flying, when one has to avoid believing what one's body is telling one. On this occasion, quite a bad crash resulted and many of the crew was killed. The potential 'skipper' survived, however, and later on went on to form another crew and fly a successful tour of operations with No 461 Sqn.

On the same night there was another prang – due to the same set of conditions, but happening in another way. This time the pilot got himself too high and slow over the flare path, and finally, after wafting along past the last flare under a lot of power and still not getting down, the nose way up, he decided to pull off power and as a result dropped like a stone – the aircraft broke up on impact and again there were casualties. A busy night for the Flare Path Officer and the rescue boats! Odd to think that we all used to hate flat calm nights, particularly on Ops with a full load – it was sometimes almost impossible to get airborne and one had to ask a power boat to rush back and forth over the take off area to create some waves to help the aircraft to fly. Quite often the last flare would disappear out of sight behind, and still on the water. Of course, there was plenty of distance available most times. How we all survived is a miracle – many of the new 'skippers', like myself a couple of years before, had only flown Tigers and

Harvards beforehand and converted to 'Boats' at Invergordon and Stranraer to then go to a squadron as a second pilot for a few months before being sent back to Invergordon to become captains with a crew of some twelve or so and a total of perhaps 200-300 hours. Nevertheless, it was an exhilarating time for us young fellows, and the lucky ones survived."

In June 1943 restriction on attacks on submarines off the coast of Norway was lifted. This allowed the Coastal Command Sunderlands and Catalina's to attack the U-boats freely and the training aircraft of No 4 OTU were often armed and sent out on patrols whilst training. On 24th May 1944 Peter Frizell was airborne with a trainee crew when an opportunity arose.

"It was during my time as an instructor that a very unusual event occurred. In June 1943 a concerted attack upon the submarine fleet of Germany was mounted and Intelligence lifted a total bombing restriction area, which had been in existence since early in the war. This was off the coast of Norway and had always been used by our

No 4 (C) OTU also trained Catalina crews. This aircraft is a RAAF serialled aircraft based in the Far East. (P Frizell)

own submarines to gain access to the area. The Germans, of course, had been aware that any submarine here was safe from attack and proceeded to use the area to pull in their forces to attack shipping during the invasion of Europe. The lifting of the restriction enabled us to attack any submarine sighted there.

I was detailed to take out a pupil crew on an anti-submarine patrol off the Norwegian coast. The crew were fellows in the process of forming up a crew, with the captain under training; I was the instructor. Some thirty mile off the Norwegian Coast, one of the gunners reported a vessel some miles away. Of course, we dived down at once and identified it as a U-boat. Operating, presumably, under the latest German orders to 'stay up and fight' it opened fire with its 4in gun and all the extra armament they had recently been issued for the purpose. This was lucky for us, as he would have had time to submerge before we could attack. This especially as the bomb racks would not extend electrically and had to be wound out by hand. The front gunner had a jammed turret into the bargain. To fix these took a little time, during which I decided to make sure the sub was always within easy reach – I was interested to discover that a sub could easily out-turn a Sunderland. When it opened fire with its 4in gun I instructed the rear gunner to call at the very instant he saw the flash and this gave me time to take violent avoiding action before the shell could arrive.

We had been trained intensively to make a quarter attack and I was determined that I would do this if at all possible. We made several passes at the U-boat, but each time we came under heavy fire and were unable to attack from the desired angle. Finally, our anticipation was correct and a full quarter attack was made. The U-boat was straddled and all gunners were able to hit their targets. The four ensuing explosions sank the U-boat within a few minutes; we were fortunate in obtaining a perfect series of photographs, which later supported a claim of sinking. We circled the area and saw bodies and wreckage everywhere, which we also photographed.

After sending the required messages we decided to leave the area as we were well within the range of fighters – also we had an engine problem and were, at that stage, unsure of how many hits, if any, we had sustained. Some hours later we reached Invergordon to quite a welcome of small craft, the Commanding officer etc.

The unhappiest part of the whole exercise, from my point of view, was on entering the mess – most of my own crew, with whom I had flown some sixty operational trips, without ever attacking a U-boat, were at Invergordon as instructors, and were sitting at a table there –

I would have given anything to have had them with me on this day, instead of a crew not yet trained, with their whole operational career ahead of them. This was only one of two cases of a pupil crew in such an attack during the entire war – I was awarded an immediate DFC, very soon after and the celebrations at Invergordon lasted for days! The whole OTU became quite well known as a result and I consider myself very lucky to have had the opportunity of realising the dream we all had, after years of training and fruitless trips out over the Atlantic. Shortly afterwards I was posted home to Australia.

U675 takes the full brunt of the attack by Frizell and his crew on 24th May 1944. (P Frizell)

The submarine attacked and sunk by Peter Frizell and his pupil crew was U675, captained by Lt Sammler – there were no survivors.

Frizell was posted back to Australia in July 1944 and on to another general reconnaissance course, subsequently he converted to Liberators at Tocumwal and joined No 102 Sqn RAAF in Queensland. After the war he joined Australian National Airways and spent the next thirty-three years as an airline captain, retiring at sixty having amassed over 25,000 flying hours. He served as the Chairman of the Guild of Air Pilots and Air Navigators in South Australia.

As a postcript to Peter Frizell's story, he returned with his wife to Invergordon in 1976 to visit a remarkable woman who had shown hospitality and great generosity to many of the aircrew based at Invergordon.

"A trip to the UK in 1976 saw me, accompanied by my wife, on a nostalgia trip to all of the flying boat bases I had flown from during the war, including Invergordon. We drove up to the house, after all these years, and I knocked on the door without giving any previous notice of our intention. Unfortunately Joey Macleod was in hospital, having suffered a slight stroke a short time before. We then drove up to the hospital and were ushered into the ward, again without having given any previous notice. Joey was in a chair, and on looking up, recognised me instantly. She greeted my wife with the words – "And you must be Pat, of who Peter used to rave on all the time." Not bad after over thirty years!

Invergordon itself was by this time virtually defunct – times had caught up with it and it was but a shadow of its former self. We hunted everywhere for signs of the base, but all that was left were a few barely discernible foundations of the old Nissen huts – and of course, the harbour was bare even of ships. It saddened me as I had many fond memories of the place."

Spy!

FRANK GIBSON – ENGINEERING OFFICER – 1943/1945

Frank Gibson had served with No 47 Sqn in the Red Sea Hills of Sudan in 1940/41 so when he arrived at Peplow in Shropshire to become the Engineering officer for No 83 OTU it was quite a change of scenery. No 83 OTU was equipped with Wellingtons, Masters and a single Oxford. The airfield a Peplow was to the standard three-runway bomber design. Frank arrived with the opening up party for the new OTU.

> "The Fleet Air Arm station at Hinstock was in full swing when six of us officers and two score airmen arrived at Peplow. They gave us every kind of assistance possible and made us very welcome in their mess. Living accommodation at Peplow was Nissen Huts, OK most of the year but brass monkeys would have found it difficult to survive in winter! Considering the civilian food rations the 'grub' for all ranks was very good. Of course, its all relative – life at a permanent station, central heating, all 'mod cons', made Peplow seem very spartan, yet relative to the Sudan it was near perfect."

No 83 OTU was closed on October 28th 1944 and was immediately re-designated No 23 Heavy Glider Conversion Unit (HGCU). Frank remained at Peplow. Other units absorbed the trainees and the next day twenty glider instructors were posted in. Albemarles and Horsa and Waco gliders replaced the Wellingtons.

> "One of the difficulties for glider pilots occurred in cloud when the towing aircraft could not be seen. An instrument similar to an artificial horizon was connected via the towing rope to the towing aircraft. I think it was called the Angle of Deflection Indicator, but known locally as 'Angle of Dangle'. This indicated to the glider pilot if the towing aircraft was above, below, port or starboard in relation to the glider.
>
> Urgent instructions came from Group to adapt Link Trainers. It was a complicated structure in an arc around the front of the Link Trainer, carrying a platform with two geared, reversible motors. One to move the platform around the arc, the second to move the towing connection up and down. I had two Links to convert (one at our

satellite airfield, Seighford). Owing to lack of materials and the time factor I thought up my own 'Heath Robinson' invention, which was easier and quicker to erect. I scrounged four American landing light motors from a nearby 'Yank' base. Fitted them to the front of the Link Trainer with slotted bars. At the intersection of the bars I fitted a cord to the 'Angle of dangle'. I wired up the Link instructor's desk so he could deflect the towing point up, down, port or starboard. When the glider pilot corrected, movement of the Link Trainer was used to operate rheostats wired to the motors to return the frame to the central position."

Shortly after the conversion of the Link Trainers Frank almost ended up being locked up as a spy!

"I had some photos taken of the contraption soon after we had converted the Link Trainers. Shortly after that I managed to rent a flat a few miles away from the station. A car was essential when applying for a petrol ration. The car logbook and other documents had to be enclosed. Having no large envelopes at the flat I hunted in my desk at camp and was very pleased to find one the right size. A week later I had a visit from the CID wanting to know what my game was sending secret documents through the post? I managed to convince them nothing sinister was afoot. Incidentally, the 'Heath Robinson' contraption worked. The link trainer instructors were pleased, as were the Chief Flying Instructor and the Chief Technical Officer. The CTO wanted photos and a write up to send to Group (hence the photos). I never heard anything more about them."

In 1945 Frank moved to No 15 (P) AFU at Babdown Farm. The AFU was equipped with Ansons and Oxfords. Whilst there Frank had an unusual engineering problem to resolve.

"A pilot increasing speed for take off noticed no airspeed indicator reading, so he returned to dispersal. The airspeed indicator and pitot head were changed and everything was then OK. A check of the original instrument found it to be serviceable. The pressure tube of the pitot head was found to be blocked by a greenish mud coloured clay. It was sent for analysis. The result returned was that it was the work of a leaf cutting bee or wasp. Two other aircraft parked in the same area were found to be partially blocked. This resulted in another strict check on Daily Inspections. I had never heard of this leaf cutting insect before or since."

"We Only Take Army Volunteers Here"

GEORGE GRAY – NAVIGATOR – 1940/1945

From 1935 to 1939 George Gray had followed a pharmaceutical apprenticeship and at the outbreak of war was working, as a dispenser with Boot's the Chemists, in Peterborough. At the end of March 1940, having volunteered to join the RAF he was sent to Northampton to commence the process of trade selection. Arriving in Northampton the evening before he sought out the Drill Hall where he had to appear the following morning.

"I arrived at the Drill hall well before the appointed time of 9.00am but I was not the first man there. I joined a queue of some ten to fifteen men in front of a plain deal table where sat an Army Sergeant, smart and crisp in a freshly pressed uniform, waxed moustache bristling as he barked questions at the would-be volunteers. As I shuffled slowly forward to the head of the queue I was suddenly struck by the realisation that the whole set-up was exclusively Army! There was the Army Sergeant and the RAMC Corporal wandering in and out of the cubicles. I was stunned! What a ghastly mistake! I was in the wrong place; Air Ministry had flubbed. It was too late to turn back as I had now reached the head of the queue that faced the sergeant. To turn away would be too humiliating but I was still a civilian, I reassured myself, and I was not going to join the bloody Army and footslog my way through mud and mire to death or glory. So I handed my letter to the sergeant.

He glanced at it but without reading it he thrust a form at me, saying roughly, "Fill this out and wait over there," pointing to the benches. I took a quick look at the form and saw it was an Army form. It was now or never. In a voice that squeaked a little from suppressed tension, I said, "Sergeant, I did not come here to volunteer for the Army."

"Don't waste my f... ing time," he responded.

"You did not read my letter. Air Ministry sent me here to join the Air Force not the Army," said I.

"We only take Army volunteers here," he said.

The sergeant's manner triggered an instant repugnance. He was not going to browbeat ME! After years of running around police stations with my police Superintendent uncle during the holidays a khaki uniform and waxed moustache was not going to put me off. So, I said: "I want to see the Officer in Charge."

Astonished by George's temerity the sergeant sent him to an office where he explained the mistake to an officer of First World War vintage. The officer explained that he should have been sent to Cardington and after a medical examination George was on his way.

"At last a doctor arrived; quickly he tapped my chest, took my blood pressure, looked for piles and palpitated for hernia; then with a terse question: "Any complaints" "No, Sir." "All right, you can dress now." It was over. He hastily jotted down some remarks on a blue form and told me to see one of the men in the office. There, I collected a 'chitty' for a free meal at a cheap café across the street and a railway warrant to take me to Cardington. By one o'clock I was aboard the train and clattering towards Cardington. The sun shone brightly, it was a beautiful day and my spirits were soaring."

After a slow train ride to Bedford in the warm Spring sun, George found a bus for the short ride to Cardington.

"Try, if you will, to visualise me now at the guardhouse at the gate of the largest RAF Reception Centre in Britain, the former home of the airships R100 and the ill fated R101, and handing my precious letter to the Sergeant. He gave it back to me and still clutching my little leather attaché case, I was led away by a Corporal, all Spit, polish and Blanco."

George next completed an application form and waited with the other volunteers for his turn to go in front of the Selection Board.

"I was in a room, facing three elderly men in uniform, seated side by side behind a large table covered in dark cloth. I found the chair in front of the table and sat down, bolt upright, tense with expectation. The room seemed dark or was it only my imagination? There was a total silence for a long time as the man in the centre read my application and then passed it to the other two in turn.

There followed a barrage of questions which I only vaguely remember; my past at school and my present job were thoroughly discussed. One of them asked why I wanted to join the Air Force. I had them there, I thought; I wanted to fly aeroplanes and airmen – I named a few for good measure – had been my interest since I was a boy. Good grief! I could see them saying to themselves – he still is. So it went on until one of them said: "Tell me the difference between a two-stroke and a four-stroke engine." I missed the boat on that one. I knew the answer but could not put it concisely and they cut me short. It was over and "Would I wait outside?"

I was left wondering why only I should be asked to wait when all the others had left without being recalled. I sweated and chafed for what seemed a long time before they asked me back. If I wanted to be a pilot I would have to wait six months but they needed navigators immediately. I had to make a snap decision. I asked if there would be a chance of changing later – I was so, so naïve. The senior man said, "Certainly." "I'll stay," said I. That was a mistake although I was not to know it for a long time.

Thus, my application stamped with approval; as the last candidate for the day, the corporal escorted me, dazed, relieved and so far, happy to a barrack block where I was to stay the night to be ready for the supreme test the following morning – the Aircrew medical Exam."

The evening, after a meal of beef stew, carrots and potatoes, George returned to the barracks hut to await the call to be sworn in to the RAF.

"There was not long to wait. The corporal arrived and bawled for silence. Like sheep, he led us to another adjoining hut; empty except for a table at the far end, stacked with books, which proved to be bibles. In ragged rows, we stood like derelicts at a Salvation Army Saturday night meeting. He distributed Bibles to us and we waited. Then in walked three officers. We were barked to a sloppy 'Attennn-Shun' by the corporal. We were to be sworn in to the Royal Air Force according to the procedure prescribed in Kings Regulations and Air Council Instructions. It was a solemn and almost religious moment and I felt as if I was in a church chanting the Nicene Creed. We were collectively congratulated on joining the RAF. It was all over. I was an airman. Irrevocably!!!"

The next day George was given an aircrew medical and, in the best traditions of the RAF, picked up a rumour from a Cockney airman that they would be going to the other side of the camp for three weeks 'square bashing'. George moved into 'B' Flight, under Cpl Bryant.

"He began his introduction slowly moving up and down the centre of the hut, every word spoken with a quiet vehemence that oozed menace. "'B' Flight, you are here for three weeks Initial Training. You will receive your kit and uniforms. You will learn to march and obey orders. You will learn to salute your officers and obey orders. You will take your orders from me and you will obey instantly or I'll hoist you by the balls up the Flagstaff!"

Following this introduction, George realised that life was not going to be free and easy anymore. Initial training consisted of drill, PT, fatigues, lectures on hygiene and Air Force Law – the only law. The last link to civilisation, civilian clothes, was packed for shipment home, to be replaced by uniforms, shaving in cold water and drill, drill and more drill.

> "In a way, I enjoyed my initial training. I could not have endured it as a way of life; I would have atrophied from sheer boredom. We were all glad when it was over but by and large we were better men. We had joined the RAF for a limited purpose – to help win the war – Initial training was a necessary beginning; it was, thank God, not to be the sum and total of our future.
>
> The personalities of the other occupants of my hut began to adjust and personal relationships began to form. Next to me on one side was a shy youth, named Fisher, who was to be an instrument mechanic; on the other side, aircrew trainee like myself, was Denis Furse, also hoping to be a navigator. Directly opposite was Jean Burnett (his mother was French.) Denis became 'Windy' and Burnett was nicknamed 'Niblick' for no real reason I can remember. The three of us became very close and we were named 'the Three Musketeers' by some bright character. We were to stay together till September of that year. Niblick had been partly educated in France. He had left school at 17 and at 26 had had plenty of experience of the vagaries of the working world. He was stocky and muscular and had a Churchillian impediment in his speech, which under stress or excitement or anger became a jaw-breaking stammer that at times rendered him totally speechless. He above all of us was a total patriot and made no secret of the fact that he had joined the RAF with one aim only – to kill as many 'f-f-f-fucking N-N-N-Nazis as p-p-p-p-possible' – he was to have his wish granted but at great personal cost.
>
> The three weeks of Purgatory ended – finally. The climax was the Passing Out Parade. It was a Saturday and the parade was to begin at 10am with a COs inspection. The hut was a hive of activity from 6am on; buttons polished and re-polished; boots burnished to a mirror shine; and an added bit of 'bullshit' instead of tunic belt, our webbing belt, blanco-ed and brass highly polished. By 9am we were assembled outside the hut in brilliant sunshine – it was going to be a damned hot

parade. A final inspection by Bryant and we moved off to march on to the parade ground and take our place in the centre between 'A' and 'C' Flights, squarely in front of the reviewing stand. We waited and waited. Finally the officers arrived. Then began the individual flight inspections and that ceremony completed the officers retired to stand to watch the WO i/c put us all through our paces. The three flights performed in unison on the huge parade ground; wheeling, marching, forming file and line from rest and on the march, all the antiquated mumbo-jumbo of the ancient drill; ending with the March Past by Flights in front of the reviewing stand where the Squadron Leader i/c Training Squadron took the salute.

Back at the NAAFI, we were even joined by Bryant who unbent enough to wish us all good luck and even said we had been better than most. We had of course practised the entire ceremony to the point of exhaustion the previous day. It had not been so bad after all."

George met Cpl Bryant again at Cranage in 1943. Bryant was now a flight sergeant AG and was flying on Beaufighters. He had had to bail out at night, been injured, and it had ended his ops career. He was awaiting a commission.

Having passed out the course waited and waited to learn their fate. They were given a 48-hour pass and on return expected postings, but still, they waited.

"Then, suddenly out of the blue, it happened. One morning as we hacked and hoed in the 'garden', Sgt Brown returned from his daily visit to the Orderly Room and casually called us to follow him to his office. Just as reluctantly, we went, suspecting some new 'fatigue'. With irritating conversation about nothing in particular, he 'dillied and dallied'; then finally told us the momentous news, that we had waited for. We were posted immediately to No 3 ITW at Hastings.

Kitbags were packed in record time, clearance 'chits' signed, Movement Orders and railway warrants hastily collected from the Orderly Room. The next morning, bright and early, we humped our kitbags, our backs bent by our heavy webbing equipment, over to the station, a mile or so away, to await the slow train to Sandy, where we caught the stopping train to Kings Cross. In the summer heat, we wrestled with all our clobber across London by crowded Underground, to Charing Cross for the train to Hastings. GOODBYE CARDINGTON!"

No 3 ITW was accommodated in a large hotel, a vast concrete structure resembling the upper decks of an ocean liner, on the seafront at Hastings.

> "A notice, signed by some Orderly Room sergeant said that hot water was limited to one hour, morning and evening; the bath had the regulation black line painted four inches up the side to conform with wartime restrictions. 'Hot' meant a temperature never more than tepid. Our entire flight of sixty was composed of cadet navigators. We were issued with white flashes to be worn in our forage caps. It distinguished us as flight cadets. We blanco-ed them diligently and wore them with arrogance and pride. It is such small things that help to cement an esprit de corps; it did not concern us greatly that we were still only AC2s, being paid the princely sum of 2/- (10p) per day; Our uniforms were shoddy, though the tailors in Hastings made quite a killing from those of us who visited them with pleas for a better fit; and all of us pressed our trousers nightly, putting them under the bottom blanket and sleeping on them."

Training at ITW consisted of Morse code, aircraft recognition and maths in a large, requisitioned underground garage beneath the Esplanade. There were several route marches and a maths examination. Failure in this exam meant return to Cardington. George had a complete blank and thought he had failed. After a 'dressing down' by the flight sergeant at which he was threatened with the withholding of his LAC badge, the flight sergeant took him to one side and told him that the exam meant nothing and was a 'blind' to enable some to be removed from the course who were thought to be unsuitable. The actual results were never announced. Only three names were removed from the course and the others were all re-categorised as LAC.

> "The Three Musketeers celebrated the results of the exam and newly sewn on LAC shoulder patches with an expensive non-rationed evening meal at one of the hotels, that is expensive for us on our newly-won 3/6d *(17 ½p) per day.*"

As the BEF began its retreat through France, George and his course moved to Torquay, away from the threat of invasion or shelling in Hastings.

"The RAF requisitioned a number of hotels, the bed and breakfast sort, that faced the bay and ran up the hill towards Daddy Hole Plain. We were assigned to the Beacon House Hotel, right on the corner, and when we were dismissed, the three musketeers, joined by Linford, 'Curly' Hillyer and Goldsmid seized a room on the second floor that had its own bathroom attached. We congratulated ourselves on our selection but were a little disappointed when we found out that our bathroom was smelly."

The routine at ITW varied little and the Squadron Warrant Officer, Flight Sergeant Richmond, regulated the cadet's lives. In August he would be promoted to Warrant Officer.

"The full Squadron Parade was to be a weekly affair; other times, we paraded as separate flights and the inspection was by King or often only by Richmond. We would then drill until 10.00am; to be dismissed for a fifteen minute break for a 'cup o' chaa and a wad' at the Sailors Rest nearby or in a café close at hand, to the annoyance of the civilians and the delight of the waitresses. Parade again and dismissed rapidly

'Niblick' and Gray about to go on parade at No 3 ITW, Torquay, July 1940. (George Gray)

to change into PT kit and jog our way up the hill to Beacon Hill Common known familiarly to us as Daddy Hole Plain. There we did PT until we were exhausted by the push-ups, leap-frogging etc., then run as smartly as we could down the hill to our hotel to change back into uniform and to the Mess for dinner. We were allowed almost an hour for the midday meal. At 1.30pm sharp, we were paraded once again by Richmond. He would march us 'At Attention' through the town to some hall or other for Morse Code practice; a short break at 3.00pm for tea, then off again to some other hall for an Aircraft Recognition or Armament lecture. Finally, he marched us back to barracks for a short drill session until 5.30pm when he dismissed us for supper and the rest of the day was ours."

The quality of food for the cadets was often a bone of contention at many training units and Torquay was no exception. In fact feelings ran so high that a breakdown in discipline occurred which was to affect several of the staff and students.

"For the first week, the food in the mess was adequate, but badly cooked and poorly served. It arrived on our plates cold! There was no variety. Each day was a repetition of the last; hard-boiled and leathery eggs and glutinous porridge for breakfast; at midday, e faced undisguised Spam, potatoes almost raw and white Navy beans, hard as brazil nuts. For supper, sausages and beans yet again. Those goddamned beans!! And Spam not even disguised! Year later, whenever I see those damned white beans, I am still obsessed by the vision of those we were expected to eat in the mess. The mess, of course, catered to the entire Squadron and after two or three days of this unappetising and monotonous diet, complaints began to surface. The NCO's response was: 'It will improve! Don't you know there's a war on!'

After a week of this, with no end in sight, hungry and broke from buying extra meals on our paltry pay, a spontaneous and quite unplanned rebellion suddenly flared up. Led by 'A' Flight, we all refused to eat the eggs and some were tossed at the servers; everyone refused to go on parade until something else was served. This impetuous action caused consternation among the NCO's; was this a mutiny? They had never had to deal with a bunch of civilians in uniform.

Richmond proved equal to the challenge. He took us aside and warned us that it was his 'stripes' and our aircrew status that were at stake and promised action if we would obey orders. He promised that there would be no reprisals. We refused breakfast but went on parade as usual. The other NCO's panicked and there was a flurry of MP action, which we smugly watched as we marched up and down and went through our daily paces. The MPs hauled off about half a dozen of the more vociferous cadets from other flights. A couple of the NCO's were reduced to Corporals and posted. The cadets were posted back to Cardington or Padgate and the bush telegraph had it that there would be court martials if there was any more trouble. But the food suddenly improved and henceforward was always excellent in quality and quantity.

From this a very close bond developed between Richmond and us. We never let him down and cheerfully did all he demanded of us. We put our heart into the drill and PT programme to achieve the ultimate in perfection. In return, he connived with us to allow us to spend hours, when we should have been stomping wearily on parade, sunbathing and swimming in Beacon Cove, cloistered from the public eye and the officers alike."

By August 1940 there was a great upheaval in Training Command with many schools closing down or being transferred overseas. All the experienced instructors were also being transferred to man EFTS's and Navigation Schools in Canada and Rhodesia. Consequently, with only a few schools like Prestwick and Jurby still operating, and the Navigation Schools in Canada not yet fully operational, many cadets had to await postings at ITW.

"We had to mark time at Torquay and we remained there long after our course should have finished. It enabled us to polish up our Morse and Aldis lamp so that we achieved a high proficiency. It stood me in good stead when I finally got to a squadron and had to 'talk' to the Navy by Aldis lamp. We even enjoyed our Morse instruction; our Corporal instructor had been in the RAF many years and regaled us with stories of life in Aden, Shaibah and Quetta; and his Morse was sweet and rhythmic as a Chopin Prelude."

Eventually the flight was informed that they were posted. In George's case it was to No 1 AONS at Prestwick, south of Glasgow on the Clyde coast. Breaking his journey at Leeds to take a short leave with his uncle, George eventually travelled by train to Scotland and was deposited at Kilmarnock to make his way to Prestwick.

"We arrived in Kilmarnock; Kilmarnock, all red brick, rose coloured sandstone, sombre granite and blue-grey slate, rain-washed clean, clear and brisk under a blue autumn sky. We tumbled stiffly off the train lugging our 100 pounds or so of kit. We organised ourselves by bus to Prestwick, to be dumped at the gates to the Scottish Aviation Ltd. Airfield. The bus conductors were hardy souls but compassionate and helped stow the mountains of clobber that servicemen always seemed to hump around. They would cheerfully sing out the names of the 'Stops' and assist the lost and the drunk.

This was no isolated airfield in the middle of no-where but right beside the main Prestwick-Glasgow road with bus stops just outside the gates. The field was grass and while we were surveying our surroundings, Tiger Moths of the EFTS were taking off, over the granite wall that separated the field from the highway and over our heads. We trudged to the buildings a hundred yards beyond the gates past the big aircraft repair building; to the headquarters, which fronted onto a large macadamised aircraft parking apron. We reported in. To our surprise civilians received us. We were to be billeted at Rosemount, a big, greystone Scottish country mansion that had been requisitioned by the government. It had seen better days and was sadly in need of refurbishing. It was in its own grounds about two miles from the field and we were driven there just in time for super. Although we had RAF rations, everything was organised by Scottish Aviation. The staff, catering and janitorial, were civilians."

After the usual scramble to secure a favoured bed, George and his companions, Bob Linford, Paddy and Niblick, explored the grounds. Soon they had wandered into Monkton past the airfield gates and on into Prestwick.

"It was less than half a mile, past the Episcopal Church, to the main street. By this time we had acquired a thirst, there were no pubs in sight but we saw a little café that seemed tempting. It was the Copper Kettle, in peacetime it had no doubt catered to day-trippers from Glasgow and Kilmarnock; it preserved an air of quiet bourgeois gentility. We found out that it was popular with the Nav students and we carried on the tradition

If our palates were jaded by the stodgy but nutritious RAF rations, we rushed there for a lunch break or, after flying schedules, we would relive the experiences over tea and cakes – Scotch scones and butter!!! The waitresses were reserved in a Scottish way but very friendly. They gave us the 'gen' on bus schedules and told us to visit the local Golf Club House which had been converted by the patriotic womenfolk of Prestwick into a sort of Airman's rest. There one could get home-baked food and tea at nominal prices to suit our limited pockets.

Section 'A', D4 Course, No 1 AONS, Prestwick, October – December 1940.
Back row: N/K, N/K, Daniels, Collinson, Goldsmid, N/K, Gray, N/K, Arkley, Hillier, N/K.
Middle Row: Inwood, N/K, Beer, Burnett (Niblick), N/K, Griffiths, N/K, N/K, N/K, Dearden.
Front row: N/K, N/K, N/K, N/K, Evans, Bulloch, Gething, N/K, Catley.

There were two Quiet Rooms to read magazines, write letter or play cards – No Gambling! I took up Bridge again with Niblick and anyone else that we could persuade to join us. On Saturday evenings there were regular dances with someone looking after the gramophone and local girls were jolly partners. We took to wearing shoes again, contrary to regulations, so for me dancing again became a pleasure."

Ending their exploration, the group returned to Rosemount to see off the previous course. They also learned that they would be the last course at Prestwick. Future courses would go to Canada. In common with all new arrivals they quickly picked up rumours and 'gen'. Among this was the information, much exaggerated, that food was poor, aircraft were always u/s and there was a lot of evening homework. George's course at No 1 AONS would last from 23rd September 1940 until 3rd January 1941 under the leadership of the Chief Instructor, Sqn Ldr Dobson. The instruction was divided into the following subjects: DR Navigation, Instruments and Radio Direction Finding, Compasses, Meteorology and Maps & Charts, Reconnaissance and Photography and Practical Navigation (Flying).

"We were divided into two sections, A and B, for lectures and spent our first morning collecting manuals, Air Ministry publications, notebooks, plotting instruments etc. and in meeting our instructors. We attended an introductory lecture by the Chief Instructor, the only RAF officer other than the staff pilots. All our instructors were ex-Merchant Navy men – First officers as we gradually learned – with a vast experience of navigation at sea; most of it gained on fast freighters, such as banana boats that plied the Atlantic to and from Jamaica, or small ocean liners.

Our Chief Instructor was Sqn Ldr Dobson. Apart from the initial lecture introducing us to the course and the final farewell talk during which he wished us well, we never saw him. He was our only link with the RAF for this period except for a very casual Pay Parade conducted informally by some Account Officer twice a month. We were of course subject to RAF discipline but as we had no Unit formation, such discipline was only applied when we appeared in public places. To all intents and purposed we were just civilians wearing the same uniform.

Our Course Leader was a Mr Tee who had been at one time the Chief Officer on the liner 'Empress of Britain'. One day he recognised this beautiful ship from the Fokker. It was sailing gracefully up the Clyde past the Tail of the Bank. All navigation practice was abandoned as we circled the ship at low altitude and Mr Tee signalled his greetings to the bridge by Aldis lamp.

Our DR instructor was a Mr Hurst; he had been First Mate on a banana boat. Meteorology was in the charge of Mr Oldfield, who handled that infant discipline with skill and flair; he had spent several years with the Air Ministry Met Office. They were good; they brought to the classroom the benefit of practical experience.

Air Navigation was in its infancy. Our bible was the Air Ministry Publication AP1234. This had been written in the 1920's with a few minor revisions and additions over the intervening years. It was completely re-written in 1943. The assumption was that an aircraft behaved like a ship and the vagaries of the wind, the equivalent of current and tides. These premises were subject to the shrunken time frame of the aircraft's much greater speed. Just as the vector of the ship's track and speed was the resultant of the vectors of speed and heading and the set and speed of currents and tides, so one could determine the track and groundspeed of the aircraft as the resultant of the vectors of course and airspeed and of windspeed and direction. New techniques were developed later as the discrepancy of an aircraft's speed increased but the fundamentals were the same. All this is now as archaic as Chaucer's English with the advent of such technological marvels as Inertial Navigation Systems, Radar and electronic computers.

Using large scale Admiralty Charts or Mercator plotting charts, we wrestled with interceptions by geometric plotting with pencil and parallel ruler and dividers. Ship to ship, aircraft to ship with the aircraft flying from a land base or moving ship base and returning. We plotted bearings and position lines to obtain Position Fixes. We plotted and found wind velocity by track and groundspeed and by the drift on three different courses. Then we practised using the Dalton Computer to find the wind velocity from the same information, until Dead Reckoning was second nature to us. This was a breeze for me; for I had staggered everyone at Spalding Grammar School by obtaining 100% in geometry and trigonometry in the Intermediate Scholarship exam. The intricacies of vectors and the relationship of angles and Lines of Constant Bearing held no terrors for me. I quickly mastered the rudiments and constantly clamoured for more simulated flights to the chagrin of the others and the annoyance of Mr Hurst. I was really very smug. Hurst finally throttled me by setting me to produce an exercise complete with all observations, an interception and a Square Search for good measure. That silenced me for several sessions. Goldsmid of all people was told to share the task with me – he was equally self confident. In the end we produced a 'dilly' which was given to the other half of the course as an intermediate exam paper. It was clear to me that Goldsmid was the man to beat. In the end he did beat me in the final standings because his log keeping was much neater than mine was and I lost marks for untidiness.

All the courses fascinated me and I found that the background of scholarship that Spalding Grammar School had given me was more than adequate to enable me to sail through all the theoretical subjects well ahead of almost everyone else on the course. I say almost everyone, because in the final exam Goldsmid topped the course and the dark horse, Arkley, whose diagrams of instruments were artistically beautiful, beat me by 2%. Third place out of fifty-two satisfied my overweening egotism. It is interesting that Gordon Arkley and I met again six years later on the Specialist Navigation Course at Shawbury. We again enjoyed the same friendly rivalry but I beat him on that occasion – just!!

Meteorology was in its infancy. Air masses, fronts, depressions and anti-cyclones were still only tentatively formulated and jet streams not even suspected. There was little literature available. Oldfield did a good job and we supplemented theory with lots of practical observations. We learned how to plot weather observations and all the symbols used and their proper position around the station circle. We drew in frontal systems and tried our hands at forecasting from data we had plotted. We discussed local weather and cloud formations over tea or coffee ad nauseam.

I had a good visual memory that enabled me to visualise the intricacies of compass deviation and magnetic variation and the instruments in use at the time – airspeed indicator, altimeter and P4 Compass were so unsophisticated that a little mechanical aptitude reduced their internal workings to the simplicity of a clockwork toy.

The study of the elegant RAF topographicals just being produced was a joy and their beautiful and artistic colouring, their accuracy of detail, plentiful but not overwhelming, soon gave me a mental picture of the features of Great Britain that I have retained to this day."

Having mastered the basics of air navigation in the ground lectures, George and his fellow pupils were keen to get airborne, but the early flight did not quite come up to their expectations. They also started to realise the difficulties of navigation in a moving aircraft.

"I did not have long to wait for my first flight. An hour long jaunt in one of the Fokker four-engined machines, to get us used to all the equipment we had to carry -- parachute, Mae West and navigation equipment and to give us a brief Air Experience. At last I experienced the long-awaited thrill of becoming airborne. A sensation that has never lost its ability to excite.

The early flights in the Fokker – twenty of us at a time – were somewhat frustrating. The only navigation instruments in general use at the time were the Tail Drift Sight and the Mk IX Bombsight. Two sets of these instruments were installed in the tail of the aircraft in what had been the luggage compartment. We each took turns to practice taking a drift, while the pilot flew various courses, so that we could calculate a three-course wind velocity. As we only flew at about 2-3,000 feet above the hills of southern Scotland and the back of the aircraft was the least stable part of the machine, our main lesson learned during the brief time allowed, was how difficult it was to attain accuracy and how important practice to develop this skill was.

The Fokker was a high wing monoplane with four radial engines embedded in the wings and a fixed undercarriage. They waddled through the air like pregnant ducks at 100 mph. They had been acquired by Scottish Aviation from KLM early in the war, although rumour had it they had been commandeered. They had had the airline fittings removed and the seats replaced with bucket seats. The centre aisle from cockpit to rear used by the instructor to supervise our efforts. He detailed us, two at a time, to go to the baggage compartment, where we lay on our belly to take the drift. The first three weeks of flying were limited to simple practices of about one to two hours duration in these large and ungainly aircraft, with each of us eager for our turn at the instruments, or frantically trying to lot the aircraft's track on a plotting board covered with Perspex and a blue grease pencil."

The problems of navigation were exacerbated by the lack of modern equipment. George and his compatriots were not aware of the development work being done by the scientists and engineers working behind the scenes.

"We realised very early in our course that the crude equipment was quite inadequate to get us to the target accurately. We did not know then that the Telecommunications Research Establishment (TRE) existed, or that brilliant minds were already working desperately to devise new and sophisticated methods. Radar was the subject of speculation and wild rumour. Not all our thoughts were occupied with navigation or flying. We had heated political discussions. War strategy was dissected and we could not understand why the mighty

British Empire was almost on its knees in that autumn and early winter of 1940. We cursed our earlier political leaders – Baldwin and Chamberlain. We raged about the bombing of the cities and thanked our lucky stars for Fighter Command. But we were secure in our little haven far from the crash of bombs and the dust and devastation of the huge fires."

At last George thought he would start 'real flying', but even this prospect was not without its drawbacks.

"We were impatient to start what we thought was real flying – individual exercises which we were to do in Ansons. These old machines, only recently retired from front line service in Coastal Command, were ideal for the purpose. Slow and reliable, easily serviced and with plenty of room for two trainee navigators. There was one great drawback, forever remembered and frequently recalled over a beer in the Mess in later years. The undercarriage was retractable but only by operating a handcrank located in the most awkward position possible, under the pilot's seat. Many have been the lurid curses muttered by grumpy navigators while churning away for 122 turns as they sweated under a Sidcot suit and parachute harness, always aware of the unspoken impatience of the pilot. There was no Elsan, so woe betide the unhappy man who had not voided his bowels before the two-hour flight. There was a crude 'piss-tube' consisting of a small funnel and a length of rubber tubing which terminated in a metal tube to the outside. The end of this tube was bent towards the rear so that the slipstream carried all away. The small funnel produced many crude jokes in which comparisons of size were made and its inadequacy called question by the more boastful of my friends. A favourite prank was to turn the outside spout to face the slipstream so that if the unwary used the funnel, he was covered by a warm spray of urine blown back at him by the slipstream. It became an essential part of the pre-flight check to ensure that no-one had tampered with this vital piece of equipment, for oddly enough, the tension of learning to navigate combined with NAAFI tea produced an overwhelming desire to urinate after an hour or so at 2,000 feet. Service pilots, both officers and NCO's flew the aircraft. Some were Poles who had learned to fly with the Polish Air Force and had escaped to Britain, or in the case of one at least, Kolodziecyck, had been a Polish airline pilot. The language barrier was in some cases insuperable and we communicated by signs and figure jotted on paper, but they certainly could fly! One or two of the English pilots were fighter pilots recovering from the strain of the Battle of Britain and hating every minute of it.

The first exercise was very, very simple – Air experience. Many of us thought that this was a waste of time as we had already done this in the Fokker. We just 'stooged' around the countryside near Prestwick for an hour and sat with a map on our lap. For me it was like sitting in a fast sports car watching the countryside flash by with a map in hand. I laid the foundation of map reading expertise, which always gave me satisfaction and pleasure"

It was not all work at Prestwick and occasionally George managed to escape for a few hours. Being young in spirit the sheltered confines of the airfield had kept the pupils away from the horrors of the war and a visit to Glasgow served as a reminder.

"We lived in a world almost totally divorced from the horrors and rigour of the war. Even rationing was only a minor irritant. Occasional visits to Glasgow only served to demonstrate to us the enormous weight of bombs that would be required to flatten a large metropolis of brick and stone. The bombed out buildings seemed so few compared to the whole built up area. A good grilled steak at the Caledonian – still available in December 1940 – drove all thought of the agony, distress and tragedy of the bomb victims from our young minds.

Flying continued in the Ansons. Like young birds testing their wings we flew further and further afield. No longer the short flights back and forth across the Firth, from Lady Isle to Arran and back to Ayr Light, but down the coast to Stranraer to photograph the Stranraers and the Lerwick sitting like swans on the waters of Loch Ryan. Down past Culzean Castle, which later became famous for its apartment furnished by a grateful government and leased on life tenure to General Eisenhower, past Turnberry to Girvan. We had other photographic exercises – Stereo Pairs and Line Overlaps – much more difficult to accomplish and the technique soon rendered out of date by Cotton's development of the automatic camera and the use by PRU of high flying Spitfires equipped with them. For us though it was great fun to lie on one's stomach counting and clicking away. It required an accurate knowledge of the wind and straight and level flying and pre-supposed non-interference from enemy fighters or jinking to avoid enemy AA. However, from 5,000 feet the pictures of Kilmarnock, Maybole, Oban and Stranraer were superb. Unfortunately, we were never allowed to keep them. None of us was ever called upon to use the skill we thus acquired.

NO. 1 A.C.N.S. PRESTWICK.

Time carried forward :- 28.40

Date	Hour	Aircraft Type and No.	Pilot	Duty	Remarks (including results of bombing, gunnery, exercises, etc.)	Day	Night
6-11-40	0915	FOKKER G/AFXR	P/O CORMACK	NAV 9	DR FLIGHT. AYR LT - STRANRAER - DALBEATTIE - AYR L.T.	01.40	
6-11-40	1100	FOKKER G/AFXR	P/O CORMACK	NAV 5	WIND FINDING by MULTIPLE DRIFTS (CLRS) LOCAL FLIGHT	01.20	
7-11-40	0925	ANSON N3440	S/P PURDON	NAV 8	ELEMENTARY DR FLIGHT. LADY L. ARDWELL PT. - LADY L	01.10	
...-11-40	1035	ANSON N3110	S/P PURDON	NAV. 5.	ELEMENTARY DR FLIGHT. LADY L. ARDWELL PT. - ADM	01.20	
12-11-40	1540	FOKKER G/AFXR	F/LT VATCH	NAV 5	WINDFINDING MULTIPLE DRIFT (CLRS) LOCAL FLIGHT	01.50	
17-11-40	1430	FOKKER G/AFXR	FLT THORAL	NAV 9.	DR FLIGHT. PLADDA - COLONSAY - LT. - PRESTWICK	02.30	
19-11-40	0940	ANSON N9739	S/P COOLING	NAV. 8	ELEMENTARY DR FLIGHT. LADY LT. MAY ISLE. ARDWELL PT.-LADY L.	01.10	
19-11-40	1100	ANSON N9739.	S/P COOLING	NAV. 8	ELEMENTARY DR FLIGHT. LADY L. PORT WILLIAM - LADY L.	01.10	
22-11-40	1430	FOKKER G/AFXR	F/LT THOMPSON	GUNNERY TEST EXERCISE		02.00	
26-11-40	0920	ANSON L 7454	P/O PALETHORPE	P. 2	STEREO-PAIR PHOTOGRAPHS of FOUR OBJECTS	01.10	
26-11-40	1520	FOKKER G/AFXR	F/LT THOMPSON	AVIATION MAP READING		01.30	

TOTAL TIME ... 45.00

There were no mid-course exams, as such, but it was made quite clear to us that the instructors made weekly progress reports and there were revision tests from time to time. The pilots reported on our conduct of the exercises in the air. About six weeks into the course three of our number were suddenly and discreetly posted to unknown destinations. They had just disappeared and we knew then that the axe had fallen. We wondered if there would be others and how many of us would pass out at the end after the week long final exams."

George's first real test of his navigational skill arrived on Christmas Eve when he was selected to fly a trip with a Sergeant Pilot with a fearsome reputation.

"I was supremely confident on the theoretical side. I felt I only had Goldsmid to beat. My assurance on the practical side in the air received a tremendous boost on Christmas Eve when I was told to go with Sergeant Pilot Cooke on a special flight to Speke and do an exercise both ways. Everyone else was off celebrating a two-day break. It was with some trepidation that I went with all my nav gear to the Pilots Room. I had not flown with Cooke, but he was notorious as the most exacting and demanding of the staff pilots. Others of the course, perhaps from a feeling of envy, said 'sooner you than me' for they had had experience of his acid tongue and belittling remarks. Some said he was bitter because he had been refused a commission in spite of his experience and Fighter Command record, others that he had had a near-fatal accident as a result of a navigator's error. We were to fly via Stranraer and Dumfries and instead of completing the usual triangular exercise were to fly on to Speke. I worked like a man possessed, bathed in perspiration in spite of the freezing temperature at 4,000 feet – the Anson had no cabin heating.

There were no comments from Cooke and no conversation except for a terse demand after thirty minutes for an ETA for Speke, a demand so unexpected that I almost rebelled. I remember clearly doing some frantic calculations then handing him a time in which I had no confidence. The knot in my stomach grew more griping and I wondered if I might even be airsick. By the time we had reached Carlisle, my assurance, bolstered by Cooke's silence and a good ETA at both Dumfries and Carlisle, had returned and I confidently gave him a new ETA for Speke, which he accepted in silence although it was a major change from my first hurried guess. Speke turned up on track and on time and I was treated to a fighter pilots approach and landing. The object of our trip was now revealed as we taxied towards dispersal where half a dozen Hurricanes were sitting. In the squadron hut, Cooke became alive as he greeted his old squadron friends. I, a mere LAC and worse, a student, was dismissed summarily to get some lunch and return by 2.30pm. I joined the greasy, oily 'erks' – the Hurricane mechanics – in their mess for food and joined in the general complaints of having to spend Christmas Eve on duty and not getting drunk – their wish not mine!

The trip home was entirely different. Cooke, his spirits lifter by a 'good natter' with his friends, was a changed man. He talked, he offered comments, and told me what he expected of a navigator, pointed out pinpoints and generally gave me a helping hand. Finally, the supreme demonstration of his confidence. He said, as the cloud closed in around us, just north of Carlisle, that he was going above it and that I had better be good and have an accurate course and ETA for Prestwick because he did not want to hit anything on the way down. Foolhardy, perhaps, but I now know that, being a good pilot who had many times flown the same route with pupils, he not only knew the ground below but also a let down on the course I had given him was quite safe. Be that as it may, it was a tremendous boost to my confidence. We dove down as my ETA approached and I gnawed my nails in silence as we flew down through a white mist that every second became greyer and thicker. Suddenly, the ground appeared below and I instantly recognised the railway into Ayr and ahead were the Scottish Aviation buildings. In joy and relief I cheerfully wound down the undercarriage – al 122 turns!! In the pilots hut he said it had been a very' Good Show' and I knew then that I would pass out as a navigator.

The euphoria produced by this short and really quite unremarkable flight lasted for a long time, made me unbearable to my friends and sustained my further efforts. I even forgot my long held grudge that circumstances had denied me a pilot's training.

We were approaching the final stages of our navigation training. The Christmas week was taken up with the final exams. Our first exam paper was on Boxing Day!! We had Christmas Day and New Years Day free. Some of my friends burnt much midnight oil cramming desperately. I, with my flaunted egotism and conceit disdained to do so and approached the exams with unusual calm. I had worked hard during the course and like a runner, who has trained for months for one race, felt that a little peace before the race would preserve the peak of preparedness. It paid off.

We were now the only trainees remaining on the airfield. We were the last course of navigators to be trained in Britain (except for Jurby). We envied the later volunteers, whom after ITW at Torquay,

Babbacombe, Paignton or Scarborough could look forward to training in Rhodesia or more probably Canada. The EFTS had also gone. Transferred lock, stock and Tiger Moths to Rhodesia. The Moths no longer staggered around or dipped and rose in the gusty winds that blew up the Firth. I had a brief letter from Gordon that made Niblick and I green with envy and sick with jealousy as he described the exotic climate and surroundings in Southern Rhodesia. Gordon had been one of my ITW friends, who with Windy, had wangled a re-mustering to pilot. I was to meet him again much later when I joined 524 Sqn in June 1944. When the war ended we teamed up as a crew to fly Liberators with 86 Sqn brining troops back from India.

Rosemount had closed at the end of November and we spent the last six weeks of the course billeted in various homes in Prestwick. Niblick, Jim Collinson, Paddy and I shared a billet at Mr and Mrs Mitchells. It was right in the middle of town and only two streets back from the seafront. We were welcomed warmly with good but simple Scots cooking. There was a comfortable sitting room where we did our evening studies, discussed our future interminably and argued the esoteric subtleties of navigation. The Mitchell's never disturbed us but spent their evenings in the kitchen.

Niblick, of course, tried to do a number with the Mitchell's twenty-year-old daughter, unsuccessfully. Even he was so caught up in the concentrated efforts we all made to succeed, that his advances were only half-hearted.

Christmas day not being really a Scottish holiday, we celebrated quietly. Our real celebration was New Years Eve. Exams were over. We, that is Niblick, Paddy, Jim and I, knew that we had nothing to worry about the results, so the evening was completely carefree. We celebrated New Years Day in similar style. We could easily have become quite drunk had we been so minded as all the men we met in Prestwick and on the bus to Ayr – we were going to a dance there – seemed to carry a little flask of good Scotch Whisky and we were each invited to pass the bottle. It was embarrassing because we had not been forewarned of this custom and could not reciprocate. The day was a fitting end to our stay in Prestwick. The following day or two were occupied in the shambles of departure. We learned the results of the course. I came third after Goldsmid and Gordon Arkley so I had no complaints. No one failed the final so that there were fifty-two of us posted to Bombing & Gunnery School. Half of us were to go to No 9 BGS at Penrhos in north Wales and the others were split between Silloth, near Carlisle, and West Freugh, not far from Stranraer. Happily for me, Niblick, Paddy Gething and Jim Collinson were on the list for

Penrhos. There was some grumbling because we were only given a 48-hour pass and as most men lived in the south or the Midlands, their stay at home would be very brief. I decided that I would spend the time in Glasgow at the Caledonian."

Penrhos was a three runway, grass airfield, in Caernarvonshire. The airfield was situated on the coast with high ground rising to the northwest close to the field. The longest, NE/SW runway was only 800yds long. The station had opened in February 1937 as an Armament Practice Camp and by September 1939 was home to No 9 AOS. By the time George Gray arrived the unit had been re-named No 9 BGS and was equipped with a collection of obsolete types such as the Handley Page Harrow and Fairey Battle.

"A local bus took me the five miles from Pwllheli to Penrhos. I was in the heart of Welsh-speaking Wales. RAF Station Penrhos had achieved a brief notoriety just before the war when Welsh Nationalists had burned down one of the barrack blocks. I was the first of our crowd to arrive. It was a bit of a shock to face once again the discipline of the SP's at the gate after three months of civilian freedom. At the Orderly Room I was told that we would be billeted in Llanbedrog, a tiny village, two miles further along the coast. I was given a name – Mrs Hughes – and an address. Back to the front gate to sit disconsolately in the steady drizzle, alone with my kitbags, to wait for another bus to appear on the road to Pwllheli. After an hour or so, the decrepit bus was still nowhere in sight. I was cold, I was hungry and I badly needed a bath and a shave. The vulgar remarks of the SP's from the shelter of their warm Guardhouse added to my discomfort. At last the bus arrived – its schedule was infrequent and the times haphazard. I dragged myself aboard with all my 'clobber'. The driver seemed in no hurry. I asked to be dropped at Mrs Hughes's. "Which Mrs Hughes?" I was overwhelmed by a flood of singsong English from several passengers. I was in no mood to appreciate the 'lilting accents of Wales'. I gruffly gave the address, badly mispronounced. Fortunately the driver, a local man, had a sense of humour and in spite of my hostile manner, let me off right by the door. I discovered that of the approximately twenty families in the village, they shared three surnames only. Hughes, Jones and Williams. Families were distinguished from one another and identified by adding the name of the house to their surname --Jones Glasfryn, or, Jones Gleny Widwe."

Having settled into the billets, it was back into the round of ground lectures followed by the flying phase. During the ground training George was introduced to the AML Bombing Teacher an early simulator device.

"There were only eighteen of us on the course. We were scattered in various billets, in homes along the single street. Each morning at 7.00am we caught the local bus by 'Jones Glasfryn', our buttons polished, boots shined and gas masks over our left shoulder, to arrive at the airfield with lots of time to spare before the 8.00am parade. It was a simple affair. Our names were called and then the NCO Discip took us through half an hour of foot drill on the tarmac in front of the hangar. We were then dismissed to classes. Our course was divided into groups of six and NCO's gave the lectures.

The first three weeks were taken up with lectures. We had Guns & Turrets, Bombs, Bombing Theory & Pistols (Fuses). We did simulated bombing using the Mk IX Course Setting Bombsight in the Bombing Simulator. This contraption was housed in a three-storey tower. There one lay prone on a platform suspended twenty feet above the floor, in the bombing position. The NCO i/c operated a film projector which projected a moving landscape on the floor below, the motion scaled to simulate correctly the view the bomb aimer would have, airspeed and wind velocity having been pre-set into the projector. In the dim light, we determined drift and calculated wind velocity. We set these parameters on the bombsight and practised dropping bombs.

When we pressed the bomb release button a light appeared on the floor to indicate where the bomb had landed and the motion of the film ceased. The instructor measured the angle and distance on the ground of the spotlight from the target. This information, together with our recorded settings was plotted later against the settings actually used by the instructor. The Mean Point of Impact (MPI) from several runs was obtained and entered in our records. It was quite sophisticated for those days and gave us some grounding in the art of bombing.

The lectures on bombs gave us detailed information on the various types of bombs in current use by the RAF at that time – High Explosive (HE), Armour Piercing (AP) and Fragmentation. The filling was Amatol but a newer and more powerful explosive was coming into service – Torpex.

Bombing Theory embraced the errors in MPI arising from incorrect settings of wind velocity or height, from inaccurate tracking and last minute violent alterations of course, to pilot errors of deviation from straight and level flight.

The lectures on Fuses included such element as construction, handling, setting and safety precautions. We also practised, with de-activated fuses, the correct arming of bombs by connection of the safety pins to the release toggle. The operation of the hydrostatic pistol in depth charges was explained. We filled notebooks with copious notes and exploded drawings.

The Gunnery lectures were equally technical. We became familiar with the Browning .303 machine gun and the Vickers gas-operated and the two types of power-operated turrets then in service in the RAF: the Fraser-Nash and Boulton-Paul. The mechani9cs of the turrets had to be known precisely and we learned to draw the hydraulics of the Fraser-Nash and the circuits of the electrically operated Boulton-Paul from memory.

Our instructors were Corporal Armourers of the peacetime RAF whose technical and mechanical knowledge and skill were developed to a very high degree. Our little squad of six were fortunate in having a Corporal who was very articulate and who enjoyed his job, so that our gunnery classes were amusing, enjoyable and very instructive. He would time us with a stopwatch as we stripped a Browning completely and re-assembled it. He would send us out of the room one at a time and when recalled we had to identify and name the part that he had hidden and so we had some mild fun as we handled these potentially lethal weapons. The penalty for failure was to pay for tea and a 'wad' in the NAAFI for the rest of the squad. Taffy and I rarely paid.

Our Corporal conducted the final exam, which in addition to the written test included a practical test of our ability to strip and re-assemble the guns. We were tested individually. The first part of the test involved naming instantly each of the many parts of the gun as he produced them at random. Then we were timed by stopwatch in striping and re-assembling the Browning. This included completely stripping the breechblock. For 'Taffy' Evans and I because of our demonstrated deftness in class, he insisted that we do the whole procedure blindfold while he stood by with stopwatch in hand. I had done the trick for a bet before. It was going to be a breeze!! I accomplished it in about a minute and a half, until I came to the final movement, which was to cock the blasted thing. Imagine my fury when the damn gun jammed! What HAD I done wrong? He taunted me for my overweening arrogance and told me to find the trouble, still with the blindfold on. As I stripped it down, I found the problem.

Corporal, the 'tricky bastard' had quietly dropped a matchstick in the works. He thought this a great joke and 'razzed' me over my discomfiture. Realising that if there had been any chance of failure he would not have played the prank, I too saw the funny side."

Range firing was practised regularly and almost became fatal to George when on of his fellow pupils became a little over-enthusiastic with an automatic pistol.

"We also had to practice weekly, firing at target on the range with the old Lee-Enfield .303 rifle. I quickly discovered a talent for this and ended up in the top three. As a left-hander, I sighted from the left shoulder, so that the bolt action was close to my face. I had to prove to the Sergeant i/c Range that this was no restriction when 'rapid fire' was ordered. One day, we had target practice of a different kind. We learned to handle the Sten gun. It was a bitch of a gun when firing on 'automatic'. If one did not press on top of the barrel, one sprayed bullets into the air like a Roman candle!

Also, we practised with revolvers and pistols of astonishing variety and age. I got hold of a Smith & Wesson .38, the standard RAF officer issue. I got some excellent results. Not so my neighbour on my left at the range. It was Inwood, who was a real dolt of only mediocre intelligence and who paid little attention to regulations. We all remembered how, when at Torquay, he had tossed his bayonet wildly into the air as we were pulling them from the scabbard to 'Fix bayonets'. It had hit a man further down the ranks. Fortunately, we could have ridden, 'bare-arsed to Berlin' on them without getting cut. Richmond had lost his temper then and had made him do a week's sentry duty outside Headquarters.

On this particular occasion, he had picked up his loaded Colt .45 while the Sergeant had his back turned and began to play with it quite contrary to all Range Orders. Before anyone realised what was happening, there was a 'Burp! burp!, burp!' and the sand was spurting around my feet. I leaped backwards, screaming blasphemy in my fear and shock. For this exciting little episode, my friend Inwood had the laughter taken out of him by being hauled before the CO and being given a week's cookhouse fatigues. – He should have had a month! I, the near-victim, had no sympathy but it did add a little zip to NAAFI 'bull' sessions for a day or two."

Eventually the flying phase commenced and George had the opportunity to relieve some of his frustration, albeit in a limited fashion, from the rear turret of a Whitley.

"We were all anxious to start flying training. This was to be done in Whitley's –the Mk II with Tiger engines – and Fairey Battles, survivors of the massacre in France in 1940. The Whitley's were used for gunnery training. Six of us squatted in the fuselage until we were airborne, then each of us in turn locked ourselves in the rear turret – a Fraser-Nash. We had then to load the single Browning .303 – it was the standard four gun turret but only one gun was mounted – with a belt of ammo, which we had earlier belted ourselves. When the drogue had been streamed from the accompanying Fairey Battle and the instructor's "OK to fire" given over the intercom, we poured bullets generously in the right direction. Our number of 'hits' was appallingly low but at least it relieved our frustrations.

The Battles were used for Practice Bombing and carried sixteen 11½lb practice bombs which we dropped from various levels at the Aberdaron Bombing Range off the coast nearby. Staff pilots, officers and NCO's flew the aircraft, English and Polish. By far the best of them was a Polish sergeant, named Steinke, only twenty years old, handsome as a filmstar and reputed to be a devil with the women! When it came to flying he had complete assurance, a delicate touch and was steady as a rock on a practice bombing run. He also flew the lumbering Whitley with equal skill – no mean achievement.

I disliked the Battle for one reason only. To aim the bombs required the bomb aimer to lie prone in the rear cockpit. A sliding panel in the floor had to be opened to the slipstream and the bombsight lowered on a retractable support into the icy blast, which numbed one's face and hands in spite of gloves. This opening was immediately behind the engine radiator which, in the ancient and decrepit machines in which we flew, always dripped oil and Glycol. This black, oily and smelly 'goo' blew backwards into our faces.

In some cases it gave us nausea as well as spattering us so that we landed looking rather like grimy loco mechanics. Soon, bombing practice was humdrum and was enlivened only once for me by the exhilaration of aerobatics. Flt Lt Turpin was one of the few survivors of the Battle squadrons that had been decimated in Northern France in 1940. At the end of a low-level bombing practice, after making quite sure that I was properly strapped in, and everything in the rear cockpit secure, he treated me to a number of split-arsed turns and a couple of rolls, all strictly against SSO's."

A reminder of the dangers of war, even in flying training, was brought home to the students one day whilst preparing for a bombing trip.

RESULTS OF AB INITIO BOMBING COURSE

Station held : No 9 B & GS   PENRHOS

Period of Course 6.1.41. To 8.3.41.

Exercise	Bombs dropped	Av. Error in yards	Type of Aircraft
H L. Group	8	105 radius	
L. Applic.	24	196	
E.	—	—	
H L. Moving	—	—	
L.	23	184	Battle
Night.			

Exam. Marks % **83.**   Course Flying Time 11   Hrs. 45

REMARKS : PASS/FAIL

Results well above average will make a good bomb aimer

_____ JWArmny. S/L. for .... C.I.

The Bombing certificate for George's course at No 9 BGS.

"There was only one serious incident and we never knew why it should have happened. One morning as we were loading the 11½lb practice bombs on the racks in readiness for our first detail, there was an explosion from another aircraft down the line. One of our number had dropped a bomb. We had dropped them before; they were perfectly safe until the safety pin was removed. What he did we never knew but somehow contrary to all SOP's he had removed the pin before the bomb was properly in the toggle. It had exploded with considerable violence. His mangled body was taken to Sick Bay then quickly transferred to a hospital in Liverpool. He did survive but was invalided out of the Service, a battered wreck. It was a sobering reminder of the hazards of handling explosives.

We had no regrets when the course came to an end. Playing with bombs had been interesting and the flying had added to the zest that I had brought to the course. It meant that at last we would, after a year of training, have chevrons to display on our arms and the coveted Flying 'O' on our left breast. It did not matter that we had no actual experience of war or any real idea of how we would cope with the actual tensions, fears and dangers of Operations. We would be joining an elite. Our pride and arrogance were immense.

We had no regrets when the course came to an end. Playing with bombs had been interesting and the flying had added to the zest that I had brought to the course. It meant that at last we would, after a year of training, have chevrons to display on our arms and the coveted Flying 'O' on our left breast. It did not matter that we had no actual experience of war or any real idea of how we would cope with the actual tensions, fears and dangers of Operations. We would be joining an elite. Our pride and arrogance were immense.

The final exams had proved to be easy and no one failed the course. I maintained my previous reputation by finishing in the first three. The gunnery marks disappointed me but everyone else had been marked down too. Goldsmid beat me again – the clever bastard. I who survived should not disparage Goldsmid, he was indeed a very good navigator and a brave man who was one of the first of our crowd to sacrifice his life. He went to a Blenheim squadron and failed to return from one of the suicidal missions over Northern France."

Just before the end of the course George and several others were put in front of a commissioning board. George was not successful. Only the public school men on the course were accepted and George entered the Sergeant's Mess. Almost the entire course went en bloc to a Blenheim OTU in Bomber Command. Niblick was one of them.

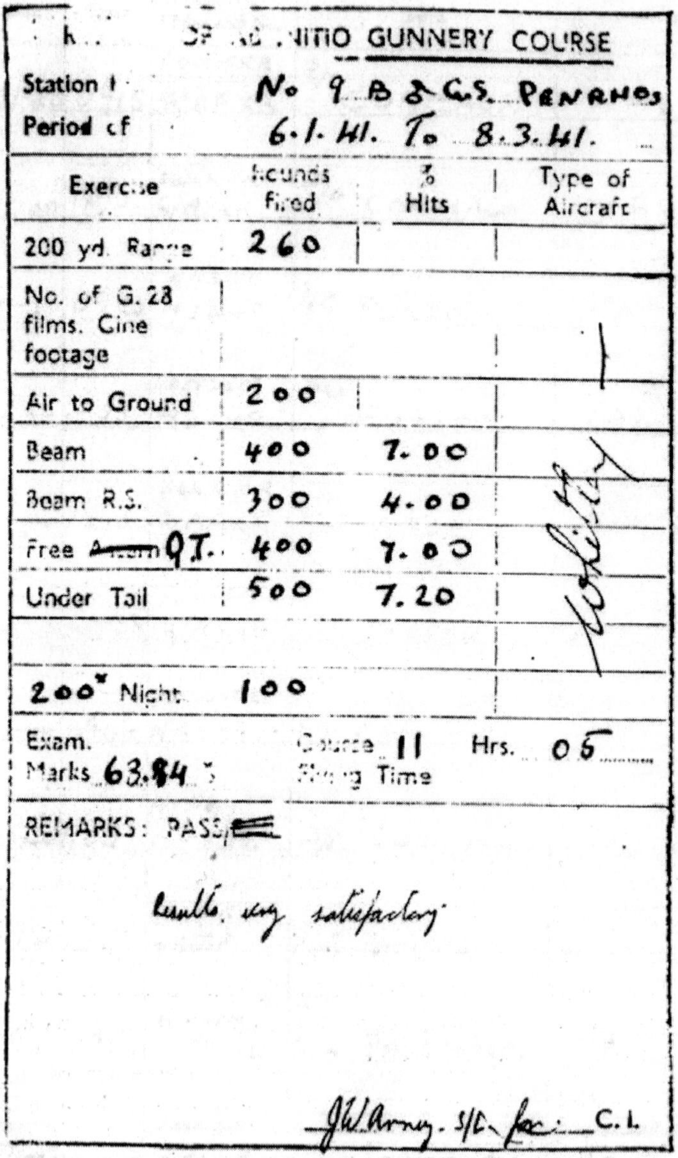

... OF ... ITIO GUNNERY COURSE

Station : No 9 B & G.S. PENRHOS

Period of : 6.1.41. To 8.3.41.

Exercise	Rounds fired	% Hits	Type of Aircraft
200 yd. Range	260		
No. of G.28 films. Cine footage			
Air to Ground	200		
Beam	400	7.00	
Beam R.S.	300	4.00	
Free A... Q.T..	400	7.00	
Under Tail	500	7.20	
200* Night	100		

Exam. Marks 63.84 %

Course 11 **Firing Time** **Hrs.** 05

REMARKS: PASSED

Results. very satisfactory.

JW.Arney. S/L. for: C.I.

The logbook Gunnery certificate from No 9BGS.

George, Bob Lindford and Paddy Gething remained at Penrhos pending a posting to an OTU, yet to be formed, at Chivenor in Coastal Command.

Chivenor had originally been the North Devon Airport, but had been taken over in May 1940 by the RAF. Work commenced to lay three 3,000-yard runways and the airfield opened in October 1940. The first occupants were No 3 (Coastal) OTU but they left in July 1941 and were to be replaced by No 5 (C) OTU, which George and the others were to join.

> "We liked the look of Chivenor, a new airfield, clean and freshly painted. It was out first sight of concrete runways and they seemed to us to go on and on forever. But there was a big snag; the station was not expecting us. We reported to the Station Orderly Room to be told to get our kit stowed away and come back the next day. So it went on. No Admin staff, no Orderly Room, no instructors and above all no aircraft. We were orphans. The station personnel wanted nothing to do with us. During the next few days a few AG's and three or four more navigators arrived from West Freugh, who brought us up to date with news of some of our Prestwick and Torquay buddies. We spent fruitless hours hanging around. Rumour had it that the Beauforts would arrive "tomorrow".
>
> One morning Paddy and I were caught by the Sqn Ldr Controller who was looking for 'bodies' to help organise the Ops Room. We volunteered our services. It was a lucky break for us. Whilst the others went on leave we worked in the Ops Room. One day the Sqn Ldr casually asked us if we would like to be re-posted for operational training on Whitley's. He told us that No 3 (Coastal) OTU Detachment, presently at Kinloss, required two navigators. We both said yes."

After a week of leave at home, George travelled by train to Kinloss, east of Inverness on the Moray Firth. Kinloss was an Expansion Period airfield. The airfield was home to No 19 OTU and No 45 MU. A detachment of No 3 (Coastal) OTU had arrived in April 1941. Also at this time Kinloss began to use a satellite airfield at Forres, a few miles to the west. Arriving at Kinloss, George was confronted with a somewhat disorganised OTU detachment.

> "A local bus took me to Kinloss from Forres station. It was a Saturday evening and only the Duty Sergeant of the Bomber Command OTU was available. He dumped me without ceremony in the changing

room of the gymnasium as a temporary billet. At least there was a truckle bed, hot water for a bath and the room was heated.

I had all the following day to get orientated. I was now adept at getting all the 'gen'. Who was the Station Commander? What units were there on the station? Where did one go on days off? Inverness or Elgin? I discovered too that No 3 (C) OTU Det was a despised lodger unit on what was a Bomber Command station. Despised because it was small, badly organised – it borrowed lecture facilities and a haphazard flying schedule that interfered with their intensive training programme. I could find none of my Coastal comrades in the Sergeant's Mess – they had all disappeared for the weekend. I was treated with some contempt (my stripes still looked very new!) and my friendly approaches at the bar were rebuffed. To escape the snide remarks of the bomber boys I took the bus into Inverness.

The role of the OTU was supposedly to enable the various components of the crew to learn to fly together as a team. No 3 (Coastal) OTU fell far short of the goal. It had advanced very little beyond being merely a unit for conversion of pilots to type. The detachment was intended to supply crews for the two squadrons of Coastal Command which were operational on Whitley aircraft – Nos 502 and 612. They had only recently converted and so had no experienced personnel to release to the unit to pass on their experience to the tyros.

The trainee pilots had no problems; there were enough experienced pilots to undertake the conversion. For the AG's and radio operators too, the problems were minor. They were already familiar with the guns and turrets and the radio equipment was little different from what they had been passed out on at Radio School. The detachment also had a Signals and Gunnery instructor.

For 'sprog' navigators like Paddy and myself, the situation was chaotic. Navigation as a full time occupation for a crew member was relatively new. The Hudson squadrons had only recently added a navigator to their crew complement – some still flew with two pilots who took turn about to do the navigation. We had no navigation instructor.

Early Monday morning I finally located the Unit Orderly Room and reported in. It was a dismal office in one of the hangars. The Adjutant had a small corner from which he surveyed a welter of files, coffee cups and the odd gasmask. There was a Corporal clerk and an AC2 'dogsbody'. The CO was not in his office and the Adjutant was quite disinterested, but he did rouse himself sufficiently from his newspaper to tell the corporal to show me my billet and to tell me that

I should go across the airfield to see the Flight Commander who would give me all the 'gen'.

It was late morning when I reached the two dilapidated wooden huts. It was a warm, sunny Spring day. There were four or five rather worn looking Whitleys parked nearby in various stages of serviceability, with fitters and riggers in oily overalls going about their various tasks. Two or three aircrew lazed about outside one of the huts, striped to the waist, sunbathing, reading Picture Post or a newspaper. One man, a Flying Officer – I noticed his tunic draped on the back of his chair – roused himself from his Daily Telegraph to look me up and down. I stood at attention in front of him. The encounter went something like this:

Me: "Sir! Sgt Gray, just arrived from Chivenor. The Adjutant sent me over to see the Flight Commander."

Fg Off: "Oh! Really!" Pause. "Do you do these?" He waved his Telegraph languidly.

Me: "Sometimes, Sir!"

Fg Off: (reading out a clue in his best Etonian accent.) "How about this one? He was against Flying Boats. Question mark."

Me: "Cicero, Sir?"

Fg Off: (turning to his companion lounging in the other chair.) "It fits! Good God! The man's a scholar. But can he navigate? Do you think?"

I am getting madder by the minute. What sort of 'Fred Karno' outfit is this?

Me: (now beetroot and stiffly at attention.) "I would like to see the Flight Commander. SIR!"

Fg Off: "OK old man, keep your forage cap on! He's flying but come inside. I'll get Sgt Whittington to put you in the picture."

Somewhat mollified, I followed him into the hut. A single room, two deal tables, one littered with cups and flying kit, parachute bags and a green canvas Navigator's bag along one wall. Three men seated at the other table, playing cards. They ignored us until the Flying officer said: "Dick, this is Sgt Gray, he's come to join us. Give him all the 'gen' will you?"

It was time to wander back to the Mess for lunch, so we talked on the way. Dick was one of the two navigators of the other two crews, just starting their second month at the unit. The apparent lack of organisation appalled me. No one seemed to give a damn. He suggested that I should collect some nav kit and gave me a run down on what I should have. He told me that Stores could be ' difficult'."

Like many others, before and since, George encountered the RAF storeman's attitude of ' I store it, you can't have it in case someone else needs it, and anyway, your not entitled'!

> "I spent the rest of the day 'chivvying' the corporal in the Orderly Room to fill out the necessary forms (in quadruplicate!) to present to Stores. I decided enough was enough and retired to the Mess with a sheaf of papers to brood until the next morning. I had to screw up my courage to face the NCO i/c Stores.
>
> The next morning, I set about getting my equipment together. I had to fight the Stores NCO's to the very end. They clutched all their stock to their potbellies with miserly avarice and after scrutinising my requisition forms with irritating reluctance, waddled down the aisles of equipment pretending there was none available. My persistence and a threat of going to the CO wore them down in the end and I collected the mass of maps, tables, drafting equipment, sextant and Longines watch that I wanted. I was alone in this minor skirmish. None of the other crewmembers had arrived and the two crews already on the course were too engrossed in their poker games or the Picture Post to pay much attention to me. I appropriated a locker for all my equipment and waited on the sidelines.
>
> I met the Flight Commander in an off hand way and bandied words with the Fg Off O had met on the first day. I had become part of the furniture. By mid-week Paddy arrived and with him the rest of the new crews. My spirits revived. I managed to tell him my tale of frustration, but he was bubbling with the news that he was getting married and was too excited by the prospect to pay serious attention to my complaints."

Having finally managed to collect his navigation kit and been reunited with Paddy, George approached the next obstacle in his journey towards an operational squadron – No navigation instructor.

> "Paddy and I found ourselves very much on our own. There was no organised programme for us as there was no nav instructor. We could have sat around all day in the warm Spring sunshine. It was a Spring of exceptional warmth and sunshine along the south coast of the Moray Firth in 1941. But animated by a restless energy and a dynamic enthusiasm. I plunged into a continuous round of flying. It was frequently unauthorised but never forbidden. Thus I accumulated a number of hours flying with pilots on circuits and landings and local flying, whether they were my designated pilots or not. I flew regularly with Vic Pope and Jonah Jones, my official pilots, but I also flew with

'Tinker' Bell and Joe Edwards who were the pilots of Paddy's crew. I was always available so that even the CO took me along as navigator for a trip to Silloth.

When in the air I busied myself with becoming familiar with every knob, tit and lever, and with every nook, cranny and crew position in the Whitley and I was soon at home with every piece of equipment on board including the dinghy and emergency pack. It was an objective I pursued with single-minded determination throughout my flying career when it came to flying in an unfamiliar aircraft.

The Whitleys that we flew in were an odd collection. All were cast-offs from Bomber Command. They were Mk V's with Merlin engines. One morning early in the course, I had corralled a LAC electrician to explain the Bombing Panel to me. It was the standard panel that we had become familiar with at the BGS but I wanted to make no mistakes. We were snugly ensconced in the nose of the aircraft – the panel was on the starboard side – and I was crouched on what was in fact the forward escape hatch. There were other groundcrew around going about their normal daily inspections. Suddenly the LAC lost his audience! To his surprise and my consternation I disappeared through the hatch to land on a very astonished fitter. The fitter had

George Gray trained on Whitley's like this one, a Mk VII, at Kinloss with No 3 (Coastal) OTU Detachment before flying in them on ops with No 502 Sqn from Limavady. (George Gray)

decided to open the hatch and bingo! I was jettisoned. His presence broke my fall and fortunately we both only sustained minor bruises but it was a timely warning. Later marks were modified and the hatch was made to open only inwards.

I watched the take-off and landing procedure from a position just behind the pilots and memorised the sequence with care. I knew the emergency drill for lowering the undercarriage in case of hydraulic failure – one had to crawl into the wing and from a very cramped position wind down each wheel separately. I watched the sequence for changing fuel tanks. In short I became an expert in everything but my own métier for which there was no opportunity other than map-reading in the short flights of the first three weeks, but I came to know every inch of the ground within fifty miles of Kinloss as well as the back of my hand.

My assiduous pursuit of every little bit of knowledge about the aircraft paid a dividend very early. Three weeks into the course came the time for the pilots to do their first night flying. I had no orders to join them for what were only circuits and landings and they never left

Liberator of No 36 Sqn at Shaibah, Iraq, 7ᵗʰ March 1946. George and crew were involved in transporting troops of the Indian Division back to India from Cairo. They landed at Shaibah to pick up fuel and food. The Liberator was capable of carrying twenty-four troops. (George Gray)

the circuit. But by now my enthusiasm (madness as Paddy called it) was acknowledged and I prepared with them for my first night flight. Anyway, I would qualify for a special pre-flight meal and I could not pass that up! There was nothing for me to do but watch the proceedings and enjoy the feeling of my first experience of flying at night."

The early stages of becoming familiar with a new aircraft type could be dangerous for a new crew and George and his crew almost came to grief when one of the pilots made a mistake.

"Kinloss, at that time, was a flat grass field with the western overshoot area running straight into Findhorn Bay, which was mostly mudflats at low tide and about six feet of muddy water when the tide was high. We took off in almost pitch darkness, the take-off path barely indicated by dimly flickering 'glim' lamps. Vic did several landings without a hitch, then it was Jonah's turn. The take-off was OK but as he turned in for his final approach he was too high and too close. It was going to be a near thing. He increased his rate of descent and tried to get his speed off. He pushed the stick forward and at the same time pulled the throttles back but he could not get the engines throttled back far enough. I sensed the urgency. There was an increase in tension as he tugged at the throttles desperately, with no response. The flare path was fast approaching and he made no effort to go around again. I grasped the situation. I knew what was wrong. So ignoring all rules, I reached over and yanked the Mixture Control into Rich. In his alarm he had forgotten this vital drill. Unless the Mixture was in Rich the engines would not idle. The landing was a bit long but we did not run out of grass!

Not all night landing practices were so successful. A minor incident, which became a joke in the Mess, involved a trainee crew from the Bomber OTU. It was revealed to us one morning as we walked across the field to our Flight huts. There, in the middle of Findhorn Bay, like some great black water bird, lay a Whitley seemingly undamaged. The crew, practising night landings had done what Jonah did – failed to put the Mixture into Rich, and too late to go around, had overshot and pancaked into the Bay. Apparently the tide was just on the point of coming in. The crew in the panic of the crash landing had launched the dinghy in the pitch darkness and had dived overboard only to find themselves stranded in knee-deep mud and had had to wait for the tide before they could paddle the dinghy ashore."

George, ever keen to learn, decided to master Astro-Navigation, and once more had to do battle with Stores.

"Astro-Navigation had not been taught at Navigation School. The pioneers of the long-range flights of the '30's had developed it. Even Alcock and Brown in 1919 had used it, but they had adapted the long and tedious methods of the sailors and had used a maritime sextant. The aristocrats of Coastal Command – the boat squadrons – had long used the marine sextant. For the requirements of Bomber Command, the Air Ministry had developed a bubble sextant for use at night – the bubble could be illuminated – with an averaging device, which reduced the errors of the bubble.

I had badgered Stores into issuing me a sextant together with such new tables as were then in print. They reduced the length of the mathematical calculations. I also obtained a Planisphere. Paddy and I had to share the sextant – Stores refused to issue another.

We bribed a Sergeant from the Bomber Command OTU – with several beers – to give us the basics of the art. In those sunny days of that extraordinary Spring, Paddy and I took dozens of shots of the sun and plotted them on a large scale Admiralty Chart until we achieved a speed and accuracy which we deemed adequate. Then we spent several nights with the Planisphere laboriously identifying the major stars and taking shots until we could guarantee a tiny 'cocked hat'. I carried the sextant into the air and while Vic and Jonah familiarised themselves with flying the Whitley, I practised taking sunshots. This was not a simple procedure in the Whitley Mk V. They had no astrodome from which to survey the whole dome of the sky in comfort. One had to lower the upper escape hatch and then flip up a narrow windshield to deflect the slipstream. One had to ensure that maps, charts etc. were well secured before doing this or one risked having everything sucked out! The draught also brought mild complaints from the pilots. Then one poked one's head into the 120mph gale to take the shot. I checked their accuracy against pinpoints on the ground."

George came across another item of navigation equipment, which excited his curiosity. It was initially drawn to his attention due to the fact that it was missing from the aircraft.

"One day I was prowling around one of the aircraft that was U/S for a minor inspection. I came across a framework directly above the Nav table. The Nav table was immediately behind the pilot on the port side and the navigator sat sideways on the starboard side. It aroused my curiosity and I grabbed an instrument LAC:

"What's this for?"

"An Astrograph fits in there. We took it out. It's all over in Sgt Cook's office."

"Lets have a look at it."

My interest was aroused. I was considered a bit of an oddball – I fraternised with the groundcrew. Sgt Cook was a careful soul. He loved his aircraft as only a Halton-trained airman could. He produced the Astrograph – it was new and still in its case! He also had the films to go with it. I was in my element. My friend the instrument man and I spent the rest of the day familiarising ourselves with its mysteries.

Its operation was in fact quite simple. It had been devised for Bomber Command to eliminate the time-consuming drudgery of starshot calculations. It was manufactured by Kodak. It fitted in the framework directly over the Nav table. The appropriate film was inserted and the light switched on. The picture projected on the table could be focused and centred by means of adjusting knobs.

There were guidelines on the film so that the chart could be properly aligned and then pinned down. The films consisted of a series of altitude curves labelled for three major stars selected to give a 'cocked hat'. One rolled the film forward or backward to align one meridian on the chart with the appropriate LHA noted on the time scale on the film. All one had to do then was shoot the selected stars and plot the altitudes on the chart from the appropriate curve. Simple! Paddy and I spent one night practising with it but we decided that we preferred the longer method. It was too tedious to keep the thing in proper focus. I never did use it on the squadron."

In one of their brief escapes from Kinloss, George and his friends had an unusual, and potentially very embarrassing, meeting in Inverness.

"Jonah spent his weekends away from us all at Blackboats on the Spey with some horseracing crony angling for salmon. He returned from one of these expeditions with a glorious 10lb specimen which, using his carefully cultivated contacts; he had put in the cooler at the Great Northern Hotel in Inverness. He called for a celebration. The following Saturday night, Vic, Jonah, Paddy and I with 'Tinker' Bell and Joe Edwards assembled there, in our best 'bib and tucker' with buttons highly polished etc., to enjoy the feast prepared by the hotel's chef at a table specially reserved –it cost each of us two or three day's pay! We had just started our meal when, from another entrance, three high ranking Air Commodores and an Air Vice-Marshal with an aide quietly took their seats in a secluded corner not far from us. Surreptitious reconnoitring by us followed and we were surprised to recognise the Duke of Kent and his entourage. I recognised him immediately, having paraded for him on his visit to Torquay.

We would have left it at that and hoped that nothing would attract their attention to us lowly sergeants. Not so, friend Jonah, with aplomb of an accomplished courtier and the assurance bred of years in the racing world, he went over to their table and asked if he might have the chef serve them some of the salmon that we were about to enjoy. We others cringed in embarrassed silence waiting for an abrupt dismissal, but no, they would be grateful and the Duke responded by sending over two bottles of excellent Chablis with his compliments."

With the course end nearing there was a rush to get all of the flying in and to learn as much as possible of what might be useful, or even essential, on operations. Even at this point there was time for a little humour and recreation, although it could lead to trouble.

"The weather continued summer-like over the whole of Northern Scotland while letters from home told tales of unending rain and cold weather in the south of England. We developed an almost tropical tan. The final weeks were a mad scramble to complete our required number of cross-country flights as a crew. These two, three and four hour day and night flights were the first real test of my skill as a navigator. They were undistinguished but I made no major blunders and gained in confidence.

Among other things, we spent a hilarious afternoon at the baths in Inverness. The Bomber OTU instructor had given a lecture on Dinghy Drill and we had a dry run at the airfield. There was also a static display in one of the hangars, where the contents of the dinghy pack and the auxiliary pack attached to the dinghy by a six-foot rope were displayed. We did a practice dinghy drill by jumping off the deep end of the baths and scrambling aboard the dinghy which we had watched inflate when we had tossed it into the water. We spent the rest of the session in some rather energetic horseplay.

Our flying training produced one minor contretemps. Our preflight briefing may have been casual or, in our over-cocky way, we may not have paid attention to the order that we must not fly over the Tay Bridge. However, tired of flying above cloud with only occasional glimpses of the ground below, Vic announced as we passed over Perth and turned onto the next leg of the cross-country and set course for Dyce that he was going to descend through a hole in the cloud deck over to starboard. Away we roared in a steep dive. The hole was small and we were soon embraced by a billowing whiteness. After about two minutes we broke through at 2,000 feet. We were way off course to starboard and heading, still in a shallow dive straight for the Tay Bridge and Dundee in what must have appeared to the Air raid Wardens, an imminent attack. We resumed our course and duly landed at Kinloss, proud of a cross-country successfully completed. Meanwhile all hell had broken loose from Dundee to Inverness and we were soon disabused of our smugness. We received a peremptory summons to the Station Commander's office and were given a severe dressing down. Our brief but exhilarating dive had caused consternation in Dundee. Sirens had sounded and two Hurricanes had been scrambled from Leuchars. We had not seen them. Vic took all the blame and was awarded three days Duty Pilot in expiation.

During the last couple of weeks we had a number of short flights for low-level bombing practice for the pilots and gunnery practice for the AG's who fired their guns from a height of 100 feet at smoke floats which I tossed out through the flare chute. I always insisted that I have a turn in the turret and practise as well. There were no objections from the gunners because I always helped with the tedious chore of belting the ammo. Firing four Brownings got rid of some of my frustrations! At the end we, that is both crews, were given a weeks leave and told to report directly to No 502 Sqn at Limavady near Londonderry, Northern Ireland.

So, you may ask, after two months of sunbathing and occasional flights, had you learned anything about your place in the crew? What part had I to play in the crew? Of course, my job was to navigate the aircraft safely and, above all, accurately. But what other requirements did a U-boat hunting crew demand of a navigator?

Paddy and I learned mostly by hearsay. We kept the log; the written record of all events of the flight, ie. Navigation data, course, true airspeed, track, fixes and bearings. We logged signals sent and received, when the fuel tanks were changed, fuel remaining, weather observations every half-hour or when a change in weather was observed, ie. Major wind velocity change or frontal system encountered.

We also had a couple of lectures by the Signals instructor on Codes and Ciphers and were introduced to the mysteries of the Syko machine – a very simple device for enciphering messages to base or de-ciphering any received. The cipher could be changed at scheduled times by simply inserting a different cipher card. The Q-Code was used for non-operational messages and the Naval Three Figure Code for ops reports reference ships, hostile sightings etc. I began to realise that I would be a very busy little man! I was also responsible for making and receiving any Aldis lamp signals to our own forces.

We all rapidly got our clearance chits signed and logbooks checked and signed by the CO. Then we all piled into a station transport, which dropped us at Inverness station. All of us that is, except Jonah, who elected to spend a short leave with his fishing pal at his home on the Spey. We caught the night train to Perth, there we parted, Paddy and I went to Glasgow where he left me for the boat-train to Stranraer and I hustled on to the crowded express to London. From London, I caught the train to Peterborough and the local bus home."

After home leave George made his way by train and ferry, fascinated by the names of the Ulster towns and villages he passed through, to Limavady.

"I was the only airman to get off the train at the 'Halt' that was the station for Limavady, but from the First Class coach, two officers, a Flight Lieutenant and a Flying Officer quickly walked into the tiny waiting room. I followed more slowly dragging kitbags and webbing equipment. I had to find some way to get to the airfield. I had my usual good fortune. I had just dumped my kit when the Flt Lt emerged from the ticket office.

"Sergeant!"

"Yes, Sir!" I clicked smartly to attention.

"You need transport?"

"Yes, Sir!"

"I have a Commer coming. You can join us. Which squadron are you?"

"502 Sqn, Sir!" I did not know there was another squadron. It was 224 Sqn, who were equipped with Hudson's.

"You're new, aren't you?"

"Yes, Sir, Just arriving from Kinloss."

"Good show! We need some more navigators."

A short wait and the van arrived, driven by a very scruffy 'erk'. I heaved my kit into the back of the van and followed it. The two officers crowded into the front seat with a friendly greeting to the driver. They were dropped off at their Mess – a requisitioned country home called Drina. I climbed over into the front seat and we set out down some country lanes to the 502 Sqn Sergeant's Mess.

I was about to arrive!"

Halifax 243/R at Khartoum, 19th October 1946. The groundcrew are seen with Flt Lt Baker, the pilot and Flt Lt Helme DFC. George and this crew were on No 2 Specialist Navigation Course at RAF Shawbury and this flight was part of a long-range navigation exercise. Flt Lt Helme, a fellow student, had been the navigator on a Catalina from Sumburgh in the Shetlands which had carried out a twenty-five hour flight to reconnoitre Jan Mayen Island. (George Gray)

'Aries II' with groundcrew at Tengah, November 1947. (George Gray)

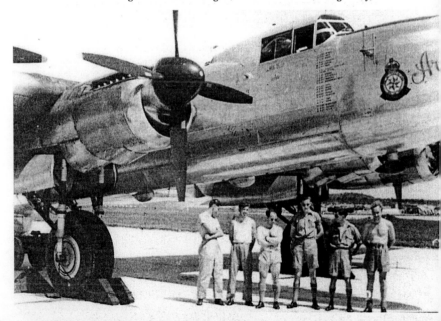

George Gray remained with No 502 Sqn until August 1942 after which he was posted to No 3 (Coastal) OTU at Cranwell as a Navigation and Bombing Instructor on Wellingtons and Whitley's. He was commissioned in October of that year and posted as Station Navigation Officer to Reykjavik in Iceland in 1943. In June 1944 he returned to ops with 524 Sqn at Davidstow Moor and Langham. In 1945 he was awarded a DFC and mentioned in despatches. In June 1945 he was posted to No 36 Sqn at Tain and later Oakington for trooping flights to and from India. In 1947 he became the Navigation officer of No 202 Sqn at Aldergrove and followed this with a course at the Empire Air Navigation School (EANS) at Shawbury. He then became the navigator on 'Aries II' on its mission to Australia, New Zealand and South Africa. After a spell in the radio dept at Farnborough he was selected for an exchange tour with the USAF in 1948. He went to Alaskan Air Command and served as Command navigator to Generals Twining, Atkinson and Armstrong. Whilst there he also flew Polar meteorological flights with the 375th BW in B-29's. In 1951 he received an AFC and retired from the RAF eventually settling in Canada.

View from the Ground

JOHN HOLMES – OBSERVER/GROUNDCREW – 1936/45

John Holmes joined the RAF in February 1936 at Uxbridge as a metal rigger. He did his 'gravel crunching' at Orpington and his trade training at Manston and Henlow. He was posted as an AC1 to No 6 FTS at Netheravon and later also flew as an Observer. From 1938 to 1940 he served with No 63 and No 40 Sqn in the AASF in France. He ended the war as a Flight Sergeant with a BEM and a mention in despatches. John's story is very interesting in that he spans the whole of the war and the period of build up to war, both as groundcrew and aircrew. He also sheds an interesting light on the work and lifestyles of pre-war and wartime personnel.

"My first posting was to No 6 FTS at Netheravon. The unit moved to Little Rissington in 1938 at which time only one barrack block and one hangar had been completed. The various rigger trades there were metal riggers, carpenter riggers, riggers balloon and fabric workers. Certain metal riggers were sent on welding courses, their certificates lasting for six months after which they did a test weld, which was destroyed to check for carbonising. Electric welding was almost unknown. In 1936 there were still five Warrant Officer II's in the RAF. They wore large brass crowns, whereas the WO I wore the 'Tate and Lyle' badge. They were riggers balloon and sundry trades and could only get promotion by re-mustering to the general Duties branch. There was also a King's Warrant Officer who had received his warrant direct from King George the Fifth in France in 1918.

He could only lose his rank by Royal Proclamation. The aircraft were various Hawker types and one Avro Anson, then designated as a medium bomber, but with no hydraulics, hand-starting engines, no armament, until a hand operated turret was fitted and fixed pitch airscrews. There were two Flights. 'A' Flight trained fighter pilots on Hawker Furies and 'B' Flight had the Hawker Audax, Hind and Hart and the single Anson. Night flying from the grass field was done with paraffin gooseneck flares about one a month. If the approach needed to be illuminated the aircraft were fitted with magnesium flares under the lower wingtips, which were initiated electrically. If these were used the aircraft had to do a fast taxy until they went out as there was no way to quench them. Control was by Aldis lamp, no R/T was carried.

In the case of the two-seaters communication was by Gosport Tube. We had one 350-gallon fuel bowser and never used it all on any one night. All aircraft were expected to be down by 3.30pm each day so that they could be cleaned and put into the hangars. Tea was at 4.30pm and the day's work was supposed to be done by 4.00pm. The hangars were locked until 7.00am when the Duty NCO drew the keys and opened up ready for the day's work to start at 8.30am after parade on the square. Breakfast was at 7.30am, parade at 8.00am followed by a march to the hangars and work until noon. March back at 2.00pm and work till 4.00pm. Best Blue uniform was breeches and puttees with peaked cap. We had two caps, one working and one best, no forage caps or berets. Working kit was trousers. Collars and ties were only worn by Sergeants who had passed their confirmation of rank exam. They also wore shoes instead of boots. Acting Sergeants wore the same uniform as airmen. The frugal Air ministry would not issue the collar and tie until the exam was passed as in cases of failure the sergeant reverted to corporal. Three attempts were allowed at this exam. Later I volunteered for aircrew duties and was interviewed by Air Cdr. Blount at Grantham."

Having passed the aircrew interview John was selected for Observer training. Per-war Observers were expected to continue in their ground trades and flew only when required.

"I was sent to No 1 Air Observer Course, No 11 ERFTS at Perth for navigation training on DH 89a's. We were not allowed to wear uniform and were billeted in civilian digs. The pilots were RAF in 'civvies', the ground instructors were civilians and in one case a retired Commander RN."

On completion of the elementary phase of his course John was posted to No 4 AOS at West Freugh, near Stranraer in South West Scotland. West Freugh had opened in August 1936 and was one of the Expansion Stations of that period.

"Our bombing and air firing was done at West Freugh at No 4 AOS. The aircraft were Heyford's. The Vickers Gas Operated was very new and we were only allowed to use it once, on one trip. At the completion of this course I was posted to No 63 Sqn at Upwood".

John stayed with No 63 Sqn for about eight weeks before being re-posted to No 40 Sqn at Abingdon. He went to France with the AASF and was based at Bethenville with No 40 Sqn. He was invalided and grounded in 1940 and spent the rest of the war on groundcrew duties. One of the units he served with was No 57 Sqn at Scampton. This unit first flew Blenheims then Wellingtons and finally Lancaster's.

"The conversion was carried out by a Manchester Flight formed for the purpose. Previously converted aircrews within the squadron did the conversion, but this method diverted both air and groundcrews from the operational strength and resulted in the eventual formation of the heavy Conversion units. Being already engaged in the Conversion business as acting Flt Sgt i/c what was loosely known as 'C' Flight and having some acquaintance with Manchester's I was posted to take over No 3 Site at Winthorpe."

The Roll of Achievement board at West Freugh showing honours and awards given to former pupils of No 4 B&GS on operational units including the award of the VC to Sgt John Hannah. (Authors collection)

Having had a busy war up to this point, firstly as aircrew in the Battle of France and then groundcrew on an operational squadron, John might have expected a rest from the pressure, but his next posting to No 1661 HCU was anything but a rest. Winthorpe was a typical Class A bomber airfield. Opened in 1940 it had accommodation for almost 1,900 personnel and sufficient hardstandings for up to thirty-six heavy bombers as well as three hangars for aircraft maintenance – one B2 type and two of the T2 type. All of the accommodation was temporary. No 1661 HCU was formed from the Conversion Flights of Nos 9, 44 and 49 Squadrons and moved from Skellingthorpe to Winthorpe on the last day of 1942.

"This unit was formed, as were the rest of the HCU's, from the squadrons which had formed Conversion Flights to convert from Wellingtons to Lancaster's or Halifaxes. In our case it was Lancaster's and we also used Manchester's for training. When I was posted in they were flying Manchester's, when enough could be made serviceable. The aircraft were at the end of their working life and suffered badly from engine failure and leaking oil coolers and radiators. The airframes were very sturdy and gave very little trouble. The hydraulic lines were fairly simple and relatively trouble free, however, spares had dried up and the aircraft were taken away and replaced by Stirling's. Some of the Manchester's of the older type had a dorsal fin in addition to the double 'Lanc' type tail, which was disposed of in favour of somewhat larger fins and rudders.

The Stirling's were in very little better shape than the Manchester's. They were old aircraft, the word 'old' being relative. They also suffered from engine failure and the electric motors, which operated the undercarriage, burnt out frequently. There were far too many electrically operated parts in a Stirling, leading to continuous earthing and other troubles. We eventually got rid of these also. A separate Flight was formed at Winthorpe to get the aircraft sufficiently serviceable to fly away, the further the better for my book. I also manage to 'collect' this Flight, which only existed for a matter of weeks. There were numerous Stirling crashes. The most spectacular at Winthorpe was a Stirling from Swinderby, whose long runway was aligned with ours, with about two to three miles separation. This aircraft took off and for some reason failed to clear some trees on a very low ridge between the fields. Leaving part of his tail in the trees he eventually crashed in our overshoot area at the town end of the runway. The aircraft burned out and all aboard were killed. It was an alarming sight to see this aircraft weaving down the runway, about twenty feet up, in the dark, only his lights giving any indication of attitude. We had no contact on R/T and were unable to establish what aircraft it was until long after the crash.

We also had a Whitley land one night. No lights, no R/T. We could not detect what type it was and the duty pilot in the aerodrome caravan was not familiar with the type. I happened to be duty engineer, a job done by rota by the engineer officers, Warrant Officers and Flt Sgt's. (It later became a one- man job and I did it for about a year with a relief about every eight days). I took the vehicle allocated to me, a Humber Snipe, and went out to see if I could find the aircraft, which had taxied into a dark patch, to establish who he was and what was the trouble. I eventually found him and guided him to a spare dispersal and brought the crew back to control. In parking I hit the tailplane of a parked Lanc, wrote off the elevator on one side and broke the windscreen. I ended up with glass in my face and the promise of a court martial – I managed to escape that later.

A Lanc landed on the runway, either with a burst tyre, or burst it on landing. The magnesium alloy wheel flashed up and the whole aircraft burnt out. The heat melted the larger part of the fuselage and wings. The pools of Duralumin keyed the relics into the concrete and had to be removed with crowbars.

Winthorpe was what was termed a temporary camp. All buildings except the standby powerhouse and one or two special buildings were of wood. The Officers Mess was in an old house in the grounds. The whole area was fairly heavily wooded. The WAAF quarters were in a separate area with some open ground between it and the main camp. The living conditions were fairly primitive, the huts and bunks were heated by tortoise stoves fuelled by coke, if and when available, and were either bitterly cold or like ovens if the black-outs were in place. The showers were in a separate building approached by a cinder path. The station had been a Polish, Battle-equipped unit. Obviously they had had better supplies of coke than us and had made paths out of it. A few of the older hands like myself recovered enough good coke to keep the fires going in our individual bunks.

One night the main fuses blew, blacking out the camp. When the duty fitter started up the standby generators, they stopped – over-loaded. Eventually the cause was discovered to be hundreds of fires, made of biscuit tins and fire elements. To accommodate the extra load nearly all billets had silver paper coated nails instead of fuses – the mind boggles! Naturally all this stopped for a time but slowly drifted back. Strangely, the fuses held and the camp did not go up in flames.

The messing was as any station at that time. Officers Mess, with batmen. Sergeant's Mess and Airman's Mess. The NAAFI was out of bounds to all above the rank of Corporal (they had a small room in the NAAFI building, fondly known as the 'Snake Pit'). Messing was carried out by NAAFI contractors, the airmen on basic rations. The Sergeants Mess levied 9d (4½p) per day extra messing. The Officers mess bills were worked in a different pattern and included wine bills and other exotic charges. The food was ver good at Winthorpe. The Sergeants Mess kitchen was run by a WAAF Flt Sgt called Ricks, known as 'Trixie'. She got the best out of the available food, which was cooked in coal fired ranges.

Being a training station the aircrew greatly outnumbered the groundcrews and on bad weather days we found it impossible to get meals and get back to work. As a result the Mess was split into two, aircrew and groundcrews. Not the best of ideas but the only available way to guarantee the ground staff could get a meal fairly quickly. As the Station Adjutant insisted I wore my brevet I was always trying to explain to aircrew and officious young groundcrew that I was not only ground staff but also the senior but one at that. I never got it finally sorted out. The population of the HCU fluctuated too much.

Aircrews came to Winthorpe from various courses specialising in their own branch and were crewed up into sevens. They commenced on 'circuits and bumps' by day and graduated to 'circuits and bumps' by night. Then a series of night exercises on bombing, air firing and cross-countries, first short and then one very long one of some nine hours. As we flew 24 hours a day and seven days a week there were always several courses going at once. There was usually a break of a couple of hours between night and day flying and about the same between day and night. From our point of view, when our courses on No 3 Site reached the long cross-country stage, or a combined bombing and short cross-country, we considered things fairly easy. The bad bit was the 'circuits and bumps' – burst tyres and bogged aircraft. Winthorpe had notoriously soft verges. The Stirling engines overheated very quickly and they were a nightmare to dig out of the mud with their very high undercarriage. We were rather the poor relations of the operational squadrons. We had superannuated aircraft and we always knew if another squadron was being formed as we were raided of such equipment as jacks and engine platforms. We were also about the last to swap our Fordson Majors for David Brown tractors and our transport had to be seen to be believed. In view of the almost continuous refuelling we had to make do with two 2,000-gallon tankers, one for each site.

Occasionally we would get a nearly new aircraft. The crews were, by and large, too raw to have an opinion. They were buoyed up with the thrill of flying and being aircrew. Occasionally I looked at them and wondered how many had any future to speak of. They were just keen to get airborne. The instructors were all first and second tour men, under few illusions, but still managed to instil into their pupils the esprit de corps, so necessary, especially in the relatively large crew of a Lanc. I never heard of anyone trying to put a pupil down or relate some of the more unpleasant things they had seen or heard. My own impression was that the standard of pupils was maintained throughout the war. The crews were allowed, within limits, to form themselves - maybe a little push here and there, just occasionally one or other would be replaced, but that is bound to occur with hundreds of men at any one time. We had one or two senior officers pass through, men who had been on the Staff and were going a squadron CO's or Station Commanders. It was, I am sure, the Command policy that their men knew what they were talking about, from a practical point of view.

The life of a senior engineering NCO was one long grind, to plan not only the day to day but ahead, to make use of the lulls in flying due to the weather, to sort out junior NCO's for various responsibilities and to coax or drive airmen according to their abilities, and dare one say it, intelligence. Wartime brought together all sorts and types, the RAF were lucky, as most of our airmen were volunteers, unlike the Army. The selection of aircrew was always, as I understood it, a careful process. I suppose in some two and a half years I had dozens of aircraft to deal with. My only object was to fill, as far as possible, the requirements of the training staff. One developed a very impersonal and distant view of any individual aircraft. On the squadrons things were different. The aircraft became either old friends or old enemies depending on their habits. One had the same aircraft for months, flown by the same crews, who grew to like their own aircraft and resented moving if it was not available. Training units did not have the same family atmosphere. Strange as it may seem, life in the squadrons was easier than on training units. I tried both and as aircrew as well. Give me the squadrons.

It is difficult to explain but the ground staff on a training unit draws together and was a unit in themselves. Once the aircraft were prepared for some special programme we had to move on to prepare other aircraft for other exercises. There were always other demands to fulfil. The aircrews did not use any special aircraft; they took whatever was allocated. We knew them slightly but never as well as a squadron groundcrews got to know an aircraft and its crew. There was always a feeling of personal loss if a squadron aircraft went missing, which was all too often. Losses were not frequent in a training unit. The stresses were caused more by long hours with old material, than by trauma. As the war progressed our groundcrews were whittled away but we were expected to produce the same amount of work. We did, in fact, do just that.

For almost two years at Winthorpe I was permanent night duty engineer doing eight days in nine, working 4.30pm to 7.00am. I was responsible for the serviceability of the aircraft at night and the preparation of the aircraft for the day programme. Also for the supply of refuelling tankers and questions of MT. It was quite a job, very exacting and interesting, but I finished up in complete exhaustion in two years. I spent fourteen days in hospital and then reverted to Flt Sgt i/c No 3 Site, from whence I had originated."

Morse Happy

NORMAN JONES – WOp/AG – 1941/43

During the middle years of the war the RAF training organisation grew to enormous proportions with huge numbers of trainee aircrew, proceeding from one training unit to another, ever hopeful of reaching the end of the courses and receiving the coveted aircrew brevet. This progress was often interrupted by a period of holding on a unit awaiting a course, or of receiving practical experience in a ground trade associated with the pupils hoped for aircrew specialisation. Norman Jones was one pupil to go through the training tunnel and reach the light at the other end.

> "Having volunteered to join the RAF in March 1941, I was ordered to report to Padgate later that year following enrolment in June 1941 into the RAFVR. I travelled by train from Bournemouth to London, then from London to the nearest station to Padgate. In the carriage with me from London was one 'Bert' Brewster, who was also joining. Bert was from Battersea and was in civilian life a rat catcher. He was in fact listed as a Rodent Operative and due to the need for people like him to keep the Underground stations in London free from rats and mice – as they were being used as Air Raid Shelters – Bert could only get into the services by volunteering for aircrew duties. He wasn't very big, but a real tough little guy and I certainly learned a lot from him, as I was fresh from the Dorset countryside. The first morning at Padgate, at some unearthly hour, we were woken up by someone shouting; 'Come on you lot! Do you know what time it is?' Bert said; 'Yes. About time you shut up and let us get some sleep!' It then transpired that he was talking to a Flight Sergeant and we all soon were told that Flight Sergeant's had almost the power of life and death over us in terms that left us in no doubt that we were well and truly in the 'Mob'."

Having arrived in the RAF to this rude awakening, Norman Jones was duly kitted out and posted to Blackpool to continue his introduction to service life.

> "From Padgate, after kitting out, we went to Blackpool to be taught how to be airmen. This meant 'square bashing' for half the time and learning Morse code during the rest of each day. A book could be

written about Blackpool alone and about the Blackpool landladies, for we were all billeted in guesthouses and some of the landladies were shockers. Bert and I were in three different guesthouses during our time there due to them complaining about little things that one or other of the lads had been doing. So, to keep the peace, the RAF chose to move us, although I know that the next lot into the house would get exactly the same again. However, we did learn to look like airmen as the Drill Instructors did their best with us. What is more amazing is that we were taught to read Morse code at up to ten words per minute within the twelve-week course. If you think about it, it was a feat. So trying was it all that a number of men had breakdowns before the course was over. There was an arcade in the shopping area called 'Feldmans Arcade' and the shops there were turned into wards to receive those who became 'Morse Happy'.

I have two special memories of Blackpool. The first is of a Sergeant Hill who was permanently billeted in the last guesthouse we were sent to. He was a Physical Training Instructor (PTI) and before the war had been a professional wrestler under the name of 'Mazurky'. Apart from being one of the nicest men, he was also very modest. Although he never mentioned it, he had been awarded a medal for rescuing people from the railway station after one of the aircraft from a nearby Polish Air Force training station had crashed on it. The second is of Christmas Eve, 1941, when Bert and I volunteered to undertake fire-watching duties and were sent to 'Woolworth's' to spend the night there in case of an air raid. We found that 'Woolworth's' had their own night watchman and, not only did he see that we had a good nights sleep, but that the café staff left us a wonderful supper of Lancashire Hotpot and some bacon and eggs for breakfast. That convinced me that if there were duties to be carried out it is always best to step forward, because the guy handing out the duties will be so impressed that he will pick the best job for the first volunteer."

Escaping from Blackpool, with his sanity, Norman Jones continued with his aircrew training. His next posting was to Yatesbury in Wiltshire, situated a few miles east of Calne. This was a large camp, housing No 2 Radio School (RS), with a small grass airfield. The unit came under the control of No 27 Group.

"After Blackpool and some leave I went to Yatesbury, which was a Radio School for WOp (Air) under training. Here we were taught basic electricity, radio theory and were taken up to eighteen words per minute, sending and receiving, Morse code. There was no flying from this Radio School, all class work. It is surprising how the instructors there taught us who had, in the main, arrived with no knowledge of radios. One of the instructors was Sgt Hannah, awarded the VC earlier in the war after staying in his Hampden aircraft, set on fire over Germany, to put out the fire and help the pilot get it back to their base. He used to pull our legs by reminding us that while he checked on parade for being clean shaven, he did not have to as the skin on his face, after skin grafting, came from regions of his body that did not produce hair.

I was taken ill at Yatesbury on the day that I was to take my final trade test and, while the medical people did not know for sure what was wrong, they did know that I had a temperature of well over 100 degrees. For some reason, probably because I pleaded so much, I was allowed to leave the sick bay and report for the trade test. Two examiners refused to come near me so it was left to a Warrant Officer to take my test. He sat as far away as he could, asked me two or three simple questions, and that was enough for him to order me back to see the MO and assure me that I had passed and would be awarded my Wireless Operator badge when I was well again. It turned out that I had acute tonsillitis, so was not too long after the rest of my course in going home on leave before my next posting."

Norman was steadily moving through the training system when he was posted into a unit for 'on the job' experience. Unfortunately it turned out to be, initially a move 'along the road' but later a full stop to his training for almost six months.

"Following training as WOp's the idea was that we all went to a Signals Section at an operational unit for a maximum of six months, to gain practical experience, before moving on to training as operators in aircraft. This didn't always work out as I met one fellow who had spent his time in the morgue of a large Bomber Command airfield – which was just what an aircrew member under training needed! I was posted to RAF Hurn, about five miles from my home, and I thought that was great. Only to be told on reporting to the Guardroom that the whole station was being moved to RAF Defford in Worcestershire in a matter of days. The move was complete in forty-eight hours due to Pickfords being brought in and every lorry they had was used in the operation. Apart from those that travelled up in the station aircraft, the rest of us were transported by train and, believe me, it was some move.

Our Intelligence Service had gathered information that the Germans were planning to drop parachute troops on the airfield and on the research buildings themselves with the purpose of destroying all the aircraft and equipment before they themselves were killed or captured. A Sqn Ldr who was in charge of security was discussing this plan in the Officers mess. He was overheard, by two young Parachute Regiment officers, saying that the plan would never work and it could be discounted. These officers then took their men up, dropped them and captured the airfield as an exercise. This prompted the rush north away from the coast. We went under canvas at Defford, as there were not enough huts to go around. The weather was against us for the fist week or so and it wasn't fun.

After a week or so I was seconded to the Air Defence Research & Development Establishment at Malvern Link, which was being run on behalf of the Army and Navy as they were into anti-aircraft equipment such as radio-controlled guns, searchlights etc. I found this to my liking as I was billeted in a private home and only had to report to Defford every two weeks for a pay parade. Added to the luxury of all this I had met a girl who later became my wife. So I spent my spare time with her and the 'boffins' used to cover for me. My job was to link the ground trials with aircraft flying as targets via R/T, so you see I never did get the W/T experience I was supposed to."

Jones was in for something of a shock when he arrived at his next post. After the relative luxury of a private house and reporting once a fortnight things changed drastically. A strong regime prevailed, and though there was still a little luxury, No 7 Radio School was a happy unit.

"In November 1942 I was posted to the Wireless Operators (Air) Maintenance Course at South Kensington. We were billeted in a block of luxury flats across from the Albert Hall and the classrooms were in the Science Museum, which had been converted by means of wooden classroom partitions. There were an awful lot of airmen who had been living in the free and easy attitude of operational stations suddenly brought back to parading three times a day under NCO's, who were Drill Instructors, and thought that the only way to control us was by piling on the 'bull'. There was very nearly a mutiny at South Kensington. It all came to a head one evening when one of the lads found a dead mouse in his evening meal. We were using the hall in the Imperial College of Science and Technology as our mess, and after this guy held up the mouse, we all struck up singing 'Three Blind Mice'. The Orderly Sergeant tried, in his Drill Instructor way, to stop us without success. Then the Duty Officer arrived and he was given the 'bird'. It all simmered for days afterwards and I am pretty certain that one or two men were singled out and charged. During that time London was still getting the odd air raid so, all in all, it did not make for a very happy station. In the end an officer arrived who had been in the Coldstream Guards. This fellow, Flt Lt Martinez, taught the Drill Instructors that maintaining discipline was not a matter of bullying, but of being fair, if hard."

Norman Jones next posting was to No 4 Radio School at Madley in Herefordshire. This RS operated a mix of De Havilland Dominie's and Percival Proctor's of various marks. The airfield had three runways and the camp was built in the wartime temporary style. Madley was home to 7,000 officers, airmen and WAAF's. It was here that Norman had his first practical experience of flying and operating radio equipment in the air. It was also here that he became the 'victim' of staff pilot's boredom, which they would try to relieve with some unauthorised low flying.

"The huts were of typical wartime airfield pattern, long enough to house about thirty 'bods' in dormitory fashion. A Canadian type stove at each end for heating and a linoleum floor that had to be kept polished. We did not have the luxury of hot water in the mornings so shaving was in cold (very cold) water. The floor polishing was carried out at night-time on a rota basis and in the morning we moved about it on pads so that we didn't mark the floor. It was inspected each day and the whole hut would be confined to camp if the Duty Officer found the place not to his liking. We were taught that we had to think of each other as a team and letting the other guy's down wasn't on.

The badge of No 7 Radio School.
The winged sandal signifies the
speed of message transmission

Training in operating radio equipment in aircraft was quite extensive and incorporated such things as tuning the receiver into a certain frequency then tuning the transmitter to match. This was not too easy because signals could be very weak from the base station and the equipment could itself cause frequency drift. We had to learn how to use the direction finding loop aerials so that we could set up the receiver to give the pilot an indicated course to steer back to the base station. There were set exercises of messages to be transmitted and received and, as we had to wear thick flying gloves, it wasn't easy to handle the tuning dials and operate the Morse key at the required speed of at least eighteen words per minute.

At the start of the flying course we went up in De Havilland Dominie aircraft, which were multi-seat aircraft, fitted out with a number of the, by then, standard radio transmitters and receivers Type T1154/R1155. These had been designated as radio equipment, general purpose – GP – so became affectionately known as the 'Jeep'. This equipment operated over what was then medium and high frequency ranges. The aerial running along the top of the 'kite' was for high frequency work and we had to lower out of the aircraft, via what was really a large centre pin fishing reel, the wire aerial of the correct length for medium frequency operation. The trick was not to forget to wind in the aerial before coming in to land. If it wasn't and was lost by catching on the perimeter fence then £1 was stopped out of pay and that meant eight days pay at that time.

After passing the standard set for operating 'Jeeps' we then flew in the single-engined Proctor where there was just the pilot and the WOp under training on board. In these aircraft we had to operate the radio equipment that had been in use before the war. This was the TR1082/1083. This was wonderful equipment as to change from one frequency to another we had to change coils. There were plug in coils wound to suit a given frequency band with the radio's variable tuning condenser. Added to the problems set by the course and the equipment, we had to contend with the pilots who, because they were bored by this type of flying, used to do such things as fly around the Malvern Hills as low as they could to 'buzz' anyone walking there. On one trip the Australian pilot I was flying with 'shot up' a courting couple and I remember the male member of the duo was a sailor. On another trip, after I had told him that my girl lived in Pershore, he took the plane there and we circled her house in tight turns for some time. This caused some problems for me as I was in the middle of a long contact with Madley when, due to the aircraft banking and the trailing aerial altering its relationship with it, the frequency drift caused them to lose contact with us and they thought we had crashed. All good fun now, but at the time my main concern was passing the course and Flt Sgt Mills RAAF wasn't helping. Having started the course in March 1943, two years after volunteering, I qualified as WOp (Aircrew) on 5th May 1943 and was half way there."

The next phase of Norman Jones' training was posting to AGS. He was posted to No 3 AGS at Mona on Anglesey. This airfield was situated a few miles west of Llangefni with the A5 running alongside. Mona had been completed in mid-1942 for a new AGS, No 6, but this unit did not form so No 3 AGS moved in from Castle Kennedy in December 1942. The airfield had the standard Class A configuration of three concrete runways. A single T1 type hangar and seventeen blister hangars provided shelter for the aircraft. The 1,700-odd personnel were accommodated in the usual wartime austerity temporary huts. No 3 AGS was equipped with the despised Blackburn Botha and Avro Anson's.

"We went almost directly from Madley to AGS only to find when we got there that we had to stand back while a course of WOp/Air Mechanics were given their gunnery courses. All these fellows were destined for flying boat squadrons, hence them being on a Wireless Mechanics course. It galled us somewhat, as these men had been with us at South Kensington and had volunteered for the additional Mechanics course from there, while most of us had refused that as we thought it would hold us up in our quest for the Air Gunners brevet to go with the WOp badge and thus be fully fledged aircrew.

When we did start our course we were split up into four groups, each with a Squad Corporal, who was selected from the trainees. In charge of each group of two squads was a Course Sergeant; again drawn from the lads, while over the whole course was a Course Flight Sergeant. It was made quite clear that, as we were to become SNCO's on completion of the course, whoever was acting as Trainee NCO had to do it properly. If anyone on the course got into trouble that could have been prevented then the acting NCO's would be judged incompetent and would not be passed out as Sergeant Air Gunner at the end of the training. I was made Course Flight Sergeant and the pressure was on. We had a guy, named Jepson, on the course and he was a real rebel. He had served in the Merchant Navy before volunteering for aircrew duties. He had one thing up his sleeve, which we hadn't – If he was tossed off the course he could insist on going back to sea, while the rest of us would have to take 'pot luck' in the

RAF. Jepson was posted to a Coastal Command squadron after passing out as a WOp/AG and refused to go saying he had joined to fly in Bomber Command and if he didn't go there he wouldn't go anywhere. He was threatened with a court martial but the 'Brass' eventually backed down and he went to Bomber Command only to be killed on his thirteenth mission.

Our gunnery training was in Anson's and Botha's and we trained by firing at drogues towed behind other aircraft. To tell if an individual was hitting the target the .303 ammunition had the slugs painted different colours, so, if one was firing red, after landing and the drogue had been dropped, the holes in the canvas with red around them were counted and one was given a percentage mark depending on the hits. The type of attack was varied so that one day the target was towed level with the gunnery plane, while another exercise would see the target coming across at right angles and so on. All designed to simulate a fighter attacking. Out of a total of 1,800 rounds fire I was allowed 100 on target. This was not too accurate as I remember. If one had more than about ten hits per 200 rounds fired then the instructors would dismiss the rest a 'pure luck'.

The rest of the course was learning how to strip and clean the Browning machine guns, just in case we ever found ourselves without the aid of an armourer in some forward base. We were quite proud of ourselves for getting through it all and only one guy fell out of the course because he could not stand up to the discipline required and when you think about it that was the object of the exercise. On 17th July we all paraded, were issued our AG brevet and Sergeant's stripes and after sewing them on that day were sent on leave as fully fledge

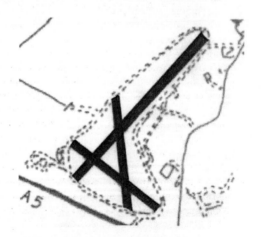

RAF Mona was the airfield used by No 3 AGS.

aircrew. When we were being addressed by our Australian Flt Sgt Instructor prior to the passing out parade he finished up by saying, "….now, when you are sitting in the turret at the back end of the kite on operations and its dark, raining and the plane is being thrown all over the sky by flak, just remember that the turret is only held onto the aircraft by four ¼ inch bolts!". That rotten so and so knew that that was exactly what I had on my mind the first time and many more times after."

Norman Jones may now have been 'fully fledged aircrew' but his training was not yet over. There was still one more hurdle to get over – OTU. Norman was posted to No 7 (Coastal) OTU at Limavady. This Coastal Command station, under the control of No 15 Group, was surrounded by hills on three sides and was the site of many accidents.

"At the outset we were flying as individuals. Crews were selected for various exercises and this went on for a period during which crews were being formed by natural selection. We were all told that we were to find ourselves a crew that we wanted to be in. I met up with a couple more WOp/AGs and they in turn had teamed up with an Australian navigator. He in turn talked to a Canadian pilot whom he had met and liked. We all met over a drink one evening and agreed that the pilot, Plt Off Bob Craig, should apply for Sgt McGuire to be his navigator and Sgts Sexty, Routledge and Jones to be his WOp/AGs. This left a second pilot needed and eventually Sgt Henry Hall joined us to make up the crew. That is how all the crews were formed except that at the end of the course any that had not found a naturally selected crew were thrown together into crews. Not a bad idea as we were mates first and that meant that we trusted each other from the start."

The OTU used many Pegasus engined Wellingtons and with the nearby Coastal Command station of Ballykelly using the same type there were many ditchings of aircraft from both stations.

"On the early part of the course I flew eight trips in Ansons with various pilots and two of these were air-sea rescue missions. One of our planes ditched and although I cannot now remember the names of the rest of the crew I well remember the name of the principal of the affair, Sgt 'Trigger' Collins. The Wellington of 'Trigger's' crew lost one of its engines while they were over the sea some miles from the Giant's Causeway. Because the Pegasus engine would barely keep the

Wimpy flying on its own and no way would it lift the aircraft the captain decided that he would ditch it as close to the coast as he could because Limavady was behind some hills inland. Having mad a really good forced landing they all piled out onto the wing and then found that the plane was apparently floating quite nicely, but some good distance off the beach. Now 'Trigger', who sensed that there might be some kudos in this, volunteered to swim ashore and alert the lifeboat. After stripping off to his pants he dived into the very cold water and started to swim ashore. After he had left and was really struggling against the tide, the captain, a very big Canadian, slipped off the wing into the water and found that it only came up to his chest. The rest of the crew jumped in and they all waded ashore, passing 'Trigger' on the way, without him knowing it, so that when he dragged himself up on the beach exhausted they were all there clapping him!"

This was only one of many incidents and Norman Jones recalls another.

"Another crash at Limavady concerned an all Australian crew. It brought me an insight into the Australian make up. We had all landed from various exercises one evening, except one crew and it was the policy of the Sergeants Mess to dish up the evening meal when all details had landed and could eat at one sitting. Standing on the steps of the Mess we watched the last aircraft come into the circuit, circle and for some reason crash straight into the side of a nearby hill where it burst into flames. It was obvious no one was going to survive it. Another Aussie then turned and said; "Well, come on then, there's an extra portion for anyone who wants it tonight." I was shocked at this until I saw tears in his eyes, but of course, it was against their tradition to be anything but the hard man. It was one experience of the war that made me grow up much faster and to this day I am grateful for having met wonderful characters from Australia, New Zealand, Canada and America and I only wish today's youth could sample the comradeship that can be built up between men from every part of the world."

Jones completed the OTU course at Limavady but was not yet to leave this Ulster station for an operational squadron.

"During September and into November 1943 this course took us and we flew sixteen exercises during four or five weeks. We were crewed up on everything from navigation trips out over the Atlantic to bombing and gunnery practice with night flying thrown in. By the time we completed the course we felt well able to take our place on an operational squadron but did not go straight to one as we went back to Limavady after passing out. The reason for this was that there was a hold up in overseas postings and, rather than us being on leave for some weeks, we went back to keep our hand in. The second period there we did two trips to ferry aircraft back to Maintenance Units (MU) which had cracks in their main spar and had to be taken out of service for repair. There was a batch of Wimpey's that developed such cracks, some doing ops over Germany too, so taking evasive action was dicey."

At the end of the OTU course crews would normally be posted to operational squadrons. This was not the case for crews destined for the Middle East. These crews had one more training stage to complete at a Ferry Training Unit (FTU). Norman Jones and his crew went to No 303 FTU at Talbenny. This airfield had opened in 1942 and was unusual in that its three concrete runways had a common intersection rather than the more usual triangle shape. No 303 FTU arrived from Stornoway in March 1943 equipped with Wellingtons. The crews would be trained in ferrying techniques and then issued a new aircraft to ferry out to the Middle and Far East. In July 1944 No 3 OADU moved into Talbenny tasked with the preparation of the aircraft for ferrying overseas.

"From Limavady we went to the FTU at Talbenny in South Wales, where among other things, we were lectured on escape routes through Europe and means of evading capture if forced down in Europe or the Middle East. We were given certain escape aids such as tunic buttons that hid compasses. The top was removed to disclose the compass by turning it clockwise. Handkerchiefs, which when soaked in water, became maps of Europe. Pencils that would indicate Magnetic North if dangled from a cord and to assist in a final escape if all went wrong, a .38 revolver and some ammunition. Also, in case we came down in the desert and were picked up by the Bedouin, a 'Goolie Chit' – the RAF slang name for a card that promised them, in Arabic, that they would be rewarded in gold if they returned us unharmed to the Allies.

We were issued with Wellington JA515 at Talbenny. When we took it over we saw the word 'Snake' painted on it and knew we were about to take it to South East Asia. Before leaving Talbenny to fly to RAF Hurn and thence to the Middle East we air tested the aircraft, tested the compass in a local flying exercise, did a heavy load take off exercise, fully lade with fuel, ourselves and all our kit. This was the final test to see if we could handle it all. The serious business of ferrying aircraft began at RAF Hurn where all the services needed to ensure that the aircraft got through safely were co-ordinated. It was quite a dicey business getting from Hurn to Gibraltar, or, as in our case, Rabat Sale in French North Africa. On the first leg 'Gerry' had a fighter squadron based near Cape Finisterre all trying to intercept planes going to, or coming from, the East."

The route to the Middle and Far East could be fraught with danger but this did not stop some disreputable characters from trying to make a lot of highly illegal cash as Norman recounts.

"At Gibraltar there was stationed a Flt Sgt Armourer who would meet the crews flying onwards. He would offer to sell them watches, Swiss and top class, for £5 each. With each watch went a name and address to contact, in either London or Cairo, who would buy the watch back at a nice profit. Added to this the Cairo contact would also offer to sell them other 'goodies' that were in demand along the route with the same guarantee of making a profit. This chain existed right out to Ceylon (Sri Lanka) and if the crew was returning, either as passengers, or bringing back an aircraft, the contact in Ceylon would sell them semi-precious stones again with a guaranteed profit in London. I met one guy who was in a crew flying an aircraft back and they poured their stones down the barrel of one of the Brownings in the rear turret, put the cap over the muzzle and tilted the guns upwards. Luckily they did not need to use them on the way back. They were met by Customs officers at Hurn and searched. The stones were not found and were taken out after the officers had gone. If as much thought had gone

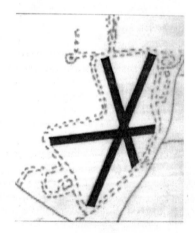

No 303 FTU was based at Talbenny with its unusual runway intersection.

into fighting the war as was used in working' flankers' it would have been all over in two years!"

Norman Jones completed a tour of operations in the Far East as a WOp/AG in 1944 before returning in early 1945 to become a Flight Sergeant Air Traffic Control Assistant at No 2 AGS at Dalcross near Inverness. During his posting there he witnessed a very unusual occurrence.

"Everyone has read or heard stories about mutiny by troops or sailors, but I wonder if anyone else, apart from the aircrew involved, has ever read or heard about a mutiny or at least an attempted mutiny aboard an aircraft. I witnessed such a happening on board an aircraft of the RAF in 1945 and recount it only now that I feel certain that the person who was involved in trying to take over command of the aircraft is dead.

I was posted to No 2 AGS at Dalcross and became a member of the Sergeants Mess and lived in quarters reserved for the permanent staff NCO's. I found Dalcross a very happy place and the Mess full of great characters from every country you could reasonably expect to have been on our side, practically everyone having had combat experience.

Among other Czechoslovakian airmen in the Mess there was one Warrant Officer 'X' and he and I became very good friends. His story, as he told it to me, was that he had been a civil airways pilot before the war and when the war eventually overtook his country he was just

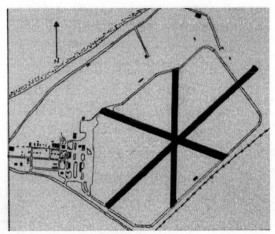

Dalcross airfield in 1998.

what both we and the Germans needed; a highly trained pilot. It seems that in aviation circles his closest friends were, because his civil airline duties took him to both countries, an Englishman and the other a German. Both put pressure on him to join their respective air forces even before the war actually started and as he hadn't taken such a step by the time his country came under German occupation, he was then in a real quandary. If he refused to join the Luftwaffe then certainly the Germans would treat him as hostile and that would have been his end. On the other hand if he took a known escape route out of his country to come and join us the Germans would give his wife and their young daughter a very hard time once she admitted that he had defected.

It happened that his closest friend was an officer of high rank in the police stationed in Prague where he lived. It was this friend who came up with an idea that would allow him to escape to join us yet fool the German authorities. He was told to make all readiness for such an escape but not to tell his wife or indeed anyone else what he was going to do. He was then told that on receiving a signal to go he was to be on his way without saying farewell and that signal came after the police had dragged the body of a drowned man out of the river and their chief had identified it as Warrant Officer 'X'. He told the authorities that he officially identified the body in order to save the wife of his best friend the task and so Warrant Officer 'X' started his journey with his wife and daughter thinking him dead. He crossed the border out of Czechoslovakia wrapped in white sheets crawling through the snow and get here he did. I met him as the time was nearing for the war to end and him and others like him to return home.

After being at Dalcross for a little while I managed to get myself accepted as Staff Wireless Operator (Air) which meant that any aircraft leaving there on a flight outside the area had me on board as Wireless Op. And there were many such flights. We had a wonderful Station Master there, Gp Capt Crauford and an equally good type as OC Flying, Sqn Ldr Rhodes and they organised navigational training flights for pilots to act as navigators so that they could brush up on their navigation. These flights coincided with the departure on leave of airmen from Dalcross so we were able to get the lads down south a lot quicker than by train and gave them extra time at home or wherever. On these flights I would spend all my time getting bearings from MF/DF stations and passing these forward to the navigator so that he could plot exactly where we were, even if his calculations didn't show us there, and thus we never once got lost. This was pretty useful, as there are a lot of mountains, or at least high ground, between Inverness and England.

The war ended in Europe and the time came for all those that could be returned to their home to be sent back as fast as possible. It was politically desirable to give top priority to getting such as Warrant Officer 'X' and his fellow Czechs back again and each of them had been given facilities to let their families and friends know that they had survived the war and were soon to return. I'll never forget 'X' showing me a photograph of his daughter, taken five or six years after he last saw her, nor the happiness he felt at the thought of being with them again.

It was arranged that 'X' and his fellow Czechs would be flown down to an airfield being used as a staging post for airmen going back to their countries in Europe and a Wellington was allocated to this duty. I remember that the pilot and captain was a commissioned officer, young and obviously with not too many flying hours experience. His co-pilot was a NCO, the navigator another NCO pilot and the crew was made up with me a wireless operator.

It was usual to fly straight down the country southwards, over the Cairngorms to southern airfields and this was known to everyone on board when we took off in very dirty weather indeed. We were in cloud immediately after take off. The passengers were sitting midway down the aircraft where they could, with the exception of 'X' who was standing up looking through the astrodome. Although I was busy getting my bearings I noticed he was getting excited and shouting and pointing outside the plane to the others. We couldn't hear what was going on, as they had all handed in their flying kit at Dalcross, they didn't have flying helmets to wear and so were not plugged into the aircraft intercom system. Because of this they did not know that the pilot had changed his flight plan and that we had turned east towards the North Sea to get away from the mountains. Not too long after take off and after wireless bearings had confirmed the navigators calculations that we were clear of land, we started to descend.

The next few seconds seemed like hours because no sooner had the nose of the aircraft pointed downwards when 'X' came rushing past me, flung open the door dividing us from the two pilots and having grabbed the aircraft captain, pulled him sideways and backwards to tear him out of his seat. Luckily the first pilot let go of the controls or else we would have gone into a nose up attitude, stalled and almost certainly have crashed. The second pilot took over the aircraft, continued our shallow dive and by the time the first pilot, navigator and one of the Czech passengers had subdued 'X' we were clear of cloud and over the sea. It was, there is no doubt, an attempt to deprive the captain of command of his aircraft and thus, I believe, mutinous.

For the remainder of the flight Warrant Officer 'X' sat on the floor, mid-way down the aircraft, with his head in his hands and one can imagine his thoughts and feelings. First, he knew that when we started to descend we had not had anywhere near enough time to clear the Highlands and no doubt he saw his meeting with his wife and daughter disappearing into the side of a Scottish mountain. Next, no matter who the RAF had put in charge of the aircraft, neither pilot was as experienced as he himself was and he wouldn't have been assured any more by the fact that the navigator was a pilot who hadn't been involved in serious navigational work since leaving elementary flying training school, all of which must have convinced him that we were heading for disaster. Then after realising what he had done he must have felt that we would accuse him of cowardice and finally if we did, and did so officially, he would be held in detention awaiting trial and again wouldn't be getting home as early as they had all been promised.

Upon landing the captain called us, his crew, together and told us that he was going to report the matter and charge Warrant Officer 'X' with attempted mutiny. Who could blame him for that, after all it was his duty to do so, apart from the slight he felt at not being trusted to fly the aircraft safely. We on the other hand set about persuading him not to take nay action on the grounds that he would probably upset the politicians, if not the RAF, as such a case would no doubt embarrass both our government and that of our ally. As I was a Warrant Officer myself by this time and therefore senior to the other NCO aircrew, I took the lead in this and now I have no doubt that I was also swayed by my friendship with 'X'. I confess that I told the captain that if he did report it I would get the other to deny that the incident had been serious and so must have myself acted illegally as far as the RAF was concerned and wrongly towards the captain. 'X' was not reported and got back home safe and sound. I still think of him with affection."

Bomber Pilot – 2

W.I. 'WALLY' LASHBROOK – PILOT – 1940/1941

Wally Lashbrook was already an experienced pilot when he was posted to No 10 OTU at Abingdon to convert to Armstrong Whitworth Whitley's.

> "I was at Abingdon flying Whitley Mk III's from 14th July 1940. The Mk III's were on the strength of 'A' Flight and because of my previous flying experience my first flights there were only check landings. These were followed by local flying, instrument flying, a weather check, auto pilot test and a ZZ procedure. More instrument flying and a dual night landing check followed this. This took about two weeks and we then progressed to 'E' Flight flying Whitley Mk V's.
>
> On 3rd August 1940 I was detached to Jurby for an air firing course, again on Whitley Mk III's. We did high and low level bombing and air firing until 21st August 1940 with 'C' Flight, which was commanded by Sqn Ldr Barrett. After about sixty-five hours flying I was posted to an operational squadron."

Lashbrook was posted initially to No 51 Sqn and then after a few months to No 35 Sqn. No 35 Sqn were converting to the Halifax and

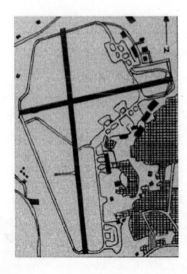

Abingdon airfield in 1999. This airfield was used by the Whitley's of No 10 OTU.

he gives an interesting insight into the training carried out by the squadrons before the introduction of the HCU's.

> "My introduction to the Halifax was fifteen minute local flying with an instructor, then I went solo. The CO at the time was Flt Lt Leonard Cheshire. In those early days the conversion training was a case of the blind leading the blind. One pilot would give another some dual instruction and then that pilot would instruct another. I did about fifteen hours training then I went on my first Halifax operation."

Surviving an attack by a fighter on the mission to Kiel on 15th April 1941, then running out of fuel and crash landing, Lashbrook remained with the squadron until November 1941. Shortly after the Kiel operation all the Halifaxes were grounded for modifications. On 3rd November 1941 Wally Lashbrook was posted for instructional duties and later served with the Empire Central Flying School. Post-war he went into civil aviation and took part in the Berlin Airlift.

'Oxbox' Incidents

HUNTER McGIFFIN – PILOT

Hunter McGiffin served for four years in Training Command after completing a Coastal Command tour of operations. Whilst acting as assistant to the Chief Flying Instructor at No 3 (P)AFU at South Cerney he was involved in the lucky escape of one pilot.

> "A pupil, who had previously trained in Canada, was flying an Oxford solo for only the second time when the outer engine bearers on the port engine broke. The engine then swung inwards and the propeller cut through the fuselage and then slightly cut the pilots flying suit before the inner bearers gave way and the engine fell off. The pilot then selected the undercarriage down and managed to land in a field near Cirencester with no further damage. We got the photo section to take photos of the plane in the field. There it was with only the engine bulkhead on the port side. It was a particularly fine effort by the pilot although he should have made a belly landing."

McGiffen moved on to command RAF Windrush, which was used by part of No 7 (P)AFU. Whilst there another lucky escape occurred.

> "An instructor and pupil were doing a night cross-country. As they proceeded the cloud gradually became lower and they tended to keep below it. Then said the pilot, 'It is closing in a bit so we will return to base. Will you keep flying on this heading until I work out a course to take us back?' One minute later the pupils exclaimed, 'We seem to be stopped!' The instructor replied, 'So we are!' In fact they had come to rest on a large flat field on fairly high ground. Neither was hurt and apart from broken propellers and slight damage to the lower fuselage the plane looked alright. Their speed was about 140 mph!"

On another occasion at Windrush, McGiffen was in his office when he received some unusual information.

> "It was usual when instructing to take another pupil as passenger and let him practice map reading. He sat on the 'step' where the main spar crossed the fuselage. One day while in my office an instructor entered and stated that, after about half an hour giving dual instruction, he had turned around and found his passenger was 'missing'. Well, I said all he could do was wait and see if any news was forthcoming.

Shortly afterwards the passenger rang up to say that he had landed by parachute on a farm near Stroud. He then took a bus and arrived back, walking into camp with his open parachute, roughly folded, under his arm. It appeared that during the flight he became in urgent nee of a 'pee'. So, he got to the door, opened it slightly and wedged his shoulder against it. At this moment the instructor, who was teaching single engine flying, throttled back the port engine and opened up the other with the result that the pupil, a Sgt pilot, was ejected.

Next day he appeared in front of me on a charge of endangering an aircraft when in flight. In the end I let him off lightly as I reckoned he had got a really good fright! It was lucky he was wearing a pilot type parachute!"

Aussie Observations

T.E. OSBORN – AIR BOMBER – 1942

Tom Osborn was one of many Commonwealth airmen who made their way to Britain to train at one of the many airfields scattered around the country. On arrival he commenced training at No 2 (O)AFU at Millom in the north of England. Completing the course in April 1942 he was then posted to No 27 OTU as a trainee Observer.

"I arrived at 27 OTU at Lichfield with a group of Observers, most of whom had been together since enlistment in early 1941. Our group was told that the 'powers that be' had decided to do away with the second pilot, have a straight Navigator and add an Air Bomber to the crew. As no Air Bombers had yet been trained as such one half of us Navigator/Bomb Aimers (Observers) would become straight Navigators and the other half Air Bombers. As the Air Bombers job was to be bomb aimer, map reader, front gunner and second pilot it appealed to me. I teamed up with Clare Taylor who wanted to navigate. Other units and squadrons used the Flight Engineer as second pilot but we were given approximately twenty hours training in the Link Trainer and on flying exercises we were given time at the

Tom Osborn and crew at 27 OTU, Lichfield, August 1942.
Left to right: Sgt Jack Kirby, Rear Gunner. Sgt Jack Murray, Pilot. Sgt Clare Taylor, Navigator. Sgt Tom Osborn. Sgt Bill Monk, Wop/AG. (Tom Osborn)

controls. I had about ten and a half hours and learned to fly the Wellington, in the air at least, as no instruction about take off or landing was given. At 27 OTU our original pilot had ear trouble and was restricted to flying below 3,000 ft so we had to wait around for a pilot replacement. Our new pilot was Jack Murray".

"The theory of my flying training was that if the pilot was unable to fly us home then I would turn the aircraft towards the English Channel, put the autopilot on and we would all bale out. My crew had a discussion and decided I should belly-land the plane in that situation, as there were a number of long runways on the East Coast especially for aircraft in distress. This was the first of many crew discussions we had in situations which allowed time for them."

Tom Osborn was posted to No 460 (RAAF) Sqn in September 1942 and completed a tour of operations including twelve ops in Lancaster AR-G for 'George' now in the Australian War Memorial in Canberra. After this tour he became a bombing instructor at No 1 LFS at Hemswell and No 27 OTU.

Bombing Section, No 27 OTU, Lichfield, July 1944.
Rear row (L to R): Fg Off Alf Dovey, Flt Lt Tom Osborn, LACW Doreen Osborn, Fg Off Geoff Webb, Margaret Watkins, Fg Off Reg Naylor, Fg Off Tony Cohen.
Front row. Left to right: Plt Off Mac Sutherland, Fg Off Roy Anderson.
(Tom Osborn)

Bullseye!

TOM OVEREND – BOMB AIMER – 1942/43

Tom Overend was one of the many aircrew who set out to become pilots and through the process of elimination ended up as navigators, bomb aimers and gunners.

"I trained originally as a pilot like many others. I did my training in this country at Brough, which was Blackburn's old airfield just outside Hull. This was a Grading School and there were Tiger Moths there. They also had two or three of the old Blackburn B.2's. We used the Tigers. At the Grading School we were restricted to about ten hours flying and you were not allowed to go solo. I think I did about five hours and was then ready to go solo. Subsequently I went to Canada and then down into the southern United States to a place called Tuscaloosa. I did not last very long on the pilots course I'm afraid. The Americans at that time had a very hard system. There was one thing I never really liked there. They had civilian instructors and I believe the Army schools were very much better. I found the civilian instructors they had were typical' bush pilots'. They were damned good pilots but a lot of them were not terribly good instructors. I always think that I would have made it quite easily in this country or in Canada.

I went back to Canada and was put on the list for a course. You had to wait for slots. They had all these failed aircrew coming back from the States and you had to fit in if you could. I stayed at Trenton for weeks and I got so fed up that when they asked for volunteers for a navigation course I did that instead. I did the navigation course at Chatham, New Brunswick and I came back from there and again hung around Trenton and almost the same thing happened again. I eventually volunteered to go on a bombing and gunnery course and went to Mountain View for that. Then I did a short radio course after which I was categorised as an Observer, which the Canadians still had at that time. So I came back proudly wearing my 'O' brevet."

After this protracted training period Tom Overend thought his future as an Observer was assured but on returning to the UK everything changed again.

"Of course when you came back here you were very quickly segregated into Bomb Aimers and Navigators and of course at that time the 'heavies' were just coming into service and they were very short of Bomb Aimers. So, if you had done a Bomb Aimers course you almost automatically became one. Although I wore the 'O' brevet I eventually had to take it down and put up a 'B' until an order came out later allowing you to wear an 'O', which I have done ever since."

On arrival in this country Tom was posted to No 29 OTU at North Luffenham a few miles from Rutland Water. The OTU flew Wellingtons of various marks from this large three-runway airfield.

"The first thing you had to do was crew up, which I did. There were ten crews on the course and I teamed up with Plt Off Joe Bowie. He was well below average height – very, very short. He had to sit on two cushions to see out of the plane, though he was a very good pilot."

Almost at the end of the course Tom was involved in a strange accident from which he was lucky to escape with his life.

"It was one of those strange incidents that you read about in books and you wonder for many years afterwards if you had a charmed life, or whether someone 'up there' was looking after you. We had a take off accident where the aircraft swung off the runway. We were going on one of the 'Nickel' exercises where you dropped leaflets on France towards the end of the course. On that particular evening, as the tail lifted, the aircraft just gradually swung of the runway and went round to starboard. So, we went round and taxied back to the end of the

The badge of No 29 OTU.

queue again. Joe Bowie said, 'This time, when we take off put full left rudder on if she starts to swing.' To this day I can honestly say that when the tail lifted I felt it going again and we had full left rudder on but it still swung to starboard. Eventually it reared up on one wheel, dug the wingtip in, cartwheeled and made one hell of a mess. We were extremely lucky that the fuel tanks did not burst. Joe was blamed for this. They said it was pilot error and at the subsequent court of inquiry, at which I had to appear, I certified that we had full rudder on. Joe was subsequently taken off the course and sent off to fighters or something they felt he could handle better and our crew was split up.

Luffenham was not a very big airfield. The approaches were not bad but it dropped away rather steeply on take off. If you ran through the fence at the far end you were due for a rough ride down the hill. The evening we piled up we were lucky to escape in the way we did. I eventually became part of my second crew. On the course was a Flt Lt Derbyshire who had been trapped in Training Command. He was a pre-war Auxiliary and had the reputation of being a martinet. His old crew at that time used to think that he beat them to death! Which he did! However, it was all for their own good and when I came on the market – I had a fairly good record at Luffenham – he promptly dropped his present Bomb Aimer and took me. I must admit that at the time I did not particularly want to go but he was a first class bloke and I always gave him credit for the fact that we survived our first tour. Of the ten crews on that course we were the only one to survive. He was one of those typical highly trained, very cool and unflappable types. When other crews were going out on Saturday afternoon we were doing dinghy drill, escape procedures and all sorts of things. We used to call him a miserable old devil at the time but it paid off. We all thought he was Methuselah. He was about thirty at the time and the rest of us were about nineteen. He was on his second log book and he had flown a lot of hours.

The sort of exercises we had at OTU were; day and night cross-countries, high level bombing and Bullseyes. A Bullseye was a night cross-country during which you did a mock bombing run on a selected target on top of which was positioned an infra red lamp. You could not see the lamp but you did a mock bombing run with the camera running and it left a trace on the print which gave your track over the target. You could not see it and you were blind bombing in a way. I remember one of the cooling towers of Newark power station had one of the lamps on it.

The problem in this country with the training was the weather and this was partly responsible for the inauguration of the training schools overseas. The remarkable thing is that most pilots on these courses had only done very basic training, which is nothing like they get today. Most of them were eighteen or nineteen with very little experience.

The course at Luffenham was generally very intensive because of the weather at the time (winter 1942-43). I still remember my first trip very clearly. We went down to St Eval in Cornwall and around the Cornish coast. It was a beautiful winter day with snow on the ground. We went on training and we did some formation flying. I do not know whose benefit that was for. It was certainly not for ours. Camera exercise, photographing selected things on the route with the F24 hand held camera, which you were marked on. Once your night flying started you did night cross-countries which lasted three to five hours. Five hours in a Wellington seemed an awful long time. There was not a lot of room and the wind used to whistle in through the fabric covering all the time. It was a good old aeroplane, very reliable and I think that most people who flew them grew to love them eventually."

To many the crewing up process may have seemed haphazard but in most cases it worked well. Once crews formed up a vital part of the moulding of an efficient crew was social activity as a group and the crews took every opportunity to find entertainment.

"North Luffenham was quite comfortable with standard barrack blocks. It was a pre-war station and had all the normal facilities and it was very good. The system for crewing up was ver haphazard. You went along to a hangar one morning and the place was seething with odd 'bods' standing around and it was largely, I believe, up to the pilots first of all to pick someone. In my case they came up and said; 'There are four of us crewed up and we're looking for a Bomb Aimer. How about it?' So I went along. That was Joe Bowie's lot. Later on old John Derbyshire decided he wanted to drop his present Bomb Aimer. He knew I had consistently good marks and his present one was a bit of a duffer. I knew the chap; he was very nice but terribly slow. So he was dropped. I did not want to go at the time but I thanked my stars later that I did.

We used to go into Stamford as a crew to one of the 57 pubs there. There was a place in Stamford; a little black market café called 'Smokey Joe's'. Where he got his supplies from no one ever knew, but you could get the biggest meal of egg, chips and even steak from time to time. It was a cellar and he had a big buxom daughter who used to serve the stuff and it was absolutely mobbed with aircrew."

On conclusion of the OTU course the next posting was to a Conversion Unit. Tom Overend was posted to No 1660 HCU at Swinderby. This airfield was south west of Lincoln. It had three concrete runways and housed the Halifaxes and Lancasters of the Conversion Unit. The strength of the station was over 2,000 personnel.

"As I remember it the Conversion Units were principally intended for the pilots and Flight Engineers rather than the rest of the crew. The pilots were converting from a twin to a four-engined aircraft and the engineer came in at that stage. The first thing that happened was the addition of two new members to your crew, a mid upper gunner and a flight engineer. We were particularly fortunate in getting an engineer who was not the ordinary run of the mill. Most of them were ex-flight mechanics. Our Flight Engineer, Eddie Sullivan, was an ex-fitter. He had worked in the aircraft engine industry before that. He was a very good Flight Engineer. I always remember when we were sitting on our beds reading books he would be sitting reading an aircraft manual. The Skipper, being something of a martinet, used to keep him up on this and regularly gave him problems to sort out. He would purposely shut something down or create a situation, which Eddie would have to handle as part of the training. Most of the younger pilots would never have thought of this. Old Derbyshire used to really put us through the hoop all the time. I think it paid off.

Initially the flying at the conversion unit was just the pilot and the Flight Engineer with a screen pilot. They started before the rest of us and would have done quite a bit of circuit flying before the rest of us flew with them. At that time at 1660 HCU we had Halifaxes. They were Merlin engined and were pretty clapped out old beasts. The ones we used for circuits were pretty battered old things but the ones we used for cross-countries were a little better. They were not pristine aircraft by any means.

We took off one evening with a screen pilot and the Skipper flying the aircraft. One of the control rods had been crossed, I am not sure if it was the aileron or the elevator. We only knew that there was an argument going on up front about this and the screen pilot was all for bailing out. John Derbyshire thought otherwise and eventually used his rank to prevail. He said he was taking over the aircraft and he landed the aircraft anyway, crossed control or not. He was supposed to be the pupil pilot but he called upon his previous experience. He had apparently had a similar occurrence before at some time.

There were several accidents at the Conversion Unit. There was one major one where they flew into the woods on the west side of Swinderby. They were all killed. Another on hit the hill coming in on the Lincoln side where there was a slight rise before Swinderby."

At the time Tom Overend was at Swinderby it was quite common for full crews or selected crewmembers to be sent on an operation as observers with a crew from an operational squadron. Tom went on one such operation.

"The culmination of the Conversion Unit training was for selected crews to fly under instruction on an operational flight. This was the pilot, Bomb Aimer and Flight Engineer. I don't think everyone did it. We had been on a fairly long cross-country and I remember getting out of the aircraft, very tired, and Wg Cdr Oxley grabbed me. He was a bit of a character in 5 Group. He said, 'You are flying tonight.' That was on the 18th of April 1943 and I went to Italy minelaying. I went from Skellingthorpe with 49 Sqn. The target was La Spezia and it took nine hours and thirty-five minutes. We flew in low level up the bay. Part of

A view of the hangars at Swinderby in 1989. (Authors collection)

the Italian Fleet was in there and there was quite a lot of flak from both sides on the way in. The old Italians used to get a lot of stick about hiding in the shelters when anything happened but they certainly did not that night."

The La Spezia raid was carried out by 173 Lancasters and 5 Halifaxes. Eight further Lancasters, one of which was Tom's, were tasked with laying mines in the harbour. One Lancaster was lost.

Tom makes some interesting comments about the relative merits of the Lancasters and Halifaxes with which the Conversion Unit was equipped. Both aircraft had their good and bad points.

"At 1660 HCU we went on to Lancasters on the 5th of April 1943. There was a Lancaster and a Halifax Flight there. The Halifaxes did not have a mid upper turret on them and the rest of the crew virtually sat down the back all of the time. I sat up the front but the training was mainly for the pilots and Flight Engineers. The Halifax was a very comfortable aircraft. For the crew up front it was more spacious than the Lanc. The Wireless Operator and the Navigator had a little cubby-hole to themselves below the pilot's platform. It was all very cosy in the front. In the Lanc it was the reverse. The Wireless Operator in the Lanc was behind the pilot and the Bomb Aimers compartment in the front. It was not as spacious as the Halifax but everyone who ever flew it thought the Lancaster was the better aircraft."

Tom Overend's crew were posted to No 9 Sqn at Bardney and after completing a tour over a six month period, in which he became the squadron Deputy Bombing Leader, he and the rest of his crew, less the gunners, were sent to Scampton to set up an Aircrew School giving ground instruction.

"On completion of our tour we were moved as a crew, less the gunners. The Skipper was promoted to Wg Cdr and we went to Scampton to the Aircrew School, which was being started. Scampton at that time did not have runways and the surprising thing is that even with 617 Sqn using the big bombs they still used the grass. Scampton was one of the oldest and probably one of the best bomber stations in the country and did not have runways until the end of 1943. During the period they were laying the runways this school was started.

Apart from the two gunners we went there to open and run this school. At this time they had an awful lot of surplus aircrew. There were far more than they could use on the squadrons and I think this was a way of keeping them together until they were posted to squadrons. They came through as crews and it was all ground instruction. There was no flying. We had to arrange lectures given by ourselves and by people brought in to give them. They got specialist lectures. I think they had realised by that time that there were a lot of little facets that were causing problems. The training was good but it was lacking in some ways. There was nothing formal about the lectures. You got a group of blokes around you and talked for a while then let them ask questions.

One major change at that time was the transfer from the old Mk 9 Bomb Sight, which we had used on the Wellington, to the Mk 14, which was a very complicated bomb sight. This was the one that was reputedly invented by a lunatic. It was a fantastic thing with about 27 different mechanisms all linked and it was virtually a mechanical computer. It did everything that electronics do now, but you gad to know how to use it. With the Mk 14 my best results from 20.000 ft with eight practice bombs was 25 yards. Most of them were a bit more than that. Some people were hopeless and never got it. Once you had the Mk 14 properly levelled for each flight- it was a simple enough job. You just put a screwdriver through a hole and centred the bubble in it – You then got the pilot to fly a very accurate course until you set it up. After that you could virtually drop bombs with the aircraft in any attitude. It was extremely accurate.

617 used a different one for some reason. They had a Semi-Automatic Bomb Sight (SABS) which I only used on two or three occasions. I still preferred the Mk 14. I remember the SABS as a large circular object, almost like a fruit bowl. With the dials on top. Again, these had to be pre-set, but once you had lined up on your target, it had a graticule reflector sight in it, it would gradually track down and all you had to do was adjust it so that the target was tracking down in the crosshair. Once that happened you just left it and all you gave the pilot was the odd correction left or right. It followed the target down and at the correct moment it released the bombs. Two pointers had to be together when it started and the first time I used it I did not know this with the result that my bombs fell nowhere near the target and landed in a field of cows. It was a very accurate sight if you knew how to use it.

They realised that a lot of Bomb Aimers coming through, although they knew how to use the sight, did not know the finer points of it. Most of them had no idea at all what they were carrying as a load. They had no idea about the fuses or pistols that the Bomb Aimer should really know about because they had never had the opportunity of seeing them. So, I acquired a whole set of sectioned fuses. On the radio side my Wireless operator, Eric Oakes, used to say, 'My God, they have a hell of a lot to learn before they go to a squadron!' You might have got away with it during training if you forgot it or did not know the right procedure, but when you were over the other side, you were on your own. So it was really just a finishing school and, I think, a way of passing a few weeks rather than send them on four or five weeks leave."

After instructing at the Aircrew School at Scampton, Tom was due for a rest period. Instead he was posted to No 17 OTU at Silverstone. This airfield, now a famous motor racing circuit, was four miles south west of Towcester. It was administered by No 92 Group and housed 2,000 personnel. Turweston was used as a satellite by the OTU aircraft.

"I went to 17 OTU at Silverstone. That was a mixed blessing and I still say it was certainly not a rest. I was back on the Wellington again and I had to fly with student crews. By this time the standard of crews was deteriorating. They were taking people for aircrew who would not have made it earlier in the war. Not all of them were bad, I hasten to add. There were still a lot of good people coming through. Some of the Canadians were a pretty wild bunch. The Colonials had nothing to lose. They were the ones who used to throw the thunderflashes on the fire. Lighting newspapers that people were reading was another favourite.

Silverstone was a wild place with nothing to do and nowhere to go. There were two service buses and no other transport. The buses went to Northampton every evening. You could get about 25 on each. You had to get your name on the list to get on. The village pub was 'grotty' and there was another pub called the 'Green ma' on the main road which served meals, and that was it.

After flying with someone like John Derbyshire, who was ver professional, it was frightening to say the least. I was at 17 OTU from June 1944 until the end of the war. While I was based at Silverstone I went to the satellite at Turweston. That was a bleak little place, just outside Banbury. I also went twice on attachments to Manby for the Air Bombing Instructors Course in August 1944 and the Bombing leaders Course in April 1945. I had been doing the job but I still had to do the course. I also did a Bombing Analysis Course and an Explosives Course at Worksop.

The Education block was three Nissen huts which formed a 'U' with the Air Gunners on one side and the Navigation and Bombing Section on the other. One day a lorry arrived and reversed into the 'U' and unloaded about thirty telegraph poles. Within seconds of the

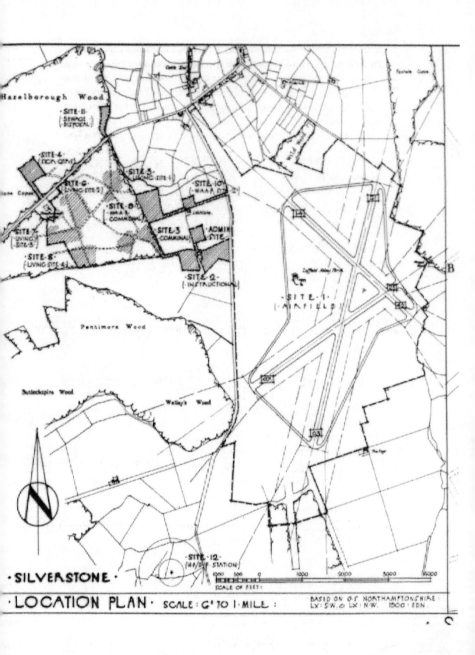

·SILVERSTONE·

·LOCATION PLAN· SCALE: 6" TO 1 MILE·   BASED ON O.S. NORTHAMPTONSHIRE.
LX: S.W. & LX: N.W. 1900: EDN.

Silverstone, home of No 17 OTU.

truck moving out two Air Gunners appeared with a two-handled saw and sawed up one of the telegraph poles. Minutes later the same saw appeared from the other side with a couple of the Navs. Within a week all the poles were gone. Months later I was Duty Officer when a gentleman from the Post Office arrived. He was a very cocky little gentleman with a bowler hat, who understood that there had been a delivery of telegraph poles and where were they? I knew what had happened and had to play dim. There was a great trade in stolen and acquired fuel for the huts. One or two had secret entrances into coal dumps and used to go out like a crowd of Commando's at night. I remember on one occasion someone tried to get a fire going in a stove with one of the aircraft destruction incendiaries. The whole stove glowed cherry red and set fire to the beds on either side."

Tom Overend arrived at Silverstone as a Plt Off and after serving in the Equipment branch for a period, which he found unsatisfactory, left the RAF as an acting Sqn Ldr.

Flying Instructor

BILL PAGE – PILOT – 1944/46

Bill Page joined the RAF in 1940 as a WOp/AG and subsequently remustered to pilot. He was taught to fly in America under the Arnold Scheme by the USAAC in the south-east USA. On completion of training he was sent to the Instructors School at Maxwell Field, Alabama and then served as an instructor at Shaw Field, South Carolina teaching American cadets. He returned to the UK in August 1943 and was sent to No 7 (P) AFU at Peterborough for UK acclimatisation and then to No 2 FIS at Montrose

"I arrived at No 2 FIS at Montrose on 22nd March 1944 for a course lasting about ten weeks during which I did about 100 hours flying the Master Mk II. Initially one had to learn to fly the aircraft from the back seat. In the Master forward visibility was very poor from the rear seat, so for taking off and landing the Perspex canopy over the rear seat could be swung open to form a windshield while the back seat was raised.

Once accustomed to flying from this rear position all the usual manoeuvres were practised, day and night, sometimes accompanied by one of the FIS staff, sometimes a fellow trainee. Great emphasis was placed on a high standard of accuracy in all flying practice. At the same time, using the RAF Flying Instructors Handbook on Advanced Flying Training as a guide, one had to learn to describe the correct technique for all manoeuvres in flight and to develop the verbal skills in describing the techniques in the air while they were being demonstrated. Also, there were ground classes to improve ones knowledge and understanding of theories of flight, aerodynamics, engine handling and so on. It was a very adequate course and twice as long as its equivalent in America."

On completion of his instructors course at Montrose, Bill was sent as an instructor to No 9 (P) AFU at Errol on the banks of the River Tay, west of Dundee.

"I arrived at Errol from the Flying Instructors School at Montrose on 14th June 1944 and remained until the unit moved to Ternhill. Living accommodation for all was either in Nissen huts, wooden huts or single level concrete buildings, the latter type was also used for messing arrangements. We used the Miles Master Mk II, which was fitted with an 850hp Bristol Mercury 20 engine and the Harvard Mk IIb. There was also a small Communications Flight on the airfield, which used the Heyford and Dakota. Oxfords of a BAT Flight also used our beam approach system and we also had a Supermarine Walrus, which was flown by the AFU staff.

I never flew the Heyford at Errol but I did fly the Walrus on several occasions. The Walrus was a little difficult to handle on the ground as it had a very narrow and poorly sprung undercarriage. I sometimes found it could not be kept absolutely straight on take off from a runway so I developed a technique of starting the take off at a slight angle so it finished up straight! In the air it was all right but tended to

Miles Master MkII of No 9 (P)AFU, Errol, 1944. (WS Page)

wallow about somewhat. The hard undercarriage certainly didn't flatter ones technique on runway landings, which were usually accompanied by a metallic bang on touch down! On water it was much more at home – however on calm water it could take quite some time to unstick on take off. The landing technique on water, which was recommended to me by an ex- Air Sea Rescue pilot, was to hold off just above the surface, keeping the nose up until flying speed was lost and the aircraft then 'fell' into the water with an impressive splash and sudden deceleration. The idea of this was evidently to avoid any chance of the nose catching a wave and pulling the aircraft under the surface. At Errol we practised water handling on the Tay Estuary but never had a rescue call.

The bulk of the flying training was for Fleet Air Arm pilots designated for fighter aircraft. However, during my time there we also had two courses of RAF pilots. I remember an inspection visit by the Group Captain from Montrose who wondered what on earth all these sailors were doing there!"

In June 1945 No 9 (P) AFU moved to Ternhill in Shropshire and was redesignated No 5 (P) AFU. Bill was posted with the unit.

The instructors of 'D' Flight, No 9 (P)AFU, Errol, 1944.
Left to right; Plt Off R Bracewell, Fg Off Bill Page, Fg Off Reg Prior, Flt Sgt
Watson. (WS Page)

"I arrived at Ternhill from Errol, along with all aircraft and flying staff of 9 (P) AFU on 25th June 1945. I served at Ternhill itself until the unit was moved to Hibaldstow on 12th April 1946. While at Ternhill we used a satellite at Atcham. Being a peace time station Ternhill was well supplied with adequate living and messing facilities and the Officers mess was very adequate.

No 5 (P) AFU flew Harvard Mk IIb and Spitfire Mk XVI aircraft and we had the Lancasters from the Maintenance Unit located on the opposite side of the airfield from the AFU which made frequent use of the airfield. When the unit moved to Ternhill the Walrus came with us but eventually I flew it down to the Isle of Wight and delivered it to the Saunders Roe factory at Cowes. It was a fun aeroplane to fly and a welcome break from the constant flying of our training aircraft. It was certainly an aircraft of great character and a 'one off' as a type.

When the unit moved to Ternhill from Errol the original four flights were combined into two large flights, 'A' and 'B', equipped with Harvards and each staffed by some twelve flying instructors. A third, smaller flight of Spitfires was also formed.

The training system was essentially a four to five week course of general flying practice for Fleet Air Arm pilots who had already qualified. Many of these would have been trained overseas and would have been unfamiliar with British flying procedures and also may have been away from flying for some time. The AFU course was designed to bring them back into current flying practice, to brush up and sharpen flying techniques and to start teaching aircraft handling appropriate to flying from aircraft carriers. The courses were divided into two sections – Fighter and Torpedo Bomber.

At Ternhill we trained the Fighter group. Most of the flying was done in Harvards while the more able students were sent off in Spitfires. Thus, hopefully, we prepared our charges for the Operational Training Units. The AFU course included navigation, some at low level, aerobatics, formation flying, low altitude circuits and low speed approach and landing, instrument flying, night flying and 'operational' low flying."

The Wellington Fighter

FRED PAPPLE – PILOT – 1943/44

Fred Papple took of for his first flight at No 21 (P) AFU at Perton on 17th August 1943. This Staffordshire airfield buzzed with the sound of Ansons and Oxfords training would be bomber pilots. Life at the training units was not all hard work however and Fred recalls one or two lighter moments.

"We used to go into the village pub and have a meal, sometimes getting eggs from the rations. One of the boys, Gus Tyson, used to play the piano so we always had a good 'sing song'. When the music stopped we always knew why – Gus's glass on top of the piano needed filling! We always rode our bikes in and one night, when we were rather merry, we lost the first rider in the village pond. That cooled him off rather quickly! Leaving the village we headed towards Perton. I was following Max Mazengarb and Gus Tyson because they had lights and I didn't. I fell a little behind them and did not notice that they had gone round an 'S' bend. Looking ahead I could see their lights OK on the other side of the 'S' bend but in the dark I went straight ahead, into a ditch and straight through a hedge. When I didn't appear round the bend they came back looking for me and found me with my head in the hedge. They dragged me out by my feet! I was most gratified, so on the bikes and off we went. It was not till we got back to the huts and into the light that we saw the scratch marks down either side of my face. I hadn't felt a thing!

One evening there was a Sergeants Mess party at Perton and even though we had paid our dues we were barred from attending as we were under training. We were not impressed and most unhappy. Whilst having tea in the Mess we decided to have our own party and were going off to the pub. We left the Mess moaning about our fate and walking past the rear of the Mess, as luck would have it, we saw two crates full of beer getting cold in the night air. We 'rescued' them, took them back to our hut and enjoyed part of the Mess party. So that the check of the Mess stocks would not be out in the morning we returned the crates and empties to where we found them"

Fred Papple remained at Perton until the end of August. After a week at No 1521 BAT Flt at Wymeswold he returned to No 21 (P) AFU, now

Year		Aircraft		Pilot, or 1st Pilot	2nd Pilot, Pupil or Passenger	Duty (Including Results and Remarks)
Month	Date	Type	No.			
—	—	—	—	—	—	Totals Brought Forward
				NO 21 (P)	A. F. U.	
AUG	17	ANSON	8723	F/SGT. CUMBUS	SELF	NAV EX. 1
AUG	18	OXFORD	663	F/SGT. REID	SELF	1.1A 2 3 4A 4B 5 6 7A 8A 9A
AUG	18	OXFORD	663	F/SGT. REID	SELF	8A 9A 9C
AUG	18	OXFORD	663	F/SGT. REID	SELF	8A 9A
AUG	18	OXFORD	663	SELF	SOLO	8A 9A
AUG	20	OXFORD	420	SGT. BLACKIE	SELF	I.F. ABCDE 18 10A
AUG	21	OXFORD	6376	F/SGT. CUMBUS	SELF	NAV. TEST
AUG	21	OXFORD	354	F/SGT. REID	SELF	I.F. A-L LMR
AUG	23	OXFORD	222	SELF	SOLO	8A 9A 4B 10B 10A 18 9C
AUG	23	OXFORD	222	F/SGT MAYBEE	SELF	I.F. DEFJKL
AUG	23	OXFORD	222	SELF	SOLO	4B 7C 8A 9A 10A 10B 18
AUG	23	OXFORD	222	SGT. OWEN	SELF	7A 8A 9A 18
AUG	23	OXFORD	222	SELF	SOLO	L.M.R. 4B 7C 9C 10B 18
AUG	24	OXFORD	3524	SGT. OWEN	SELF	I.F. 4B 7A BC 8A8 98C 10B 13 15
AUG	24	OXFORD	668	SGT. OWEN	SELF	I.F. AL-MN
AUG	25	OXFORD	6653	SELF	SOLO	4B 7C 8B 9BC 10B 15A
AUG	27	OXFORD	354	F/O RICE	SELF	NAV 2A
AUG	27	OXFORD	EL	SGT. OWEN	SELF	I.F. 1A LA 17.
AUG	28	OXFORD	420	SGT. OWEN	SELF	LMR I.F. (A-L)

GRAND TOTAL [Cols. (1) to (10)]

Hrs. _____ Mins. _____

Totals Carried Forward

An extract from Fred Papple's logbook whilst at No 21 (P) AFU, Perton, August 1943. (F Papple) at Wheaton Aston. Completing his training there at the end of October 1943, he was posted to No 15 OTU at Harwell in November.

"At Harwell we crewed up. All except the Flight Engineer, Sandy McDonald, a Scotsman, who joined us at HCU. My selection was done over a beer, talking at mealtimes and at social events. My crew was Dick McLean, our Bomb Aimer and a fellow Australian. Bob Gunstone, the WOp and two gunners, Tom Dakin and Bob Burns were all English. The Navigator was from Sierra Leone.

I had all my crew selected but was still looking for a navigator. I was called into the Flight office regarding this and asked if I was 'colour conscious'. I said no and was then told of Ade Hyde. He was with another crew, some of whom had a colour bar, and things were not working out. Would I be interested in him as a Navigator? I said I had no objections and asked about his skill as a Navigator. He had topped the course. I said I was prepared to have him but would discuss the matter with the rest of my crew, as I did not know their feelings. The matter was discussed and they were all happy. They all asked me what he was like as a Navigator and when I told them they said it was OK. We got on very well together and Ade was nicknamed 2359 (RAF Midnight)."

Having assembled his crew Fred Papple began training on Wellingtons at Harwell. The course lasted from mid-November 1943 until almost the end of March 1944.

"My first flight in a Wellington was on 13th November with Flt Lt Morris. We got on OK together, except for landing. He said I came in too low over the end fence. He liked to be higher. I liked to use all the runway but he would take over on the approach then hand back just before touch down and if it was a bit rough he would blame me for the landing. It was then that I made up my mind that if I ever became an instructor I would talk my student into correcting his error and only take over if he was endangering me.

The day I went solo we had just landed and he called me the dumbest Aussie he had met and told me to do another circuit. I saw red and was furious. I lined up on the runway and took off doing a steep climbing turn soon after lift off. Around the circuit I went, lined up on the approach, came in low over the end fence and landed. He said, 'That's better, you can go solo.', to all the crew's amazement, including mine! The crew always said I frightened the shit out of him, so he got out. He gave me a wave to take off and I had just started to taxy, not knowing Flt Lt Morris had walked behind the aircraft until the Rear Gunner, Bob Burns, called, 'Skipper, the bastard's behind you. Open her up and fix him!' I did so and heard a great laugh from 'Burnsie', 'You've fixed him, he's now chasing his hat!' There were no repercussions. We flew twice more with Morris and nothing was said, so he must have been satisfied."

Whilst at Harwell Fred was hospitalised, but apparently made a remarkably quick recovery.

"I was in hospital at Harwell on New Years Eve. A few of the boys called to cheer me up and Max Mazengarb produced a large bottle of whisky. We started to partake then the Sister came in, saw what was going on and blew her top. Max smiled back, said, 'Happy New Year, have a drink!' She did and all was well. It did me some good too. I was out of hospital on the third!"

Fred Papple and crew with Halifax Mk II at 1658 HCU, Riccall, Spring 1944. Rear L to R; -?-, Flt Sgt Dick McLean, Bomb Aimer, -?-, Sgt Ade Hyde, Navigator, -?-, Sgt Bob Gunstone, WOp, -?-. Front L to R; Sgt Bob Burns, Rear Gunner, Sgt Tom Dakin, Mid Upper Gunner, Flt Sgt Fred Papple, pilot, Sgt Sandy McDonald, Flt Engineer. (F Papple)

About three weeks later Fred and his crew carried out a slightly unusual Fighter Affiliation practice. Fred remembers it thus;

"We had a very good fighter pilot today. He was out to get us. I had to do some effective evasive action. I tightened up my turns till I heard, 'Rear Gunner to pilot. Something just flew past my turret!' I assured him it was not a wing but investigation showed we had torn a large piece of fabric from the wing. I called the fighter off and returned to base landing at increased speed in case of an early stall. We landed OK. Later we got the fighter pilots report – 'Damn good evasive action. It's the first time I have had a dogfight with a Wellington!'"

At the end of March 1944 Fred Papple and his crew passed out from the OTU and were posted to No 1658 HCU at Riccall in North Yorkshire. Fred had this to say about the Halifax;

Flying Officers Fred Black, Bill Mullens and Fred Papple. 'D' Flt, No 1652 HCU. Marston Moor with snow covered Halifax Mk III in background. Winter 1944/45. (F Papple)

"My first flight was in a Halifax Mk II, as second pilot, on 27th March 1944. The instructor was Plt Off Jenkinson. They are big bastards, heavy at the controls, but damn nice kites."

Two weeks into the course one of the crew almost came to grief, not in the air, but in bed!

"We came home from York merry and bright and went to bed at about 11.30pm. We left Dick McLean smoking in bed. At 3.30am Bob Burns arrived home and couldn't see in the hut for the smoke. Something was wrong and he raised the alarm. We awoke to find Dick, still in bed, wriggling with the heat. His 'biscuit' mattress was alight. We got him out and put out the fire. He was lucky he had not rolled onto the fire. He smelled like smoked bacon for weeks!"

Fred's crew continued training until the end of April, when, on almost the last trip of the course, they very nearly came to grief.

"We did a bombing and homing practice today. In the afternoon we had a briefing for a cross-country and Bullseye. We took off at 10pm and went on the Bullseye first. Got coned in the searchlights over Hull and turned the kite inside out trying to lose them. The ailerons jammed but righted Ok during the cross-country. Then the starboard outer played up, temperature rising. I told the engineer to keep me informed and half an hour later there was a loud bang followed by another and flames from a motor. Without looking, Sandy McDonald sung out, 'There she goes, Skipper!' I replied, 'You stupid bastard, that's the port inner!' It looked as though we were in for a two engine landing, on one side, at night. Luckily, the starboard outer was just within limits so I didn't have to feather it. We got down safely but were lucky. The Engineering Officer told us it wouldn't have gone much longer before it packed up. You can be lucky, sometimes 25% skill, 75% luck."

After a tour of operations with No 460 Sqn RAAF Fred later became an instructor at No 1652 HCU. The HCU was based at Marston Moor and was equipped with various marks of Halifax. The airfield, of standard three-runway layout, was No 74 base in No 7 Group and was home to almost 2,400 personnel. Rufforth was used as a satellite airfield.

"I was in 'D' Flight commanded by Sqn Ldr McEvoy. When I arrived I was grabbed for 'D' Flight as they were mainly Aussies and before I left we had all Aussies except for McEvoy. We were a mad bunch, so the other Flights said, because whenever we did air tests, most time to class the aircraft fit for dual only, we often waited for the weather to clear playing bridge where the winners prize was cod live oil capsules!

The Flight Commander never rode his service motorbike at night due to ice and snow but he would let us borrow it to go to the local. It was supposed to be parked outside the mess at night. This all stopped when he was questioned as to how he used so much petrol just driving around the unit!"

ROYAL AIR FORCE
HARWELL

Best Wishes

for

Christmas and the New Year

RAF Harwell Christmas card, December 1943. (F Papple)

"Prangtoft"

DON CALDWELL-SMITH – PILOT – 1944/5

Don Caldwell-Smith was a member of the RAAF and trained as a pilot. He arrived at No 27 OTU at Lichfield in Staffordshire in April 1944 and flew Wellingtons there until mid-June 1944. From there he moved to Sandtoft in Lincolnshire. Sandtoft was the home of No 1667 HCU and had a fearsome reputation.

> "One thing that does stand out was my period at 1667 HCU at Sandtoft. In Bomber Command this station was known as 'Prangtoft' because of the loss rate when flying the Halifax Mk V with Merlin XX engines. It was quite a 'joke' to say you had been awarded your 'Sandtoft Survivor medal' on completion of the course. The aircraft could not hold height on three engines and there seemed to be quite a few mechanical problems. It was a station I was very pleased to say I had finished the course."

Extract from Don Caldwell-Smith's logbook for July 1944. (D Caldwell-Smith)

Crash!

CHARLES F SCANDRETT – GROUNDCREW · 1944/1945

A pre-war airman, Charles Scandrett was a Sergeant by the time he arrived at No 1656 HCU in 1944. This HCU was based at Lindholme in Yorkshire and was controlled by No 7 Group. The airfield had three concrete and tarmac runways and dispersals for up to thirty-six heavy bombers in addition to five 'C' type hangars for maintenance and storage. The accommodation was pre-war permanent buildings to accommodate over 2,500 personnel.

> "Initially we were equipped with Halifaxes but later converted to Lancasters. I well remember one night when three Halifaxes crashed within a short time of each other, all fairly near to base. One crashed at Dunsville on to some farm buildings, just missing the house and its occupants. The 'Halibag' took the top off a tree growing at the roadside and it seemed to be that which caused the aircraft to veer to starboard, thus missing the house. The talk in the camp at the time was that the pilot, distracted by the sight of one of the other crashes, lost height and crashed. The resultant fire gave no chance to the crew aboard, but the Rear Gunner was flung out and found wandering dazed nearby. I returned home still carrying the smell of burning human flesh."

The groundcrews on a busy bomber station also had duties that were not without risk. Refuelling and 'bombing up' the aircraft could be risky ventures and accidents sometimes occurred.

> "A Lanc was being de-bombed and a flash bomb went off accidentally, setting fire to a tyre. The flames travelled up through the engine nacelle cutting off the line of escape of the airman refuelling outboard of the engine. He escaped by running along the wing and jumping off. His feet suffered considerable shock on landing!"

Airmen working in the relative comfort of the servicing hangars were not immune to danger.

> "A fire occurred on an aircraft in the Aircraft Servicing Flight hangar, which seemed to have been caused by a spark, caused by a hammer

blow on steel. All tradesmen were warned of this risk, but nobody ever thought it could really happen!"

Whilst at Lindholme, Charles had cause to become involved with Station Sick Quarters.

"We operated four Flights, dispersed around the airfield and I was in 'B' Flight. Initially I lived in the Sergeants mess but being married and having a young baby I was anxious for my family to join me. We took some rooms in Dunsville, which turned out to be quite unsatisfactory, so as soon as possible we moved to Thorne, which was just the reverse. Whilst living in Dunsville I had a bout of the flu and had to take to my bed. My wife rang up to report the fact and after a couple of days in bed I was about ready to report for work again when an ambulance turned up and whipped me into Sick bay! The MO messed about with me and discovered I had an enlarged spleen. That necessitated a journey to hospital in Doncaster for a blood count. Finally I was released from SSQ but had to walk back to Dunsville, because that was where my bike was!"

Much of the grouncrew's work was carried out on the dispersals, the aircraft only being towed into the hangars for major servicing. Once the aircraft and crews had departed on training flights the groundcrews turned to other activities to keep themselves busy, although it was sometimes difficult to get across the airfield at night.

"Working conditions were as good as one could expect operating from a dispersed site. As the aircraft were away for quite some time there were often long periods of free time. I got involved in constructing a garden around our dispersal hut. The hardest bit was doing a turn on night flying after a full day's work. I well remember one night when the aircraft were recalled early due to impending fog. By the time I had prepared all my aircraft for the next days flying, all the runway and perimeter track lights had been switched off. I got lost on the runway, pushing my bike, hoping to get across and so *take* a short cut to the main road. Fortunately, I came across the NCO from 'B' Flight, equally disorientated. Eventually we got our bearings by going into, round and out of every dispersal pan!"

Working conditions for groundcrews could be cold, wet and miserable. They often worked long hours on windswept dispersals, struggling into cramped and confined spaces to carry out their work only to have to start all over again when the fault re-occurred. Several men would work on the aircraft at the same time and it sometimes took a lot of patience as one man clambered passed or over another to get to the area they need to work on.

> "The aircraft were in quite fair condition when coming to the Flights. All acceptance checks and major work was done in the ASF hangar. The Halifax had a very complicated hydraulic system, which took a bit of getting used to. I had great trouble changing a Bomb Aimers windscreen out on dispersal on a particularly cold day. Apart from the weight of a large lump of bulletproof glass, there were an enormous number of screws to be removed and refitted. Then an extra tweak or two on these screws to ensure a good fit and suddenly there was another crack and it meant starting all over again!
>
> The feature I recall most of the Lanc was the electrician working on a main fuse panel situated near the main spar. The poor fellow had to shut it up every time another tradesman wanted to pass forward to the cockpit and then, shortly afterwards, to return!"

With the end of the war in Europe several groundcrews were given the opportunity to fly over Germany and see the devastation wrought by the bombers. Charles did not go on these trips but has cause to remember the VE Day celebrations.

> "I remember VE day as for some reason – I suppose to stop celebrating aircrew from doing something sill – we had to immobilise all the aircraft before having the day off. I was suffering from shingles at the time but, because of my previous experience of SSQ, I decided to suffer – if not entirely in silence!"

Shortly after VE Day Charles was posted away to duties in Technical Training Command.

"Sir, Do You Mind...?"

A.G. STEWART – PILOT – 1942/45

Selected for aircrew AG Stewart was posted for grading to No 11 EFTS at Perth before moving on to Canada for training.

> "At the end of 1942 we had some diabolical weather during which I was taken up by one of the instructors in a Tiger Moth. We took off and got to about 500ft at the other end of the airfield. He cut the motor and the wind was so strong that we flew backwards. He then opened up the motor and we landed without having made a circuit!"

Returning from Canada as a Pilot Officer, Stewart was posted to No 15 (P) AFU.

> "The unit comprised three stations. We were posted to Babdown Farm. You could literally step out of the huts onto the old Roman road, Fosse Way, which was right on the airfield boundary. We did the ground school at Long Newnton and then we went to Castle Combe for the flying. One day we went down to the airfield and saw a 'Wimpey' hanging over the road which went down to Castle Combe village. The road was in a gully lower than the airfield. The 'Wimpey', returning from ops on fire made a forced landing and ended up there. All that was left was the geodetic frame. I believe the crew were OK."

Following AFU, Stewart moved on to No 13 OTU at Bicester.

> "At 13 OTU they had a favourite trick of squirting petrol lighter refills onto someone's back and putting a match to it. The funny thing was that it never damaged any of the uniforms, but it singed the back of your hair quite a lot! This happened often in the Officers Mess. You had to walk around with your back to the wall for protection."

On completion of his training, Stewart was posted to No 625 Sqn at Kelstern and took part in the bombing of the coastal gun batteries in Normandy on the night before D-Day. Following his tour of ops he was posted to No 1 Beam Approach School at Watchfield.

> "I did a beam course at Watchfield in August '44. That covered about 10 hours flying and a further five in the Link Trainer. We flew Oxfords and I recall one incident. Two Oxfords collided. They were supposed

to be flying 500ft apart but they met in mid-air. The top one was hardly damaged at all, but the rudder and fin was knocked off the lower one. Of course, they went straight into a dive and they baled out. The weather was really pretty foul and both officers had flown with their raincoats with the parachutes over them. They landed safely and proceeded to the nearest farmhouse. They knocked on the door and said, 'Excuse me, we've just come down by parachute.' The little old lady in the house did not believe them. The Oxford had a bit of a whip in it occasionally on landing, but it was never any real trouble. I remember one Sunday, it was the Arnhem assault, and I was off on a cross-country. Out to the east I saw all the Dakotas towing gliders. It was a lovely day and I can still picture it."

After the course at Watchfield Stewart went to No 3 AGS at Castle Kennedy for a short period.

"I was only at Castle Kennedy from 10th October to 16th November 1944. One Saturday afternoon on my first circuits and bumps in an Anson I took off. It was a quite reasonable day and then we got showers and wind shifts and heaven know what. I was airborne for an hour and fifteen minutes and coming back I had to land over this hill. On approach I thought, 'That's funny, there is no runway control caravan?' and I could not see it anywhere. They had gone and put it away down on the left, more into wind on the grass and I had not been told this. The intention was that we should land on the grass. I got a rocket when I landed. It was a bit of a dicey landing I'll admit. When I got back there was a crosswind and they were all sitting in the Ops Room waiting for me to do a ground loop. It was very gusty but I got down safely."

Stewart was next posted to No 12 AGS at Bishops Court in Northern Ireland, but first had to complete a conversion course at the Wellington Conversion Flight at Jurby on the Isle of Man.

"We did about 12 – 15 hour at the Wellington Con Flt on Mk III's and Mk X's. The Mk III was underpowered but the Mk X was a lovely aircraft. I was in 'D' Flight at Bishops Court and we received Wellington Mk X's in April 1945. I remained with the AGS until we closed down in June 1945. When we finished as an AGS all the staff pilots went up as passengers in the Wellingtons. We went to the rear turret and fired off the guns, which we had never done before. I remember the pilot we went up with made us weightless and all the muck from the floor went up in the air. We had Martinets there and one crashed on a little island just off the coast at Bishops Court. He almost made it back to the airfield but was killed."

With the war in Europe over many aircrew were without jobs and Stewart was destined for a job in Air Traffic Control, but this was not to be.

"We were all made redundant and I had done a Pilot/Navigator Instructors Course at Halfpenny Green before going to Watchfield. I did an Air Traffic Control Course but they were short of a navigation Instructor at Watchfield so I stayed on and being an Anson pilot I did quite a lot of flying, taking students on visits to units all over the country. Kelmscott was the satellite and we used it for training runway controllers. I spent a lot of time doing landings at Kelmscott in 1945. Watchfield was run by Air Service Training and the groundcrew working for them were very good at maintaining the aircraft. The CO was Wg Cdr Jenkins and the Chief Instructor was Sqn Ldr Webb who was a director of AST.

The Anson was a lovely plane to fly. The only problem was the undercarriage, which had to be wound down manually. This took 64 turns of the handle. I was flying with a Group Captain who was on the course. He was a director of AST and Avro and we were going up to Barton. He was sitting next to me and I said to him, 'Sir, do you mind winding up the undercarriage for me?' He did. I was a little taken aback."

Wild Colonial Boys

JOHN T. SPILLANE – AIR GUNNER – 1944

John Timothy Spillane arrived from Australia in the middle years of the war and crewed up with an all-Australian crew at No 27 OTU, Lichfield. They commenced training in mid June 1944 with 'C' Flt, also flying with 'A' Flt and amassing the huge sum of 82 hours during the course. The Australians who travelled across the world to fight seem to have had a certain flair with the girls and a streak of indiscipline in them. The Spillane crew was no exception.

> "I did my OTU at Lichfield in Staffordshire and I have fond memories of finding the town of Tamworth some miles from the station. It was full of females who worked in the nearby munitions factory. I visited there as often as I could and made many friendships, however, the arrival of the Americans put a finish to that. Our crew did dinghy drills at the public baths at Burton on Trent and we made a number of trips into Nottingham and Derby where further friendships were made, mainly with females. We were an all Australian crew comprising; Flt Sgt Niall Sullivan, pilot, Sgt Archie Creswick, Bomb Aimer, Sgt 'Blue' Cruikshanks, Navigator, Sgt J Chaplin, WOp, Sgt J Lugenga, mid-upper gunner and myself as rear gunner."

On completion of the OTU course the crew were posted to No 1652 HCU. Between the courses they went to No 4 Aircrew School, Acaster Malbis for another course and had their first crew change.

> "The period between finishing OTU and starting HCU was spent at Acaster Malbis near Bishopsthorpe for physical fitness training, unarmed combat and so on. It was here that we lost our mid-upper gunner, Lugenga. He was found to be in possession of a quantity of missing equipment, including guns! He was replaced by Sgt John Merkel who had just finished a six week stretch at Sheffield which was the disciplinary centre!"

After just over three weeks at Acaster Malbis the crew arrived at Marston Moor and No 1652 HCU. Things went well until mid-September 1944 when yet another crew change occurred. The wild colonial streak was showing through again.

"The Skipper was Niall Sullivan (by now promoted to Warrant officer). He was a big man and could make an aeroplane do just about anything. Our Air Gunnery (Camera) sorties were flown against Thunderbolts and Sullivan used to enjoy chasing them around. Following a number of incidents he was transferred and the rest of the crew enjoyed an extended stay at Marston Moor with our new Skipper, Leo Britt. As a Flying Officer he was the only officer in our crew. We had to repeat previous exercises for his benefit and eventually completed HCU on 17th November 1944."

The Britt crew were posted to No 462 Sqn in No 4 group and stayed with the squadron when it transferred to No 100 group.

Divine Providence

PETER TATHAM – PILOT – 1944/45

Peter Tatham and his crew 'crewed up' at No 15 OTU at Harwell in Oxfordshire and on completion of training were posted to No 90 Sqn. They took part in the D-Day operations dropping dummy paratroops from their Stirling and then converted to Lancasters. On completion of his first tour Peter volunteered for Pathfinders and survived 55 operations, receiving a DFC.

In February 1944 I was stationed at No 15 OTU at RAF Harwell having 'crewed up' and very busy with our training schedule. We were equipped at that stage of the war with Wellington Mk X aircraft. These were excellent aircraft with two Bristol Hercules engines, an enormous improvement on the old Mk Ic models.

An incident occurred one day which could have been a major disaster, but which, thanks to divine providence and a lot of quick action by the ground staff was controlled. A young Flt Sgt Engineer who had completed his first tour of operations was showing a group of keen young Air Training Corps boys the mysteries of the mighty Wellington. With commendable clarity he ran through all the controls in the cockpit explaining the operation and function of each. He finished his excellent address to them by stating proudly, '…and this is the fuel jettison toggle!' He then must have had one of those terrible mental aberrations that we all have at some time in our lives. To emphasise the point he said, '…and this is how you operate it." And he gave the toggle a sharp tug.

The result was instantaneous. Two thousand gallons of high-octane aviation spirit crashed onto the tarmac! If this had happened at some dispersal bay around the aerodrome it would have been bad enough, but this aircraft had just been serviced and was standing in the centre of the main hangars, surrounded by aircraft in various stages of repair.

To their great credit and no doubt realising the danger much more quickly than we young trainees, the ground staff sprang into action. All fire fighting equipment arrived in record time. The Service Police ringed the area and warned anyone smoking not to approach.

After about three hours the petrol had been washed away and any persistent residues were sprayed with foam. What could have been a major disaster had been successfully defused. I left the unit shortly afterwards so I never learned what happened to that poor young Engineer. However, I think it would be a safe bet to say that he never reached the rank of Group captain!"

Catfoss Capers

DAVID THOMAS – GROUND WIRELESS OPERATOR – 1940/41

David Thomas was stationed at Catfoss in East Yorkshire from October 1940 to August 1941 as an 18-year-old ground wireless operator. The wireless operators were a vital link between the aircraft and the station and played an important part in the training of the WOp/AGs.

"I was a ground wireless operator at the HQ Signals Section. We were on shift work and mostly used Morse code and sometimes R/T. The station callsign was 'Dolphin' and the aircraft used 'Parker' The crews trained on Ansons, Oxfords, Battles and Blenheims and always kept in communication with us as a part of their exercises.

The Signals Section consisted of a large rectangular room with three receivers, two Morse and one R/T. The transmitters were a few miles down the road towards Hornsea. There was also a teleprinter room, general office and Signals Officer's office, complete with bed. As this was for the WAAF cypher officer (there were two) who had to be on duty all the time, there was always a rush of volunteers to wake her in the morning!

About every three weeks a batch of WOp/Ags would be posted to us for their final wireless exercises before the 'real thing'. They were all sergeants. The course consisted of six exercises, each one getting more difficult. Each morning our signals Flt Sgt would complete a large blackboard with the details of the day's ops.

On a busy day it was not unusual to have six or seven up at the same time. One of our Morse receivers was used for all the Anson and Oxford work, you can imagine how busy it got. On Exercise No 1 the chap had to call us up, ask if his frequency was correct and the signal strength, then ask to close down. All in his grounded aircraft. Easy? You'd be surprised.

The signals used were from a code book of 'X' numbers, for example; X112 meant interrogative, X257 I have no message, X259 I have a message, X285 signal strength. Thus, X112 + X285 = What is my signal strength? These numbers covered every eventuality. There were numbers for 'Your Morse is good' or 'Your Morse is bad'. Exercise 2 consisted of Exercise 1 plus taking off and doing it again in the air. Exercise 3 included 1 and 2 and sending a coded message, made up by themselves. Exercise 4 included 1,2 and 3 and so on. They would have to change frequency to HF/DF and come back again to our frequency. If you can imagine sitting on a set with the earphones and half a dozen aircraft, all on different exercises, at the same time – you will know what I mean!

The two most awkward things that would happen would be the WOp would forget to 'listen out' before calling us up and bash straight in on the top of another aircraft already transmitting and secondly, changing to another frequency and not being able to change back to us again. Rather like listening for him on Radio 1 and he's come back onto Radio 2. We were not allowed to search the dial for them. They just failed the exercise."

Life at a training unit could be routine but danger was never very far away as David Thomas was to find out.

"Callsigns were changed every day. Sometimes they would go up with the wrong callsign. We were forbidden to answer – it might be a 'Gerry'. Some went up using the same callsign as another aircraft. All very confusing. On one occasion when I was on the set an Anson had just told me he was coming in to land. I heard an aircraft approaching

David Thomas and crew of an armoured radio car
of No 3 ASU, Damascus, 1942. (D Thomas)

past the Signal Station and I said to the lads, 'here comes my Anson.' I looked out of the window and horror of horrors it had German markings all over it and was dropping a stick of bombs near the runway! The German bomber got away. I think it must have been a one off hit and run raid. It came in and went out over the coast before we knew what was up. One of the bombs exploded after going through the roof of the Sergeants living quarters – straight through someone's bed! As no one was in the hut at the time we all thought it was very funny.

When Hull was heavily bombed for two nights running we would stand in our slit trenches and watch the black shapes going over. Apart from the one bomber there were no other attacks on Catfoss whilst I was there. The perimeter of the airfield did have one or two light Ack-Ack guns but I never heard them fire."

Entertainment at wartime RAF stations could be hard to find and the isolated location of an airfield often meant long journeys to find it. Once found the little perks could be short lived when the authorities stepped in and placed the location out of bounds.

"Living and messing conditions for all 'other ranks' including NCO's was in Nissen huts not far from the main road. Ablutions were also in huts, only larger. There was a small parade ground and a guardroom/orderly room at the entrance. The Duty Pilot had accommodation next to the main hangar at the side of the runway. The mess was another Nissen hut. SNCO's and aircrew had their own mess. There was also a small NAAFI, which was pretty useless! Across the road, opposite the Guardroom, was Chandlers Café which had an everlasting supply of tea, egg and chips etc. as well as cigarettes and stationery. This became so popular that it was made 'out of bounds' during morning breaks while the NAAFI was open!

There were also Married Quarters – very nice. The families vacated these new houses and all the Signal personnel, including myself, were installed. This was a real bonus as we were on shift work --nights as well. When coming off duty at eight in the morning we could have breakfast and go to bed in peace without the awful noise of the Nissen hut occupants.

All Officers accommodation and the Officers Mess was a couple of miles down the road at Brandsburton village. We were very much out in the wilds. There was one double decker bus, especially directed to stop at the camp gates, every three hours and very little chance of a hitchhike. This bus took us to Beverley and another bus to Hull. You can imagine the free for all to get back in the evening. Civilians were just swept aside! There was usually an extra bus at night. In January and February 1941 the camp was completely isolated by snow and we were down to hard biscuits and 'Bully Beef'!

When new Wireless Ops were posted to HQ Signals one would always be delegated to man the R/T set. This was because it was not so busy and far easier to cope with than the Morse code. However, there was one big snag. Each 'raw' operator was warned not to deal with Parker 14 but to shout for help. Parker 14 was the number of the Chief Flying instructor. Not only did he use this number when flying, but he also had a receiver/transmitter in his office near the runway. So when he came on the air one never knew whether he was up in the air or not. His name was Wg Cdr McCarthy and he was an absolute so and so as regards signals procedure. He would listen in most of the time when there were exercises and butt in if he heard a word out of place and give the unfortunate offender a mouthful!

The Blenheims would go up in a group and go through the usual routine of contacting us. But we used to have our moments – even on the R/T. A typical group might be Parker Red Leader, Parker 23,

David Thomas while with No 3 ASU in Sicily, 1943. (D Thomas)

Parker 24 and Parker 32. Well, that's how they might start off and one could recognise a voice to fit the number. During the exercise Red Leader would call us to say, 'I am now going to be Parker 32 and Parker 32 will be Red Leader.' Of course this message had to be conveyed to the others. Now, if the message was misheard? One could tell from their voices who was supposed to be which number, but it often ended up in a complete muddle with two numbers the same, or no Red Leader! Then, of course, there was always the possibility of Parker 14 butting in and we poor HQ operators had to take it all.

The switches on the flying helmets were on a toggle for send/receive. When the switch was to 'send' the chappie could not hear you – so having said what he wanted to say, the switch would be put over to 'receive'. But if he forgot you could not tell him. On one particular occasion I had just finished speaking to him, but I did not hear the 'click' of the switch. I called him back, but there was no answer. The next minute he burst into song! It blotted out everybody else and we couldn't stop him for over ten minutes. On a second occasion I had come on watch to find a group gathered around the R/T set. The operator was working three or four Parker's. He had picked up an extra Parker and was in jovial conversation with him, against Parker 14's orders – he wasn't listening. He sounded farther away than normal and was not using the normal Parker numbers of the day and he spoke with a German accent! He soon went off the air.

Apart from the R/T set and the 'Anson & Oxford' set we had a third receiver for the Air Ministry Broadcasts. They were sent out every hour throughout the day and at night at Midnight, 0100, 0200, 0330 and 0500. The messages consisted of 5 figure groups and the length could vary from 10 to 800 groups. So one always had to have plenty of message pads and pencils at the ready. The contents were all administration messages and they would come through at normal speed, say 18 words a minute and was then repeated immediately at 25 plus word per minute. Even this work had its moments. The signal would start bashing out a few minutes before time with the callsign GFAZ. One night, whilst taking the 0330 call, I turned up the volume, reception was very clear, and hung the earphones around my neck and let the callsign bash away. When the message was about to start – 'NW' – Now – would be sent umpteen times. On this occasion the callsign lulled me to sleep and when I came to the message was being bashed out. Now this was ver awkward, though luckily it was 'first time round" I did not know how many groups there were and I didn't know where to start on the message pad. I used scrap paper until the message started round again. This was because, when decoding, each line of groups except the first was subtracted from the line above, so the positions of the groups were all important. However, if any snags did occur on this set, we could always contact Driffield or Leconfield by teleprinter, though it was a last resort.

We worked eight-hour shifts and after a while a further duty befell us which entailed losing our long break every now and again. A flashing beacon was put into operation, to be manned by a wireless op and an electrician every night. This large beacon was mounted on a four wheeled trailer hauled by a 3 tonner and towed out to one of three sites – 'A Apple', 'B Bellboy' or 'C Cut-throat'. All were situated in a farmer's field a few miles from the camp. Our equipment included an R/T Transmitter/Receiver TR9, a large wooden, collapsible 'T' fitted with white electric light bulbs, a 12v battery, a rifle each with five rounds, a tin of cocoa and sugar, a packet of sandwiches and a tent. The farms were to provide hot milk. The beacon, which would revolve and flash the 'letters of the night', was a guide to aircraft in distress, who would make a prearranged signal by lamp, which we would recognise. The electrician would have to be woken up to light up the 'T' which we hoped we had positioned pointing to the airfield. It was also hoped that if 'Jerry' came over, he might attack the beacon, mistaking it for the airfield!

Bearing in mind it was wintertime and of course a black out (no lights in the tent) it was no fun sitting up all night whilst the electrician and the driver went to sleep! Every now and then Dolphin would call, just to see if we were awake, or alive! The roads to the farms were very narrow and I had the dubious privilege of being the first to take the beacon to 'Cut-throat'. We left the camp an hour before dusk. After about a mile we got stuck on a crossroads trying to turn right. We were no very popular with the other traffic. In trying to extricate ourselves, the local telephone wires got wrapped round the top of the beacon! Happy days! Next time a different route was used."

After leaving Catfoss David Thomas moved to Uxbridge and No 11 group for six months before being posted overseas. His duties took him with a unit of the Desert Air Force known variously as No 3 Air Support Unit, 50/51 Mobile Signals Unit and No 2/5 Army Air Support Control through Syria, Egypt, Libya, Tunisia, Malta, Sicily, Italy and Austria ending up in the Russian Zone there. His adventures would fill a book of their own.

"To Hell With Your Bloody Orbit!"

JACK THORNTON – PILOT 1942/45

In early 1942 the RAF introduced the first four engined heavy bombers and with them the crew constitution was changed. No longer would there be two pilots. There would now only be one pilot assisted by a Flight Engineer. It was during this period that Jack Thornton began his aircrew training.

> "I began my flying training on Tiger Moths at No 9 EFTS at Ansty. We had just finished ITW and they sorted us all out and sent us on this course. It was only ten or twelve hours flying and the idea was that you had to go solo within that short time. If you did you had a pretty good chance of being selected for pilot. If you did not you would probably be made a Navigator or Bomb Aimer.
>
> After the course we proceeded to Heaton Park and we hung around there for several weeks till they finally announced to us what our trade was going to be. At the time they did not need many pilots as Bomber Command had decided to have one pilot per crew, so 50% of their pilots were surplus. They did not really want pilots but Bomb Aimers, so I was very lucky to be selected for pilot training."

'Lucky' Jack Thornton was over the first hurdle on the way to becoming a bomber pilot. Posted to No 11 (P) AFU at Shawbury near Shrewsbury he found the Oxfords flown there to be quite different from his experience on Tiger Moths.

> "The Oxford was a very delicate plane. It was very good for training as you had to 'fly' it all the time. It did not suffer fools gladly; any mistake and it showed you all right. It was a very good training aircraft. The Tiger Moths at Ansty were quite different. You flew them with a finger and thumb and you touched the controls very gently. The slightest bit too much and off you would go. They were both excellent aircraft for training and if you could fly those you could fly anything."

Like most trainees Jack was posted to many units and did many courses so it is hardly surprising that almost fifty years later some recollections are a little vague. His next posting was to No 1524 BAT Flt at Prestwick.

> "I do not remember much about this course but I was quite good at SBA (Standard Beam Approach) so I must have had some good training! I used to swear by SBA. I would rather have SBA than anything else. You could rely entirely upon yourself, whereas, with some other equipment like BABS you had to rely on your Navigator. With SBA you had Fan Markers, an Inner Marker and an Outer Marker. If you were off the approach to one side 'N' was transmitted and 'S' to the other side in Morse. If you were on the beam they combined to give a steady tone. It was not easy to stay on the tone. If you got off to one side you were constantly snaking down trying to get back on and it was hard to line up again."

Sometimes there would be a delay between flying courses for one reason or another and, whilst waiting, trainee aircrew were often sent on other courses to fill in the time. Jack completed one such course before being posted to No 21 (P) AFU at Wheaton Aston.

> "Many courses would be just killing time. There would be no room on the OTU you were waiting to go to so they would put you on these little courses to familiarise you with flying in the UK. One course at

Wheaton Aston in June 1993.
(Authors collection)

Wratting Common was a sort of 'commando' course. We were rigged out in army boots and so on and dumped out in the wilds and told to find our own way back.

At AFU we did beacon crawls on night flying. They used to have these beacons flashing various codes, the codes used to change every so often, which were sited on different aerodromes and all you did was set course from one aerodrome to another, quite close to each other, and crawled round the beacons."

By late 1943 Jack Thornton was at No 83 OTU at Peplow in Shropshire. Jack was not very keen on the RAF system of 'crewing up' and held back during the scramble to pick crews. His experience showed that selection of a crew was not easy and sometimes clashes of personality would occur later in what had been thought to be a good crew selection.

"Crewing up is a long story. The idea was that various members of the crew all congregated at the OTU and you were supposed to get together. The pilot was supposed to go around and say 'Would you like to join my crew?' – very embarrassing, I thought. So I decided, 'To hell with it, I'll just take what's left.' I stood back and waited till they had all crewed up and I took the remainder. Surprisingly enough I got a very good crew. I was very fortunate with the Navigator because he was one of the best navigators on the course. There were two Squadron leaders there for one of whom a crew had already been prepared. However, both of them selected their own crews and this crew was left surplus.

The WOp was rather a 'drunken bum' whom nobody wanted but he was really an excellent bloke. My rear gunner had wanted to go on the same crew as his, who was also a gunner, but he had not been selected, so I got him too. He was a Lancashire lad and also excellent.

I finished up with a really good crew with the exception of the Bomb Aimer. He was a most peculiar bloke with a triple barrelled name and four initials to go along with it. He had a peculiar wizened look on his face and looked about ninety, though he must have been in his thirties. We went through the OTU and had finished the whole course with the exception of one trip. The Bomb Aimer could not get on with the rest of the crew for some reason. We had one Night Bombing exercise to do and they sent us up on this thing at 3,000 feet. We climbed to that height could not see so went to 9,000 feet. It was December and bitterly cold. They were not warm aircraft by any means and it went to my bladder and I was bursting for a 'pee'. The

Bomb Aimer was supposed to be able to take over the control but I daren't move. So, I called for someone to bring me something to 'pee' in but I could wait no longer, so I pee'ed over to one side, all over the Bomb Aimer! I forgot he was down there. He was outraged and, of course, it was so cold it froze over him. This was the final straw. He was not getting on with the rest of the crew anyway and said he wanted a change. I said, 'That suits me fine.' We lost him and got a Canadian, Jack Ross, an excellent bloke too. I finished up with a really first class crew."

On 22nd December 1943 Jack Thornton received a Green Endorsement to his logbook following a 'Nickel' operation to Loen in France. This was one of 21 OTU sorties carried out that night whilst Bomber Command attacked two flying bomb sites between Abbeville and Amiens with fifty-one aircraft. 'Nickels' were leaflet-dropping raids carried out by OTU crews nearing the end of their course. The endorsement read thus:

"On the night of 22 Dec 43 while on a Nickel exercise the aircraft in which Sgt Thornton was pilot and captain was engaged by accurate and heavy flak near Boulogne. The aircraft suffered extensive damage and inter alia the hydraulic systems were put out of action and all interior lighting. Nevertheless he carried on and successfully completed his mission and on return to base skilfully and successfully executed a flapless landing without cockpit lights and despite the fact that the wind was appreciably off the runway in use."

Jack Thornton's version of the story is as follows:

"On a 'Nickel' raid you only carried leaflets and they sent you over on your own. Two of us went that night but not together, about half an hour apart. You crossed the coast and went half an hour or so inland, dropped your leaflets, took a photograph of where you dropped them and came back again. We were supposed to have crossed the coast south of Boulogne by about ten miles. My navigator said we were early, so he said we better make a dogleg. After doing two minutes one way and two minutes the other we were still early. He said, 'You better do an orbit.' I daren't as we were practically over Boulogne. Anyway, I started circling over Boulogne and they opened up at us with heavy flak. We were the only ones there so we got the lot. I said, 'To hell with your bloody orbit!' And dived down over the coast and shot inland. We started checking the damage. The gunners found they could not use their guns, the hydraulics had gone and all the lights had gone in the cockpit. One of the engines was playing up a bit and when we opened the bomb doors they stayed open. Anyway, we brought it back OK.

The navigator was Sgt Killeen. He was a very good navigator except that from time to time instead of saying, 'Steer 090' he would say, ' Steer 190'. So we would fly along for a while and he would suddenly realise it was not right and say, 'Where do you think you are going?' and I would say, 'You said steer 190' and he would reply, 'I did not. I said 090!' He did this several times so I memorised the courses so I always knew when he was out."

The pressures that many of these young men under training were put under had unusual effects. Many men had premonitions of impending disaster, or bad dreams, or a feeling that their 'number was up'. Jack Thornton had one such dream, which affected him.

"I had just done my first night solo and a couple of nights later I dreamt that I had taken off at night and suddenly the engine cut on take off and the aircraft swung and headed straight for the control tower. I could see a WAAF officer sitting there with a cup of tea in her hand and a look of horror on her face as I was hurtling towards her. I woke up in a hell of a sweat. The dream was so vivid that I was dreading my next take off. I was due for solo circuits that night, so I went out and was allocated an aircraft. I tested it and decided there was something drastically wrong with it, so, I did not take it and did not fly. The next night was the same and the following night. This went on for five nights. There was always something wrong with the aircraft. They were all pretty clapped out. The Flight Commander got a bit fed up. 'I don't know what's the matter' he said, 'I'll put an instructor with you and see that you definitely get up tonight.' He gave me a Sergeant pilot instructor and we went to six different

The Badge of No 1651 HCU. The motto is 'Thus trusty and strong.' It refers to the large and heavy aircraft operated by the unit.

aircraft and they were all u/s. The next night the Flight Commander said, 'We'll get you up in the air tonight. I'll go with you myself tonight.' So we got out to the airfield and suddenly a Very light went up and flying was scrubbed. The following night I got airborne but it had been a terrible week for me after that dream."

After his adventurous time at OTU, Jack and his crew were posted to No 1651 HCU at Wratting Common in Cambridgeshire. This airfield was a standard three-runway wartime bomber station with temporary accommodation for 2,400 personnel. The HCU operated Stirlings.

"The Stirlings were big aircraft. It felt big; everything was big about them. It had four big throttles, which I could only just cover with my hand. I sat on one parachute to see out with another behind my back so I could reach the pedals! It was more like a ship than an aircraft! I did not like them because they did not react immediately. When you pulled the wheel over it was three or four seconds before the plane would react and when you went back again the controls were crossed. With the Lanc it was different, you had instant reaction.

There was a raid on 16th March 1944 and we were sent out as a diversion. We went out over the North Sea, two or three hundred of us from the HCUs and OTUs to draw the fighters in the hope that they would attack us and the main Force would go off in another direction. About half way across the North Sea we turned back."

Having finished the HCU course, Jack and his crew were awaiting posting when he was called into the Flight Commanders office. The adventures were not yet over.

"When I'd finished the course the Flight Commander said, 'it's a pity about your crew.' I asked why and he continued, 'Well, we take the best crew on the course and give them H2S training. Your crew is exceptional with the exception of one member.' I asked which one and he said, 'The Bomb Aimer.' I said, 'The Bomb Aimer? There's nothing wrong with my Bomb Aimer!' He named my previous Bomb Aimer and I said, 'Oh! I haven't got him anymore. I have Jack Ross, a Canadian.' He replied, 'In that case you are easily the best crew.' He recommended us to carry on with H2S training. I wish we had not. The last flight there we crashed our Stirling. A tyre burst and we wrote the thing off!"

The training was almost over for Jack's crew now. One more course to complete at No 3 LFS at Feltwell and then a posting to a squadron.

> "This course only lasted about five days. I got one dual practice, then I was off solo. We did not get much instruction really, as the Lanc was such a beautiful aeroplane. The Lanc was a real lady. It was a much more comfortable aircraft than the Stirling. It was like sitting in an armchair. The controls were close to and the throttles were easy to reach. It was a warm cockpit, you were never cold. I never wore flying kit, you did not need it."

From LFS Jack's crew were posted to No 115 Sqn and after completing a tour there did a short course at the No 8 Group Navigation Training Unit before joining the pathfinders and No 7 Sqn for a further tour. Jack returned to the training world after his pathfinder tour and was posted to No 85 OTU at Husbands Bosworth.

Jack Thornton flew Stirlings like this one at HCU. N3638 was the fourth production Mk1 first issued to No 7 Sqn before serving with Nos 15 and 149 Sqns and No 106 Con Flt. It then became an instructional airframe, 3013M at No 4 STT. (Authors collection)

The Badge of No 85 OTU.

"I was supposed to be an instructor. When I got there they asked me what I wanted to do. I said, 'I want to fly the Hurricane.' They had one on the OTU for fighter affiliation and everyone wanted to fly it. I did not really do very much instructing, I just sat with my student for a few circuits then sent him off on his own. I had done the Bomber Command Instructors Course at Silverstone. You learned how to give instruction there.

I remember my last trip at 85 OTU was taking a Wellington to Kirkbride when the unit was closing down. All the aircraft had gone except one. It was a clapped out old thing. I flew it up with just a WOp and I had to fight it all the way. The brakes were not very good when we taxied out. On the way up I dived down on Blackpool Tower and when I tried to pull out it would not come up. Luckily I missed the tower. When I landed I managed to stop near the end of the runway and as I taxied round the brakes were getting weaker and weaker. On one of the turns of the taxiway the Wellington would not take it and |I was braking like mad. It carried straight on. Ahead of me was a hedge and I thought about whipping up the undercarriage to stop but I did not want to write off the aircraft. I thought it was only a hedge so I carried on. On the other side of the hedge was a ditch and barbed wire. The prop picked up the barbed wire and wrapped it around the cockpit as we went into the ditch and the WOp ended up with a gashed head."

Thus ended Jack Thornton's instructional career!

Early Bird

G.A. WRIGHT – OBSERVER – 1938

In 1938 it was obvious that war was imminent. The RAF was expanding rapidly and within the expansion No 1 Air Observer Navigation School (AONS) was opened at Prestwick. The school operated Ansons and the instructors were all civilians. GA Wright was an early student at this school.

"Each entry was comprised of about 26 young men and I was a member of the second entry, the course lasting from 6th November 1938 until 4th February 1939. We came straight from civilian life and were known Direct Entry Observers. All our service numbers like those of similar pilots began with the prefix 580. It was an odd situation in that although part of the RAF we wore civilian clothes during our course apart from flying clothing.

We only donned uniform of a LAC when we were posted to RAF Uxbridge when, in the space of three weeks, we suffered the agony of being turned into smart young airmen. Our bedrooms were on the first floor of the building with our classrooms being on the ground floor. Our 'matron' was a retired Warrant Officer and every morning we were on the tarmac at 6.30am for PE and drill. The flying aspect of the course was carried out by Scottish Airways pilots who, when not flying on the routes in De Havilland Rapides, piloted us on our cross-country exercises, the crew of the Anson being two students and a pilot. We soon became acquainted with the surrounding terrain of Arran and Ailsa Craig, the whole area being ideal for navigational exercises. Whilst there I saw a Tiger Moth flying headlong into a gale with a groundspeed of 0mph. When it managed to land it tipped up onto its nose. Another aircraft crashed into the Galloway Hills. Rumour had it that there was a mysterious area where planes were sucked down to their destruction!

The Glasgow Herald did a feature on the course including a large photograph of students and instructor in a classroom. The headline was 'Airmen in the making'. The instructor, shown in RAF uniform, was Lt Cdr Campbell-Waters. The course was very intensive and the urgency became clearer at the end of the year, but Wednesday afternoons were given over to sport. We were members of the local league playing against such teams as Ardrossan, Troon and Saltcoats.

Every match took on the nature of an England v Scotland contest and fortunately the referee was able to exert rigid control. Saturday nights saw us going to Ayr to a dance hall known as Green's Playhouse."

After Prestwick and 'square bashing' at Uxbridge, Wright was posted to No 1 Air Observers School (AOS).

"We were posted to North Coates in Lincolnshire for a course on air to air firing and bombing, flying the wonderful old Wapiti biplanes. Then we were detailed off to various operational squadrons both at home and overseas. I was posted to No 61 Sqn at Hemswell flying Hampdens. I was the first Direct Entry Observer they received and with three stripes on my arm was known as the first of those 'jumped up ——', the normal length of service being fourteen years before becoming a sergeant."

One Hour Fifty Minutes at LFS

J.L. MACFARLAND – NAVIGATOR – 1941/45

J.L. MacFarland joined the RAF in 1941 and initially served on Air Sea Rescue launches at Invergordon in Scotland. He decided to apply for aircrew as a navigator and after selection went to the ACRC and then on to ITW at Scarborough. From there he was sent overseas to No 5 ANS at Winnipeg and arrived back in the UK in October 1943. His posting was to No 2 (O) AFU at Millom.

> "I only have hazy memories of Millom but I do remember the accommodation was very basic – especially after Canadian hospitality! We flew fourteen training trips in the month I was there. I flew ten of my trips as First Navigator. My first flight was to Jurby when a Sqn Ldr Morton urgently hailed me and said that he needed a navigator – regulations required it – but he knew the way! We took off in overcast conditions and soon were into 10/10ths cloud. I gave him a course and ETA. We broke cloud at a few hundred feet exactly over the runway at Jurby! Quite elated!
>
> The pilots were an assortment of experienced men and conscientiously flew the course given. Most flights were around the Scotland, Northern Ireland and isle of Man area but some were from base to a Dead Reckoning (DR) position, to another DR position and back to base to test our navigation."

MacFarland then had the unusual experience of missing out the OTU stage of his training altogether and was posted directly to No 1657 HCU at Stradishall. He was never given an explanation for this.

> "I joined a New Zealand crew at Stradishall, pilot, WOp/AG and Bomb Aimer. I think the New Zealand navigator had been washed out at OTU. I had no idea why I had missed OTU and I was certainly not my choice as we all looked forward to being 'crewed up' with he folk you liked. When I heard later the casualty rate at the OTU was shocking I didn't mind."

After HCU MacFarland's crew were posted to No 75 (New Zealand) Sqn and, as the Stirlings had been withdrawn from Main Force operations, concentrated on mining operations around the enemy

No 4 Sqn, D Flt, Orleton School, No 17 ITW Scarborough, Yorks. Aug 10th – Oct 21st 1942. Flt Cdr – Plt Off H Walker. NCO i/c Flt – Cpl Dunkley. CO – Sqn Ldr R Whittingham. (JL MacFarland)

ports and sea-lanes. At the end of March 1944 the crew were sent to NO 3 LFS at Feltwell for an incredibly brief conversion to the Lancaster.

> " Our Skipper flew a few take offs and landings during the day and we flew one hour and fifty minutes at night as a crew before flying a Lancaster back to Mepal the next day!"

The crew then flew some Lancaster operations before volunteering for one more Stirling op to Kiel. A night fighter shot them down over Denmark. The pilot, flight engineer and two gunners were killed. Macfarland was to become a POW. Forty years later he was invited to a remembrance service for his crew in the small Danish village near where his Stirling fell.

No75 (NZ) Sqn – March 1944. From left: Fg Off Jim Merry, JL McFarland, others unknown. This photo was taken for a press visit. The Stirling, EF181, served with No 75 and No 218 Sqn until written off in a crash at Woolfox Lodge on 12 June 1944. (JL MacFarland)

Contractors at Work

PETER WESTON – CIVILIAN ENGINEER – 1941

In 1941 Peter Weston was working as an engineer for the Cunliffe Owen Aircraft Co Ltd and was engaged in the assembly and modification of a wide range of aircraft types including Blenheims, Hudson's, Tomahawks and Airacobras. His experience with Hudson's was to find him in a company work party detached to the Hudson OTU at Silloth.

> "It was late Summer 1941 and Hudson's appeared to be having certain problems. Having worked on them before I was part of a group detached to Silloth to try and solve the problems."

Cunliffe Owen despatched the team by rail to Carlisle an on to Silloth and Weston had his first taste of wartime long distance rail travel - which was not to his liking!

> "We arrived and were taken a few miles down the coast from Silloth to a hotel, standing alone, right on the beach at Allonby. This was to be home for nearly a year. The meals were very good and the whole place was comfortable. The Cunliffe Owen party were the only guests! Our leader quickly ascertained the problems and we all got down to fix them."

The first problem the team had to deal with was an engine-starting problem.

> "The airfield at Silloth was right on the Solway Firth and prone to cold air and heavy, damp mists sweeping in from the sea. It was concluded that the engine oil around the pistons and in the oil tanks was thickening up. The aircraft were never kept in the hangars and engine covers were rarely put on. The solution to the starting problem was to fit an oil dilution kit to the engines to thin out the oil prior to starting. They were also advised to start fitting the engine covers."

The second problem the team had to deal with was leaking petrol tank which, due to their position, were potentially very hazardous.

> "This was the most difficult job of them all. The training aircraft often suffered heavy landings and these were not always reported. The top of the main undercarriage leg is fastened to a large, strong mounting

firmly affixed to the side of the fuel tank. The fuel tank is integral to the wing and could not be removed. The large rivets holding the brackets were weakening and were not tight enough to prevent slight leakage of the high-octane fuel. This could be fatal near the hot engines. To solve the problem the fuel tanks were emptied and the upper wing access panels were removed to allow access to the interior wall where the problem lay. After some deliberation some of the rivets were replaced by bolts and the remainder replaced by a different type. All the Hudson's were modified and orders issued that pilots should report heavy landings. It apparently worked out fine."

The next modification was the fitting of a small Astrograph table at the rear of the crew compartment and this was followed by work to improve the ditching capabilities of the Hudson. Hudson's which had been ditched were reported by their crews to have sunk very quickly and Cunliffe Owen were asked to remedy the situation.

"Inspection of recovered Hudson's showed that the bomb bay doors were crushed in and that the glass panel in the nose situated in the floor had been pushed inwards. Silloth had a reputation for so many ditchings that the local populace had renamed the Solway Firth 'Hudson Bay'. Two of the runways were aligned out to sea and into the prevailing wind and were most often used. If an aircraft had a problem on getting airborne someone could look forward to getting their feet wet. Many planes were lost low level bombing on a target anchored half a mile offshore. We partly solved the problem of rapid sinking by strongly reinforcing the front glass with an inner frame and two cross bars. In between the two bomb bay bulkheads a strong girder was fitted so that the bomb doors would close upon it along their entire length. Nothing of course could prevent a quick sinking if hitting the water with great force. We did have favourable reports later, informing us that the modifications had worked out very well, which pleased us."

In 1942 Peter Weston volunteered for RAF aircrew and was accepted. He went to ITW at Bridgenorth and trained as a radio operator and later a radar navigator passing through No 4 RS at Madley, No 9 (O) AFU at Llandwrog, No 26 OTU at Wing and then on to No 1669 HCU at Langar before being posted to No 90 Sqn at Tuddenham. He remained in the RAF after the war and served through the Korean and Malayan conflicts.

Conversion Crash

RON ALLEN – NAVIGATOR – 1944

No 1663 Conversion Unit was formed at Rufforth on 7 February 1943 with three flights equipped with 24 Halifax Mk V. The Halifaxes were fitted with Rolls Royce Merlin XX engines and were a particularly sorry lot, most of them being retired from operations after many flying hours or repaired after battle damage or crashes. The role of the unity was to convert crews from twin engined aircraft such as the Wellington to the four-engined Halifax. Ron Allen, a navigator, arrived at Rufforth for training with his crew in 1944.

Training at the HCU was fairly routine, a heavy bomber crew transferred from a twin engined aircraft to four engines and increased from six members to seven with the addition of a Flight Engineer, to relieve the pilot of some of the more mundane dial watching and other duties. This period of training was of most importance to the pilot and the Flight Engineer. Navigation exercises were similar to those at OTU but of longer duration and at faster airspeed. All was going smoothly with Ron's training until September 1944 when he and his crew almost came to grief in Halifax DG407.

"The flight plan for 2 September 1944 was to have been fighter affiliation and night bombing practice. The former involving a rendezvous with a fighter, the practice of evasion tactics based on the commentaries of the two gunners and for the latter, dummy target practice. Afterwards we were to fly on to a local bombing range to drop small practice bombs.

The pilot carried out the basic checks on starting up the aircraft's engines and the subsequent taxiing out for take off. I have a vague recollection that the port outer engine appeared to have an oil pressure problem on starting up but this cleared as we proceeded to the runway in use. The aircraft started to roll down the runway and was gathering speed when it started to veer to port – because of a loss of power in the port outer engine, presumed later to be due to it oiling up.

The aircraft drifted off the runway onto the grass and the port undercarriage leg broke off. The tail gunner uttered some appropriate exclamation as the aircraft overtook the wheel rolling along the grass!

I have no doubt that the pilot was at this time taking action to stop the aircraft whilst informing us over the intercom of what was happening. The wireless operator and myself sat in the main spar area for every take off, this being no exception, and were anticipating escape action.

When the undercarriage leg snapped the aircraft belly flopped and everyone in the crew took appropriate crash landing action. While this action was being taken there was a flash from the accumulators behind the Flight Engineer's bulkhead. I saw no more as the wireless operator and myself had the upper escape hatch open and were evacuating the aircraft with great haste!

We must all have had the idea of self preservation in our minds as all seven crew members were racing hell for leather away from the burning aircraft, which had ammunition and practice bombs as well as fuel on board. That was it. All that remained in the grey light of dawn was a solidified pool of aluminium and fragments of engines."

Ron Allen went on to serve with two No 4 Group squadrons in Yorkshire, Nos 578 and 77 Squadrons.

Gunnery Gaffes

GEORGE STALKER – AIR GUNNER

Sgt George Stalker arrived at Rufforth with his crew to begin conversion to the Halifax. In his role as Air Gunner George began training in the mid-upper turret and was soon to learn the problems his use of the turret could cause other members of the crew.

> "I had arrived at Rufforth and along with the rest of the crew was eventually allocated a 'Halibag'. Because the 'Halibag' was a new experience I was a little unfamiliar with the mid-upper turret, which was fitted with four .303 Browning machine-guns and was electrically operated. Also in the turret was a clutch, which allowed the turret to

Sgt George Stalker standing at the tail turret of a Rufforth based Halifax of No 1663 HCU. (George Stalker via Ian Foster/57 Rescue)

freewheel. I'm not sure why the clutch was fitted but I'm sure I discovered the reason the first time that I engaged it!

During a flight over the East Coast of Yorkshire it was the gunners responsibility to test the guns. I checked mine while pointing over the starboard beam and, without warning anyone, I pulled in the clutch to see exactly what it could do. Immediately the clutch was pulled in the slipstream took hold of the guns and whipped the turret round 180 degrees to face over the port beam, spinning my body with it but leaving my head and neck to catch up! This in turn had an adverse effect on the handling of the 'kite' and our Skipper wasn't impressed when his flying controls started bucking about without reason, until I owned up and was duly chastised."

George's gaffes were not over and later in his conversion course he was in trouble again.

"I was again testing our guns, when I accidentally shot off our antenna mast. I was on the point of reporting this over the intercom when our wireless operator suddenly came on and told the Skipper that the wireless had suddenly packed up.

I tried to tell the wireless operator what I had done but there was no reply. About twenty minutes later he came on the intercom sounding rather confused and explained to the Skipper that he had stripped the wireless down and still could not find the fault. It was then that I spoke up and told him that I had shot off the antenna, to which came an irate reply about where he would like to put my guns when we landed!"

George Stalker survived the war and remained in the RAF finally retiring in 1975 with the rank of Flight Lieutenant.

Rufforth Recollections

RALPH FARMILOE – FLIGHT ENGINEER – 1944/45

Ralph Farmiloe arrived at No 1663 HCU at Rufforth in Yorkshire on 5 December 1944. He has fond memories of the station.

"The accommodation for the trainees was basic but as it was all that we had we had to make the most of it. The billets were situated across the road from the airfield, up a little lane and quite some distance away. The Sergeants Mess was almost the first building that you came across, situated in a field and out of view from the roadside. The living accommodation consisted of Nissen huts, which were a further distance from the Mess, also out of view from the road.

I used to travel to and from the airfield in just about the standard way for all aircrew – on a borrowed pushbike. This was a really useful piece of equipment in those days and I'm sure it saved me from trouble on more than one occasion through being late for duty.

The control tower had a flowerbed at the base of its walls and used to display a huge board, which was visible to the pilots flying in. On it were large numbers, which indicated the runway in use at the time. The most frequently used runway was 24, the SW/NE, which was also the longest of the three runways at Rufforth."

On 4 March 1945 Ralph witnessed the demise of two of the units Halifaxes in a collision. The aircraft were MZ561 and NR278. The incident was caused by the pilot of NR278 taking off on the wrong runway.

"During a night flying exercise a Halifax was coming in to land and as the aircraft touched down, another Halifax came out from one of the other runways and both aircraft collided at the intersection. One of them broke a wing clean off and careered away, eventually coming to a standstill. The other aircraft burst into flames on the runway. Luckily both crews escaped injury, except for one of the pilots who suffered a broken foot."

Ralph recalls that even the daily routine could hold hidden dangers and both air and groundcrews had to be 'on guard' at all times.

"After we had been out on a flight and returned to base, the ground crew and armourers would be waiting at dispersal for us with long trains of bombs trolleys. This was an ominous sight because, should anything go wrong as we swung around on the 'frying pan' there would not be much left of us if the bomb trolleys went up – out of the frying pan and into the fire! It must have been an awful experience for the rear gunner as we swung about on the dispersal, because the pilot would suddenly run up the port outer engine and, at the same time, apply the starboard wheel brake, which in effect got us to turn about 180 degrees.

When the aircraft were parked at dispersal it was common practice to leave the fuel tanks empty, so as not to place undue stress on the wings. When the weather turned foul, as it often did, we then had to anchor the wings down with some large, purpose built concrete blocks, which would fasten to the wings with steel cables. As well as anchoring down the wings, if the weather worsened, the groundcrews had to manhandle the aircraft to face into the wind."

On the night of 3 March 1945 Ralph and his crew were to witness the last serious attempt of the Luftwaffe night fighter force to use intruder aircraft over the British Isles. The horrors of the war and the future possibilities of death on operations were brought starkly home to them.

"We were carrying out a night bombing practice over Spurn Point, off the Humber Estuary, when without warning the range lights went out. The usual chatter over the intercom said that we had scored a direct hit on the chap below who operates the range. This was in fact not so. The 'Ack Ack' from Hull opened up nearby. This caused us to worry and not wishing to be brought down by our own defences, we beat a hasty retreat back to base.

As we were on approach to Rufforth, we could clearly see the exhaust flames from another Halifax going in to land at Marston Moor, which was only a stones throw away from Rufforth. Suddenly the Halifax going in to land burst into flames and crashed onto the airfield. In the glow from the flames, we briefly spotted a German night fighter which had picked up the aircraft coming back into base, followed it until it had become vulnerable on its final approach and shot it down. We cheered when the Halifax crashed - not because we were glad to see one of our own aircraft destroyed, but because we were glad that it was not us who had become the victim of the Luftwaffe."

Just over a week later Ralph and his crew were posted to No 102 Sqn at Pocklington.

Incident Report

No. 23 OTU – PERSHORE – 1941

The following is a report from the Operational Record Book (RAF Form 540) of No 23 OTU based at Pershore. The accident was to Wellington R1662, a Mk Ic, built by Vickers at Chester between August 1940 and May 1941. No 23 OTU was the only unit to use R1662. The pilot, Flt Lt BR Ker, was highly experienced, with over 3,000 hours in his logbook and in addition held a Ground Engineers licence. The report highlights the dangers faced by crews in training, even in a relatively new aircraft.

To: Officer Commanding, Training Wing, No 23 OTU, Pershore.
From: F/Lt BR Ker, RAFO.
Date: 28th June, 1941.
Accident to Wellington R1662.

Sir,

I have the honour to report that the above aircraft has been lost as the result of a forced landing on the 27th June, 1941, near Finningley aerodrome.

As Flight Commander, I arranged four cross country Flights of six hours duration, for which the crews were briefed by me and the flights authorized in the normal way. I took off in R1662 at 10.45, and the flight proceeded without incident until approximately one hour after leaving base, when the aircraft suddenly yawed to port. I was in the amidship position at the time and immediately went forward to the cockpit. I checked the instruments and told the pupil pilot to open up both throttles, and put the airscrews in "Fine". The port engine instrument read as follows: At full throttle in fine pitch --Boost = 4 revs. 2200 Oil temp. 65 9against other 75) Oil, pressure 75 Cylinder head temp. 120 (against other 180). I set up the right hand seat and took over control of the aircraft. The aircraft was now 90 deg off course, and I turned back on the course, and instructed the Wireless Operator to obtain QDM's for Linton. The port engine was now giving no power, but I was maintaining height nicely on one engine at 1,500 feet, but conditions were bumpy and I judged it prudent to instruct the pupil pilot to open the balance cock. The port engine gave a burst of power, and then both engines cut, and as the airspeed was only about 120mph, we lost height rapidly. Finningley aerodrome lay ahead about two miles, but the countryside is dotted with wood and nearly every field had hedgerow trees. I decided to come down at once rather than risk being forced to land in a wood. I instructed the pupil pilot to order the crew to crash positions. There was a small filed ahead, and I judged it possible to fly the aircraft between two of the trees and land in the next field. I dived the aircraft at ground to obtain speed and succeeded in manoeuvring between two trees. Unfortunately, the port wing caught a branch, and the aircraft swung to the left over the North Road, carrying away three telegraph poles. I saw the pupil pilot was alright and he opened the hatch. We fell out as the cockpit was tilted to the right. I saw other members of the crew jump from the astro hatch, and all were uninjured, but the tail gunner was trapped, his right leg being caught. Fire broke out and spread rapidly, and it was impossible to keep the flames away from him. The turret door had evidently been swung outward, but had been turned back in the crash. The fire tender arrived in about twenty minutes, and the flames at the stern of the aircraft were put out. The gunner was still alive, and the MO attended him in the turret, but it was not until a civilian break-down lorry arrived that the turret could be lifted to free his leg. The gunner was admitted to Doncaster Infirmary, but died about midnight.

As I hold Civilian Ground Engineers Licence on Pegasus engines, I am able to give an opinion as to the cause of the engine failure. I consider that the port engine failed because of a broken or punctured petrol pipe on the pressure side. Opening the balance cock (which is normal action to take in the event of engine failure) caused the petrol from the starboard engine to escape through the leak rather than the PRV on the starboard engine which is set at two lbs. Per square inch, thus starving the starboard engine and causing it to fail.

In conclusion, I much regret that I lost one member of the crew and the aircraft, but circumstances were against me, and I am able to report that the other seven members of the crew were uninjured.

I have now completed over 3,000 hours flying, and this is the first major accident in which I have been involved. The aircraft was completely burnt out, and it is unlikely that investigation will reveal the cause.

(signed) BR Ker, RAFO.

PART THREE

BRIEF UNIT HISTORIES

This section of the book deals with selected unit histories. As there were a huge number of training units of all designations a selection of the various types has been selected. Each history is brief with information on locations, equipment and incidents. Some of the histories are short due to the lack of available accurate research material.

The badges of Nos 92 and 93 (OTU) Groups. No 92 Groups role was operational training and No 93 Group was responsible for training of heavy bomber crews.

No.1 Air Armament School

No 1 Air Armament School formed at Eastchurch, Kent in April 1922 and was at Manby in August 1938 equipped with relatively modern Wellingtons and Battles and a mixture of other antiquated types such as the Fury, Wallace, Gauntlet, Hind, Hart and Demon. With the outbreak of war No 1 AAS remained at Manby and provided specialist armament courses for Air Gunners, armourers, armament officers and Bomb Aimers.

Losses were common from the beginning of the war and the Battles suffered several including K7598 which force landed on 10 October 1939 followed three days later by K7593 which crashed on Theddlethorpe ranges on the 13th. Theddlethorpe ranges were administered by Manby and used for course training. Battle K7658 crashed whilst attempting a forced landing at South Cackerington Grange, Lincs on 19 December 1939 and in the new year one of the ancient Wallaces, K3911 crashed at Skidbrook–cum- Saltfleet on 2 January.

By 1942 the unit was now using Hampdens and Blenheims in addition to the Wellingtons. Several other types were also in use, such as the Hudson, Hurricane and Master, albeit in small numbers. Lysanders were operated in the target-towing role. Several Wellingtons, Blenheims and Hampdens were to come to grief whilst operating with No 1 AAS. Another old survivor Gauntlet Mk II K5334 ended its days at Manby when it crashed on 29 November 1940 and Blenheim Mk IV crashed on landing at Manby on 14 July 1941. The

The badge of No 1 Air Armament School.

unit lost Wellington Mk Ia N3008 when it caught fire running up at Manby on 30 May 1942 and in September another, P9235 was lost when it crashed into a hill south east of Louth on the 7th. The Hampdens fared little better, N9070 diving into the sea near Saltfleet on 7 June 1942 and P1161 following it to a watery grave north of Mablethorpe on 16 August.

Caistor was brought into use as a Relief Landing Ground (RLG) in December 1942 mainly due to the very busy circuit at Manby. The size and number of specialist courses increased as the war progressed and the losses continued. The Blenheims had a high loss rate in 1943 and included T1878, T1958, T1985. Blenheim Mk IV V5449 collided with N3613 over Theddlethorpe ranges on 2 May and crashed and V6120 hit trees and crashed at Irby on Humber on 27 December. Just over a week before Z6338 had been abandoned in bad weather west of York. In July 1944 No 1 AAS was renamed the Empire Air Armament School.

Bases

Aug 38 – Jul 44	Manby
Dec 42 – Jul 44	Caistor (RLG)

Aircraft types used	**Examples**
Battle	K7566 N2083 N2086 P2322
Blenheim Mk I	K7086 L1358
Blenheim Mk IV	P6927 R3681 T1802 V5457
Botha Mk I	L6190
Demon Mk I	K5726 K5740 K5741 K8202
Demon (Turret)	K4496 K5900 K5902 K5904
Fury Mk I	K1928
Gauntlet Mk II	K5280 K5329 K5334 K5342
Gladiator	K7933
Hampden	N9080 P1242 X3123 AD853
Hart	K2995
Henley Mk III	L3338
Hereford	N9093 N9096 N9104
Hind	K6653 L7216

Hudson Mk I	P5147
Hudson Mk I TT	T9352
Hurricane Mk I	L1750 P3613 P3679 V7059
Lysander Mk IIIa	W6939
Lysander TT Mk III	T1448 T1768 T1769
Lysander TT Mk IIIa	V9614 V9789 V9808 V9856
Manchester Mk I	L7464
Master Mk I	N7544 N7550 N7637 T8610
Moth	AW162
Moth Minor	X5121
Wallace Mk I	K3675 K3911
Wellington Mk Ia	N2685 N2868 N2874 N2887
Wellington Mk Ic	P9295 R1048 R1254 X9741
Whitley Mk I	K4587
Whitley Mk II	K7221 K7234 K7248 K7254
Whitley Mk III	K9006
Whitley Mk IV	K9038
Whitley Mk V	N1363

No. 1 (Observer) Advanced Flying Unit

No 1 (O) AFU was formed at Wigtown in Kirkcudbrightshire on 1 February 1942 by renaming No 1 AOS. The unit was equipped with Ansons but Bothas replaced these in July 1942. The Botha proved unpopular as it was unreliable and underpowered and the type was replaced once again by the Anson in 1943. Wigtown came under the control of No 29 group and the airfield housed some 2,500 personnel in temporary accommodation. The AFU was also responsible for mountain rescue in the area.

The Ansons of the unit suffered heavy losses due to the mountainous nature of the surrounding terrain. Anson Mk I W2630 flew into a hill at Cairnsmore on 17 April 1942, N4995 flew into Cain Hill near Barn, Ayrshire on 3 February 1943 and AX177 flew into high ground on the Isle of Man whilst in cloud on 13 November 1944

Wigtown photographed in June 1993. This airfield was home to No 1 (O) AFU for almost four years. (Authors collection)

The Irish Sea claimed several victims from the unit, AX143 flew into the sea east of Kirkcudbright in July 1942 and the following month N5082 collided with Lysander T1446 and crashed into the sea of Whithorn on the 3rd. Several other aircraft were ditched and some just went missing such as N5272, W2637 and AX173.

With the end of the war No 1 (O) AFU held a Battle of Britain open day for the local population and ceased flying in mid-October, finally disbanding on 12 November 1945. An example of the unit codes used is Anson Mk I W1770:W-L3.

Bases

1 Feb 42 – 12 Nov 45	Wigtown

Aircraft types used	Examples
Anson Mk I	K6160 K6182 R9645 AX145
Botha Mk I	W5030 W5035 W5157 W5162
Magister Mk I	N3798
Manchester	R5788
Tutor	K4817

No. 1 Air Gunners School

No 1 AGS was formed at Pembrey in West Glamorgan on 15 June 1941 and was equipped with Blenheims. The unit also operated Lysanders for target towing and Martinets for fighter affiliation. One of the unit's first losses was Blenheim Mk IV Z6242 which dived into Carmarthen Bay on 1 August 1941. The early part of 1942 saw several other losses including Lysander TT Mk III P1863 which force landed at Broughton Burrows in Devon on 4 January, Blenheim Mk IV V5891 which was hit by V5965 which overshot on landing at Pembrey a month later. The following month Blenheim Mk IV V5745 flew into the ground at Bryneglin Farm, Carmarthen after catching fire in the air. April saw the loss of another Mk IV when Z6253 force landed at Burry Green on the 15th.

In May 1942 the unit detached 34 Blenheims to Upwood to take part in the 'Thousand Bomber' raid on Cologne but they were not used and returned to Pembrey. By this time the unit was beginning to re-equip with Ansons but the Blenheims soldiered on until at least August 1943. Some of the unit's aircraft were detached to Carew Cheriton between July and October 1942. By the end of 1942 the Blenheims were distinctly war weary and the losses continued. In November 1942 Z6074 had an engine failure and bellylanded on the beach at Kidwelly. The summer months of 1943 were bad with the losses of Z6348 crashing in the circuit at Pembrey on 11 May, V6514, Z6258 and Z6349 all crashed on take off during July and August saw the loss of Z6351 on the 2nd and V6518 which went missing and is presumed to have ditched in Carmarthen Bay on the 13th.

Wellingtons began to replace the Ansons in September 1944 and Spitfires, which were better suited to the fighter affiliation role, supplemented the Martinets. One of these Mk V AR320 was among the last aircraft to be lost by the unit when it crashed on 26 January 1945. During its existence the AGS used number or individual letter codes such as Anson Mk I MG404:3, Spitfire Mk IIa P8035:22, Spitfire LF Mk Vb BM211:7, Martinet MS673:21, Wellington Mk III X3945:W and Wellington Mk X JA346:M. The unit disbanded on 14 June 1945.

Bases

15 Jun 41 – 14 Jun 45	Pembrey
Jul 42 – Oct 42	Carew Cheriton (Detachment)

Aircraft types used	Examples
Anson Mk I	N9601 MG404
Audax	K4859
Blenheim Mk I	K7050 K7125 K7129 L1218
Blenheim Mk IV	N3536 P4833 R3688 T1800
Lysander Mk III	P9112 T1467 T1505 T1634
Lysander TT Mk III	P1683 R9017 R9021 R9110
Lysander TT Mk IIIa	V9809 W6944 W6945
Magister	T9672 T9893
Manchester	L7484
Martinet	MS673
Master Mk II	DL289
Spitfire Mk IIa	P7503 P7521 P7851 P8035
Spitfire Mk Va	W3253 W3608 W3820 W3823
Spitfire Mk Vb	AB812 AD464 AR320
Spitfire LF Mk Vb	BM211
Wellington Mk III	X3875 X3945 X4000
Wellington Mk X	JA346

*The badge of No 1 AGS shows
a dragon for Wales holding
and arrow in its forepaws .*

No. 1 Air Observers School

Pre-war No 1 AOS had been based at North Coates in Lincolnshire equipped with Henley's, Harrows and Westland Wallaces, but on 2 September 1939 the unit moved to Evanton. Shortly afterwards it was renumbered No 8 AOS.

The AOS was reformed at Wigtown in the Scottish borders on 19 August 1941 equipped with Bothas, which arrived in September. The unit also used Ansons, two of which were lost in January 1942. R3409 crashed at Brant Hill, Galloway on the 7th and on the 13th AW850

The badge of No 1 Air Observers School presented to the unit at North Coates in December 1938.

lost its tailplane attempting to recover from a dive and spun into the ground near Wigtown. Due to the airfields susceptibility to flooding it was closed in October 1941 to have runways built and in February 1942 No 1 AOS was redesignated No 1 (O) AFU.

Bases

2 Sep 39 – Sep 39	Evanton
19 Aug 41 – 1 Feb 42	Wigtown

Aircraft types used | **Examples**

Aircraft types used	Examples
Anson Mk I	K8755 N4886 W2629 AX115
Battle Mk I	L5252 P2301
Botha Mk I	
Harrow	
Henley	
Moth	AW147
Wallace	K3569 K3676 K3677

No. 1 Blind/Beam Approach School

No.1 BAS was formed at Watchfield on 28 October 1940 with six Ansons to train pilots in Blind Approach flying techniques. Courses lasted two weeks and included twelve hours flying. The number of trainees steadily increased and on 1 September 1941 the establishment was increased to 12 Ansons. This changed, however, and the first three Oxfords to re-equip the unit arrived on 17 September 1941.

By this time the course had been cut back to twelve days and a new course arrived on the unit every four days. From March 1941 the unit had been training Wireless Mechanics and by September the unit was operating 24 hours a day. The school was renamed No.1 Beam Approach School in October 1941.

Four De Havilland Dominies were added to the strength in February 1942 and by March another flight of Oxfords had been added. More Oxfords arrived in May 1942 and Synthetic Night Flying commenced the same month. Kelmscott came into use as a satellite on 17 October 1942 and by using beam approach equipment at other airfields in the area, the course length was reduced to 1 week. On 7 December 1942 Oxford V4051 dived into the ground at night one mile northwest of Watchfield. V4049 was lost after it was abandoned in bad weather over Otmoor in Oxfordshire on the 6 of January 1943 and V4053 crashed on landing at Kelmscott on 28 May.

In July 1943 Wanborough was being used as a second satellite and training continued at all three airfields. On 22 October 1943 a severe storm damaged a hangar and three of the Oxfords, one of them being lifted ten feet into the air. The BAS continued to train until it was disbanded on 1 January 1947 after training over 8,000 pilots in beam approach techniques.

Bases

28 Oct 40 - 1 Jan 47	Watchfield
17 Oct 42 - 1 Jan 47	Kelmscott (Satellite)
Jul 43 -	Wanborough (Satellite)

Aircraft types used: Anson Mk I / Dominie / Oxford Mk I / Oxford Mk II

No.1 Elementary Flying Training School

No 1 EFTS was formed at the outbreak of WW2 by renaming No 1 Elementary & Reserve Flying Training School (E&RFTS) at Hatfield. The unit was equipped with Tiger Moths. Students at this early stage of their training were inexperienced and prone to accidents. One loss in 1939 was N6620, which was crashed in fog trying to land at Hatfield on 11 December. A very busy circuit exacerbated training at Hatfield and several aircraft crashes occurred here and in the surrounding countryside. October 1940 being a bad month with the loss of N6453 which force landed at Steeple Claydon on the 10th. Two weeks later several aircraft were lost; R4920 hit HT cables at Brickenden Bury on the 22nd followed by N6589 which force landed north west of Redbourn on the 23rd and the next day N9327 hit trees near Welwyn Garden City.

By June 1941 Holywell Hyde had been brought into use as a satellite to ease circuit congestion at Hatfield and the training losses continued. There were at least another five Tiger Moths had crashed by the time the unit moved into Holywell Hyde completely in September 1942. That month also saw the loss of T6821 which hit the ground whilst low flying south west of Aylesbury on the 18th.

In September 1943 the airfield was renamed Panshanger and No 1 EFTS was operating as a grading school. Training continued till the end of the war and some of the final wartime losses were N5444 and N9330 which both crashed on landing at Panshanger on 24 July 1945. The unit continued to train reserve pilots after the war and in May 1947 was renamed No 1 Refresher Flying School.

Bases

Sep 39 – Apr 43	Hatfield
16 Jun 41 – 7 Sep 42	Holywell Hyde (Satellite)
7 Sep 42 – 5 May 47	Holywell Hyde (Panshanger from 13 Sep 43)

Aircraft types used	Example
Tiger Moth	N5470 R4748 T5379 T5414

No.1 Flying Instructors School

No 1 Flying Instructors School was formed from No 2 CFS at Church Lawford in Warwickshire on 19 January 1942. The unit had an establishment of 60 Airspeed Oxfords, 30 Avro Tutors and a single Monospar. Instructors were trained for SFTS, (P) AFU and OTU's.

One month after its formation the unit lost Avro Tutor K4823 when the pilot flew into the ground near Offchurch, Leamington on 19 February. Several other Tutors were lost during the unit's short existence the last being K3461 which undershot landing at Hockley Heath on 11 October 1942. No 1 FIS used two RLG's, Warwick and Hockley Heath, both of which were small grass airfields. The units Oxfords also suffered losses and Oxford Mk II R5956 dived into the ground at Debdale Woods, Warks on 5 June. Oxford Mk II N4768 crashed whilst overshooting at Warwick RLG on 12 July as did R6059 on 4 Aug 1942.

No 1 FIS was absorbed by No 18 (P) AFU which formed on 27 October 1942.

Bases

19 Jan 42 – 27 Oct 42	Church Lawford
Jan 42 – Oct 42	Warwick (RLG)
Aug 42 – Oct 42	Hockley Heath (RLG)

Aircraft types used	Examples
Anson Mk I	R3587
Blenheim Mk V	
Hurricane	
Monospar	
Oxford Mk I	X6789
Oxford Mk II	N4847 N6341 P1860 V3147
Tutor	K3348 K3450 K4823 K6105

No. 1 Glider Training School

No 1 GTS was formed at Thame in Oxfordshire on 4 November 1941 to train army glider pilots. The unit was equipped with Hotspur gliders towed by Hawker Hector biplanes. The hectors were worked hard towing gliders and among those lost were K9765 which crashed on landing at Thame on 26 April 1942 and K9755 which lost a wheel on take off and was written on in the subsequent crash landing at Thame on 29 June 1942.

A RLG at Kingston Bagpuize was brought into use from 9 March 1942 but the unit moved to Croughton (Brackley) between 22 July and 3 August 1942 due to the unsuitability of Thame. Shortly after the move the Hectors were replaced by Miles Masters for towing.

The technical site at Kingston Bagpuize photographed in April 1993. This airfield was used as a RLG by No 1 GTS in 1942. (Authors collection)

The unit disbanded at Croughton on 24 March 1943 and was absorbed into No 20 (P) AFU but was to be reformed, still at Croughton, on 1 November 1944. In August 1945 the unit began to use Gaydon and Master Mk III's were introduced for towing. No 1 GTS ceased flying on 25 May 1946. No 1 GTS used individual letter codes, eg. Hotspur BT990:S.

Bases

4 Nov 41 – 1 Aug 42	Thame
9 Mar 42 – 19 Jul 42	Kingston Bagpuize (RLG)
22 July 1942 – 24 Mar 43	Croughton (Brackley)
1 Nov 44 – 25 May 46	Croughton
Aug 45 – 25 May 46	Gaydon (Satellite)

Aircraft types used	Examples
Audax	
Halifax	
Hector Mk I	K8111 K8122 K8161 K9687
Hind	K5511 K5515
Hotspur	BT990 BV134
Kirby Kite	
Lysander	
Master Mk II	
Master Mk III	
Tiger Moth Mk I	K4254 N9464

No. 1 Lancaster Finishing School

No 1 Lancaster Finishing School was formed at Lindholme in November 1943 to convert crews to the Lancaster after training on Stirlings and Halifaxes at HCU. The unit was made up of the Lancaster Flights from No 1656 HCU at Lindholme, No 1662 HCU at Blyton and No 1667 HCU at Faldingworth. These flights became A, B and C Flights respectively. The unit HQ was based at Lindholme. B Flight moved back to Blyton and C Flight to Faldingworth soon afterwards and this situation was to remain until HQ and A Flight moved to Hemswell in January 1944. No 1 LFS disbanded at Hemswell in November 1944.

The unit used several other airfield in the area for training including Caistor, Riccall, Sturgate and Syerston and its first loss was Lancaster Mk I R5866 which crashed in January 1944. Another Mk I, W4312 was lost in February and just over a month later Mk I, R5851 crashed on overshoot at Syerston. In total the unit lost ten aircraft in crashes, the last being Mk I, R5866 which crashed on 25 September 1944.

No 1 LFS used the codes 3C and CE and examples are Lancaster Mk Is R5500: 3C-K, R5507: 3C-D, R5609: 3C-F, R5631: 3C-H, W4790: 3C-O, W4890: 3C-T,

Bases

23 Nov 43 – Jan 44	Lindholme (A Flt & HQ)
Nov 43 – 44	Blyton (B Flt)
Nov 43 – 44	Faldingworth (C Flt)
Jan 44 – Nov 44	Hemswell (A Flt & HQ)

Aircraft types used	Examples
Lancaster Mk I	L7541 R5549 W4154 ED310 LL748 ME583
Lancaster Mk III	W4990 DV165 ED536 EE133 JB559 LM391

No.1 (Coastal) Operational Training Unit

This OTU was formed by renaming the Coastal Command Group Pool (CCGP) at Silloth on 1 April 1940. The unit was equipped with a selection of coastal aircraft including Hudson, Botha, Beaufort, Anson and Blenheim and later a solitary Halifax. One of the Ansons was kept bombed up at all times as a defensive measure. During May 1942 Hudson's of the OTU were detached to Thornaby. There was another detachment to Thornaby on 25 June 1942 during which twenty-four Hudson's raided coastal targets while the Main Force attacked Bremen in the 'Thousand Bomber' raid on that city. One aircraft from the OTU failed to return.

From April 1940 Hudson's of the unit used Kirkbride as a Relief Landing Ground (RLG) for night flying training. A detachment of Blenheims used Prestwick from 9 August to 1 November 1940 and a Hudson detachment went to Speke during July 1940.

Like all training units No 1 (Coastal) OTU had its fair share of flying accidents. On 26 October 1941 Hudson P5116 overshot on landing at Silloth and crashed. There were several other Hudson

The large airfield at Kirkbride photographed in May 1994. No 1 (Coastal) OTU used this base as a RLG between 1940 and 1943. (Authors collection)

crashes including P5136 which crashed overshooting at Kirkbride on 31 January 1942. T9383 collided on landing with N7307 which had stalled in at Silloth on 24 February 1942. T9374 crashed on take off at Silloth on 9 June 1942 and N7207 flew into the ground whilst making an approach to Silloth on 30 November 1942. P5134 stalled and crashed on approach to Scorton on 9 June 1943.

On 10 March 1943 the unit moved to Thornaby, replacing No 6 OTU, which moved to Silloth. The aircraft of the unit used a letter/number code combination during its existence, eg. Hudson Mk I T9327:A34 and Oxford Mk I V3992:C11. The unit disbanded at Thornaby on 19 October 1943.

Bases

1 Apr 40 - 10 Mar 43	Silloth
1 Apr 40 - 10 Mar 43	Kirkbride (RLG)
Jul 40	Speke (Hudson detachment)
9 Aug 40 - 1 Nov 40	Prestwick (Blenheim detachment)
25 May 42 - 27 May 42	Thornaby (Hudson detachment)
25 Jun 42	Thornaby (Hudson detachment)
10 Mar 43 - 19 Oct 43	Thornaby

Aircraft types used	Examples
Anson Mk I	K6188 K6191 K6203 K6226
Beaufort	
Blenheim Mk I	K7091
Blenheim Mk IV	N3595 N3596 N3597 R3695
Botha	
Halifax Mk II	
Hudson Mk I	N7206 P5134 P5136 T9327
Hudson Mk II	T9369 T9374 T9383 T9384
Hudson Mk IV	AE632
Hudson Mk V	AE646 AE648 AE653 AM520
Oxford Mk I	N4602 N6234 V3992
Oxford Mk II	N4835

No. 1 (Glider) Operational Training Unit

Formed at Kidlington on 1 January 1942, this unit's role was to train glider pilots to operational standard after they left the Glider Training School (GTS). The unit was equipped with Hotspur gliders towed by ancient Hector biplanes and came under the control of No 70 Group. During February 1942 the unit was renamed No 101 (Glider0 OTU.

Bases	
1 Jan 42 - Feb 42	Kidlington

Aircraft types used: Hector / Hotspur

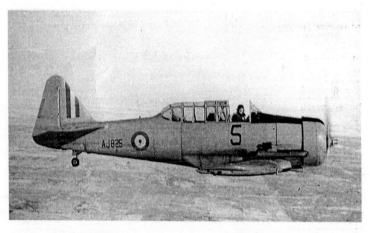

Harvard Mk II AJ825:5. Harvards were operated by many of the SFTS both at home and overseas. (WD Park)

No. 1 Service Flying Training School

No 1 SFTS was formed at Netheravon in August 1936 equipped with a mix of hawker Hinds and Hectors. By 1939 the unit was also using Harvards. The unit's main role was training of pilots for the FAA. Early unit losses included Harvard Mk I N7074, which spun into the ground at Oare Hill, Marlborough on 11 September 1939 and Mk I N7043, which dived into the ground near Netheravon on 13 November. The older types also suffered losses with Audax Mk I K2021 stalling on approach to Netheravon and crashing on 22 February 1940 and on 21 July 1940 a Messerschmitt Bf 110 shot down Hart Trainer K6485 over Old Sarum.

Shrewton was used a Relief Landing Ground from July 1940 and the Harts, Hinds and Audaxes of the unit operated there. One loss at Shrewton was Hind K4561 which crashed attempting a forced landing on 12 October 1941. No 1 SFTS was disbanded in March 1942.

Bases

Aug 36 – Mar 42	Netheravon
Jul 40 – Mar 42	Shrewton (RLG)

Aircraft types used	Examples
Audax Mk I	K2001 K2006 K3059 K3699
Hart	K3852 K3880 K3972
Hart Trainer	K3757 K4761 K4764 K4768
Harvard Mk I	N7011 N7042 N7044 N7045
Hector	
Hind	K5369 K5372 K5374 K5376
Seal	K3485
Tiger Moth Mk I	K4725 K4246 K4247 K4249

No.1 Signals School

No.1 Signals School was formed by renaming No 1 Electrical & Wireless School at Cranwell in September 1940. The unit operated from Cranwell North airfield with a mix of Wallaces, Valentias and Tiger Moths. Several Wallaces were lost during training including Mk II K6037, which flew into HT cables at Kirkstead on 4 September 1940. Three weeks later K6023 was lost in a crash landing at Cranwell and on 4 October K6061 also crashed at Cranwell. No 1 SS role was the training of ground and air wireless operators.

From November 1940 the unit was using Proctors, Whitley's and Dominies. Several Proctors were lost whilst serving with the unit including Mk I P6301 which crashed when the control column came loose on take off from Cranwell on 19 December 1940 and Valentia K3603 hit trees and force landed near Skellingthorpe on 6 April 1941. Proctor Mk III R7530 lost a wing whilst taking avoiding action and crashed at Sudbrooke on 22 October 1941. No 1 SS was renamed No 1 Radio School in January 1943. No 1 SS was allocated the aircraft code numbers 101 – 199.

Bases

Sep 40 – Jan 43	Cranwell North

Aircraft types used	Examples
DH 86b	AX795
Dominie Mk I	R5298 R5930 X7323 X7514
Harvard Mk I	N7100
Proctor Mk I	P6229 P6234 P6235 P6236
Proctor Mk II	Z7198 Z7205 Z7219
Proctor Mk III	R7531 R7532 R7534 Z7216
Valentia	K3603 K8850
Wallace Mk II	K6040 K6078 K6079 K6080
Whitley Mk II	K7219 K7224 K7248 K7256
Whitley Mk III	K9009 K9011

No.1 Torpedo Training Unit

No 1 TTU was formed at Turnberry on 1 January 1943 and was equipped with Beauforts and Hampdens. The role of the unit was training of strike crews for Coastal Command. The Hampden was not well suited to the strike role and several were lost by the unit during training. AN151 hit the water during a practice torpedo attack at night on 12 October 1942 and Sgt G Howell and three crew were killed. On 18 April 1943 AT125 collided with Wellington LB328 north east of Ailsa Craig and Sgt Cordingley and crew were killed. The Wellington landed safely. P1198 flown by Sgt Batchelor crashed into the sea off Lady Isle after a misjudged practice torpedo drop. The crew was picked up unhurt. Three other Hampdens were lost AT117 in May 1943, and X3026 and P5341, both lost in August.

A detachment of the unit moved to Abbotsinch from January to April 1943 due to overcrowding at Turnberry. In September 1943 No 1 TTU absorbed No 2 TTU, which moved from Castle Kennedy but was itself absorbed into No 5 OTU on 25 April 1944.

Beaufighters similar to those seen here were operated by No 1 TTU.
(Authors collection)

No 1 TTU reformed in August 1945 at Turnberry and moved to Tain on 12 November 1945. By this time the unit was using Beaufighters and Wellingtons. The unit's final move was to Thorney Island in November 1946 where it disbanded in October 1947. During its existence the unit used the codes TU and 9K, eg; Beaufort Mk I W6494:TU-Z, Beaufort Mk I N1001:47 and Beaufighter Mk X RD485:9K-K and RD507:9K-K.

Bases

1 Jan 43 – 25 Apr 43	Turnberry
Jan 43 – Apr 43	Abbotsinch (Detachment)
Aug 45 – 12 Nov 45	Turnberry
12 Nov 45 – 13 Nov 46	Tain
13 Nov 46 – Oct 47	Thorney Island

Aircraft types used	**Examples**
Beaufighter Mk VIc	JL636
Beaufighter Mk VI/ITF	JL951
Beaufighter Mk X	RD485
Beaufort Mk I	N1042 W6469 X8936 AW210
Botha	W5104
Hampden Mk I	P1243 X2904 AD793 AT153
Lysander Mk I	R2587
Lysander Mk IIIa	W2587
Moth Minor	X5122
Tiger Moth	N9213
Wellington Mk VIII	LA895
Wellington MK XI	HZ246

No.2 (Coastal) Operational Training Unit

No 2 (Coastal) OTU was formed at Catfoss on 1 October 1940 with an establishment of twelve Blenheims and five Ansons. Later equipment included Beauforts and Beaufighters. From December 1942 till February 1943 the unit used Lissett, a few miles to the north, as a RLG. The unit was responsible for the training of Coastal Command Beaufighter crews. Losses on this unit were quite high, especially on the Beaufighter, which was a difficult aircraft, even for experienced pilots. Anson Mk I N4893 was lost in a forced landing near Rotherham on 22 December 1940. Blenheim Mk IV N3595 crashed near Bridlington on 21 June 1941. T3231, a Beaufighter Mk Ic was lost when it spun in on approach to Catfoss on 7 March 1942. |Beaufighter Mk If R2198 flew into high ground near Broughton, Yorkshire on 28 April 1943. Beaufighter Mk VIf X8060 lost power and hit some trees near Kilham in Yorkshire on 5 February 1943 and Beaufighter Mk VI T5102 flew into the ground near Filey on 18 March 1943.

Aircraft of No 2 OTU carried single letter codes initially, eg. Beaufighter Mk Ic T3333:Z. later the unit used a letter/number combination, eg. Beaufort Mk I JM575:3-Z. No 2 (Coastal) OTU disbanded on 15 February 1944.

Bases

1 Oct 40 - 15 Feb 44	Catfoss
Dec 42 - 5 Feb 43	Lissett (RLG)

Aircraft types used	Examples
Anson Mk I	N4890 N4911 N5367 N5369
Beaufighter Mk Ic	T3231 T3241 T3244 T3245
Beaufighter Mk If	R2152 R2153 R2198 R2199
Beaufighter Mk VI	T5102 T5105 T5109 T5130
Beaufighter Mk VIf	X7938 X8060 X8064
Beaufort Mk I	N1042 W6469 W6498 W6500
Blenheim Mk IV	N3595 N3596 N3599 N3602
Blenheim Mk V	AZ861 AZ869 AZ870 AZ945

No.2 Tactical Exercise Unit

On 17 October 1943 No 58 OTU was renamed No 2 TEU. The unit operated a mix of Hurricanes, Spitfires and Masters and was controlled by No 2 Combat Training Wing. The unit operated from Grangemouth near Edinburgh with a satellite at Balado Bridge in Fife. No 2 TEU's role was to give pilots being held in reserve realistic air combat training and there were several losses during its short existence. Master Mk III W8845 was flown into a hill at Dunnygask in bad weather on the last day of 1943 and exactly a month later another Mk II W8702 crashed at Balado Bridge after an engine failure.

During 1944 a detachment of the unit was sent to Hutton Cranswick in Yorkshire for a period. Spitfire Mk IIa P7427 was lost when the pilot lost control and abandoned the aircraft south of Dunfermline on 17 February 1944 and a pair of Hurricane Mk Is were lost, AF970 flew into a hill in cloud near Castle Carroch, Cumberland on 20 March 1944 and W9180 crashed attempting a forced landing north west of Thornhill in Stirlingshire on 17 May 1944. No 2 TEU is known to have used the codes PQ and XB on its Spitfires and the unit was disbanded on 25 June 1944.

Bases

17 Oct 43 – 25 Jun 44	Grangemouth
17 Oct 43 – 25 Jun 44	Balado Bridge (Satellite)
44 – 44	Hutton Cranswick (Detachment)

Aircraft types used	Examples
Hurricane Mk I	N2616 P2987 T9519 AG101
Hurricane Mk X	P5196
Martinet	
Master Mk I	T8330
Master Mk III	W8702 W8845
Spitfire Mk I	P9371 P9501
Spitfire Mk IIa	P7908 P8075 P8235 P8650
Spitfire Mk Va	R6960
Spitfire Mk Vb	W3835 AB241 AR504 AR552

No.3 Bombing & Gunnery School

This was a fairly short-lived unit formed by renaming No 3 AOS at Aldergrove on 1 November 1939. The unit trained observers, air gunners and was also tasked with training Fleet Air Arm personnel. To carry out its role it was equipped with a mix of obsolescent pre-war types including Gauntlets, Demons, Heyford's and a few naval types such as the Swordfish and Shark. The unit also operated Westland Wallaces, one of which, K3672, crashed near Langford Lodge on 4 March 1940. Four months later on 11 July 1940 the unit was disbanded.

Bases

1 Nov 39 – 11 Jul 40	Aldergrove

Aircraft types used	Examples
Battle Mk I	K7646 N2225 N2226 N2228
Botha	L6288
Demon	K8196
Gauntlet Mk II	K5279 K5280 K5282 K5283
Gladiator	N5592
Henley Mk III	L3308
Heyford Mk III	K6857
Shark	
Swordfish	
Wallace Mk I	K5074 K5076 K8696 K8699
Wallace Mk II	K6083

No.3 Lancaster Finishing School

No 3 LFS was formed at Feltwell on 19 December 1943 to train No 3 Group Lancaster crews. The unit was equipped with a mix of Lancaster Mk Is and Mk IIIs. On 17 June 1944 the unit lost two Lancaster's when W4581 and ED376 collided and crashed. W4851 came down near Lakenheath and ED376 crashed near Southery in Norfolk.

In August 1944 the one Flight of the unit used Woolfox Lodge for training and on the 13th Lancaster Mk I W4271 crashed on landing at Swannington. Another collision occurred at the end of the year when R5674 and R5846 collided over Northwold, Norfolk on 18 December. During the January 1945 'A' Flt used Newmarket as a satellite. The unit's final loss was on 29 January 1945 when ND598 crashed near Barnham, Suffolk. Two days later the unit disbanded.

No 3 LFS used the code A5 on its Lancaster's, eg. L7532: A5-P, L7544: A5-T2, L7566: A5-Z, R5542: A5-M, R5631: A5-T, R5690: A5-S, R5756: A5-L, R5846: A5-K, R5906: A5-J, W4248: A5-I, W4249: A5-N, W4851: A5-R2, W4885: A5-L, ED425: A5-U, ED437: A5-Q, JB281: A5-O, JB319: A5-I and ND623: A5-F.

Bases

19 Dec 43 – 31 Jan 45	Feltwell
Aug 44 – 28 Aug 44	Woolfox Lodge (Satellite)
1945	Newmarket (Satellite)

Aircraft types used	Examples
Lancaster Mk I	L7532 R5514 ED376 HK541
Lancaster Mk III	ED437 JB319 LM348 ND747

No. 3 (Observer) Advanced Flying Unit

This unit was formed by renaming No 3 AOS at Halfpenny Green on 11 April 1942. The unit was equipped with Oxfords and Ansons. Course lasted four weeks and covered acclimatisation and familiarisation for graduates from the overseas training schools not used to the conditions of flying in European weather.

A record number of hours, 3,917, was flown by this unit in June 1943. Many aircraft wee lost from this unit both a Halfpenny Green and in the surrounding hills. Anson Mk I AX408 crashed in a forced landing on Malltraeth Sands on Anglesey in August 1942. N9917 crashed off Gt Ormes Head in December. 1943 saw the loss of N5382 which ditched in the Irish Sea, N5379 which crashed into high ground near Kidderminster and R3381 which overshot on landing a Halfpenny Green, all in March. Other losses included N9855, K8731, and N4925, which collided with EG185 and N5327 all in 1943. N9738, R3381, AX538 which collided with MH109 and AX562 all in 1944. 1945 saw the loss of N9618, which was hit while parked by N5293. N5064 was also lost when it crashed into Craigoul Hill, Forfar on 23 June 1945. Five of the units Ansons were damaged on 13 December 1944 when an Oxford crashed into them. Training continued until the unit was disbanded on 11 December 1945. The AFU used 'Q' as one of its codes as on Anson Mk I EF927:Q-4

Bases

11 Apr 42 - 11 Dec 45	Halfpenny Green

Aircraft types used	Examples
Anson Mk I	K8731 N9973 R3328 AW781
Dominie	X7392 X7404
Oxford Mk II	W6630 NM482
Tiger Moth	DE254
Tutor	K6096

No. 3 Air Gunners School

No 3 AGS formed at Barrow (Walney Island) on 17 October 1941 but quickly moved to Castle Kennedy on 27 October. The unit was initially equipped with Lysanders but the airfield was closed in December 1941 to have runways laid. The AGS reformed at Castle Kennedy on 20 April 1942 and remained there until it moved to Mona on Anglesey on 19 December 1942. Several aircraft were lost whilst at Castle Kennedy. Battle P6644 collided with Botha L6173 on approach on the 28 August 1942. In October Botha W5021 force landed at Sandhead and in November Battle P6632 force landed in Colts Loch at Castle Kennedy. After the move to Mona Botha W5029 crashed on landing on 15 February and two weeks later Botha W5024 also crashed at Mona.

The badge of No 3 AGS. The castle refers to the unit being based at Castle Kennedy in 1941/42.

By this time the unit was flying Blackburn Botha's which were in turn replaced by Ansons before the unit moved back to Castle Kennedy in November 1943. The unit also flew some Miles Martinet target tugs and had a mixed bag of other types for training and ground instruction.

The courses at Castle Kennedy consisted of about 90 pupils flying about 16 hours each interspersed with ground training over a seven-week period. Luce Bay was used as an air to air firing range. Training continued until 21 June 1945 when 3 AGS disbanded. The unit used a letter/number code combination as on Anson Mk I LT304:3 and LT362:T-13, Tutor K3387:M-7 and Wellington Mk X LP929:X.

Bases

17 Oct 41 - 27 Oct 41	Barrow
27 Oct 41 - Dec 41	Castle Kennedy
20 Apr 42 - 19 Dec 42	Castle Kennedy
19 Dec 42 - Nov 43	Mona
Nov 43 - 21 Jun 45	Castle Kennedy

Aircraft types used	Examples
Anson Mk I	N5103 N5115 LT304 LT362
Anson Mk XIII	MG415
Battle	K7565 P6617 P6618 P6619
Battle Trainer	R7361 R7362 R7364 R7366
Botha	L6173 W5020 W5021 W5022
Defiant Mk I	N1552 N1742
Lysander TT Mk III	T1425 T1641
Manchester	R5829
Martinet	HN976
Moth	X5127
Queen Martinet	HN909
Tutor	K3387
Wellington Mk III	X3373 X3399 X3866 X3875
Wellington Mk X	LP929

T2 hangars at Castle Kennedy in 1986. This airfield was the base for No 3 AGS in 1941, 1942 and 1943 to 1945. (Authors collection)

No.3 (Coastal) Operational Training Unit

Formed at Chivenor on 27 November 1940, No 3 (Coastal) OTU was equipped with Ansons, Blenheims and Beauforts to train coastal crews. The unit remained at Chivenor for only six months, disbanding on 20 July 1941. During its stay the unit lost Beaufort Mk I N1113 when it crashed on landing on 19 June 1941 and Blenheim Mk IV N3562 the previous month when it crashed on Saunton Sands.

The OTU reformed at Cranwell on 6 August 1941 with Whitley's. Ansons were also operated and in May 1943 these were joined by Wellingtons. Training included cross-country and oversea flights of long duration and several aircraft were lost on these flights including Wellington Mk Ic R1278 which crashed on landing at Skellingthorpe on 29 September 1941, Whitley Mk VII Z6960 which ditched in the sea 12 miles north east of Spurn Head on 18 June 1942 and Wellington Mk VIII Z8708 which also ditched in the North Sea on 20 December 1942. While at Cranwell the unit also operated some Martinets for target towing duties.

In June 1943 the unit moved to Haverfordwest in Dyfed continuing its general reconnaissance training. The Ansons were moved to a satellite at Templeton and were operated by 'O' Flight until being phased out at the end of 1943. More Wellingtons eventually replaced the Whitley's but the unit disbanded on 4 January 1944. This unit used the codes KG, eg. Whitley Mk V T4177:KG-M and letter/number combinations as on Beaufort X8932:L2.

Bases

27 Nov 40 - 20 Jul 41	Chivenor
6 Aug 41 - 23 Jun 43	Cranwell
23 Jun 43 - 4 Jan 44	Haverfordwest
Jun 43 - 4 Jan 44	Templeton (Satellite)

Aircraft types used	Examples
Anson Mk I	K6226 K6231 K6282 N9606
Beaufort Mk I	N1009 N1043 N1044 N1114

Blenheim Mk I	K7087
Blenheim Mk IV	N3562 N6205 R3745 R3760
Martinet	
Wellington Mk Ia	N2871
Wellington Mk Ic	N2737 R1276 R1277 R1526
Wellington Mk III	X3278 X3636 X3881 X3986
Wellington Mk VIII	Z8708
Whitley Mk V	N1392 N1505 P4971 P5049
Whitley Mk VII	Z6960 Z6962 Z9121 Z9122

The remains of the technical site and hangar bases at Wig Bay photographed in May 1994. (Authors collection)

No.4 (Coastal) Operational Training Unit

No 4 (Coastal) OTU was formed from the Flying Boat Training Squadron (FBTS) on 16 March 1941 at Wig Bay (Stranraer) with a mixed bunch of Singapore's, Lerwicks, Londons, Stranraers and Catalans. While at Wig Bay Stranraer K7298 crashed on landing on 12 June 1941.

In June 1941 the unit moved to Invergordon (later renamed Alness) but a detachment returned to Wig Bay from 11 March to 10 November 1942 to concentrate on the initial training of flying boat crews. One of the aircraft of this detachment was lost when Catalina Mk II AM269 crashed on take off on 15 August 1942.

By the time it arrived at Invergordon/Alness the unit was also flying Sunderlands and was training about ten crew per month. This figure increased to about twenty crews per month by mid-1942. The older types were all withdrawn by the autumn of 1942 but some of them did not survive that long. Stranraer K7298 crashed on landing on 12 June 1941. London Mk II K5913 caught fire after a heavy landing off Cromarty on 12 September 1941 and two Stranraers, K7300 and K7302 sank in a gale on October 20 1941.

Sunderland serviceability was poor in 1942 but by 1943 the situation was much improved and in October 1944 the unit was involved in 'Operation Uplift' in which nine Sunderlands ferried personnel to and from Iceland. The Sunderlands and Catalans were not immune from accidents and the unit lost Catalina Mk I Z2145 when it sank after a heavy landing on 16 May 1943. Sunderland Mk III W4027, Mk II T9083 and Mk I N6138 were all lost in flying accidents.

Whilst at Alness the unit operated a target towing flight at Evanton with Oxfords and Martinets. The TT Flt moved to Tain on 12 December 1944. The OTU moved to Pembroke Dock on 15 August 1946 and again to Calshot in 1947 where it was renamed No 235 OCU in July 1947.

Aircraft of the unit used the code QZ and TA. Later the unit used a two letter combination and duplicated letters, eg. Stranraer K7300:TA-Y, London Mk II L7043:TA-K, Lerwick Mk I L7256:TA-V, Catalina Mk I AH568:TA-H, Sunderland Mk I P9606:TA-E, Sunderland

Mk III W3980:TA-S and Sunderland Mk V RN302:TA-H, Sunderland DD838:AB, Sunderland T9049:A, Sunderland W6009:DD.

Bases

16 Mar 41 - Jun 41	Wig Bay (Stranraer)
Jun 41 - 15 Aug 46	Alness (Invergordon)
11 Mar 42 - 10 Nov 42	Wig Bay (Detachment)
Jun 41 - 12 Dec 44	Evanton (TT Flt)
12 Dec 44 - Aug 46	Tain (TT Flt)
15 Aug 46 - 47	Pembroke Dock
47 - Jul 47	Calshot

Aircraft types used	Examples
Catalina Mk I	W8406 W8408 W8410 Z2143
Catalina Mk II	AM264 AM266 AM268 AM269
Lerwick Mk I	L7526
London Mk I/Mk II	K5257 K5259 K5261 K5910
Martinet	
Oxford	T1041
Singapore Mk III	K4578 K8565 K8567
Stranraer	K7295 K7298 K7300 K7302
Sunderland Mk I	N6138 N9024 N9044 N9045
Sunderland Mk II	T9083 T9088 T9115 W3980
Sunderland Mk III	W4027 W4028 W4031 W4033
Sunderland Mk V	RN302

No.4 (Night Fighter) Operational Training Unit

This OTU was formed at Church Fenton on 16 December 1940 to train night fighter crews destined for Blenheims and Beaufighters. The unit's initial equipment was Blenheims, Defiants, Havoc's, Masters and Oxfords. It was redesignated No 54 OTU on 21 December 1940

Bases

16 Dec 40 - 21 Dec 40	Church Fenton

Aircraft types used: Blenheim / Defiant / Havoc / Master / Oxford

The aircraft dispersals at Wig Bay photographed in May 1994. No 4 (Coastal) OTU used Wig Bay for one of its detachments in 1942. (Authors collection)

No.5 (Fighter) Operational Training Unit

No 5 OTU was formed from No 12 Group Pool at Aston Down on 15 March 1940. It was equipped with Blenheims, Spitfires, Hurricanes, Battles, Masters and Defiants. Spitfire Mk I R6640 caught fire and crashed at Kemble on 1 July 1940 and a Spitfire of the unit shot down a Ju 88 on 25 July 1940. Hurricane Mk I N2606 stalled and spun into the ground at South Cerney on 26 August 1940. The unit only had a short existence being renamed No 55 OTU on 1 November 1940.

Bases

15 Mar 40 - 1 Nov 40	Aston Down

Aircraft types used	Examples
Battle Mk I	V1202
Blenheim	
Defiant Mk I	N1577 N1580
Hurricane Mk I	N2428 N2438 N2522 N2548
Hurricane Mk X	P5187
Master Mk I	N7479 N7687 N7780 N7781
Spitfire Mk I	N3054 N3106 N3281 P9361

No.6 (Coastal) Operational Training Unit

No 6 (Coastal) OTU was formed at Thornaby from No 2 School of Army Co-operation on 19 July 1941. It's main equipment being Hudson's of various marks. Crews were trained in bombing and navigation and a satellite airfield at West Hartlepool was used for circuit training. During the night of 25/26 June 1942 twelve crews from the unit took part in the 'Thousand Bomber' raid against Bremen. All twelve returned safely, one making a wheels up landing. Other crashes occurred and some crews were not so lucky. Hudson Mk II T9368 overshot on landing at Thornaby and the undercarriage collapsed on 28 January 1942. Hudson Mk III T9395 crashed on take off on 13 March and Hudson Mk I N7206 hit low wires whilst low flying at Gainsford in County Durham on 1 May 1942.

During March 1943 the unit moved to Silloth replacing No 1 (Coastal) OTU which in turn moved to Thornaby. By this time the unit was also using Wellingtons and Ansons. No 1429 (Czech) Operational Training Flight was absorbed into the OTU in March 1943 but the Flight was disbanded in August 1943.

The Wellingtons used Longtown as a satellite airfield from October 1943 to January 1944 and a detachment was sent to Ballykelly in Northern Ireland during the summer of 1944 for anti-submarine patrol work. Whilst at Silloth Wellington Mk III X3986 was lost when it ditched in the sea off Silloth on 20 August 1943.

July 1945 saw a move to Kinloss. The unit was now mainly equipped with Mosquitoes and Beaufighters. Two weeks after arriving the unit was redesignated No 236 OCU. The unit used a letter/number code combination.

Bases

19 Jul 41 - 10 Mar 43	Thornaby
Jul 41 - Mar 43	West Hartlepool (Satellite)
10 Mar 43 - 18 Jul 45	Silloth
20 Oct 43 - 5 Jan 44	Longtown (Satellite)
44 - 44	Ballykelly (Detachment)
18 Jul 45 – 31 Jul 45	Kinloss

Aircraft types used	Examples
Anson Mk I	K8723 N4834 N4890 N5314
Beaufighter Mk X	RD709
Hudson Mk I	N7206 N7215 N7225 N7228
Hudson Mk II	T9368 T9372 T9376 T9378
Hudson Mk III	T9395 T9403 T9404 T9406
Hudson Mk IV	AE627 AE634 AE636
Hudson Mk V	AM523 AM532 AM574 AM619
Mosquito Mk VI	RF908
Warwick	HG115
Wellington Mk Ic	R1000 R1403 R1412 R1771
Wellington Mk III	X3881 X3986 Z8707
Wellington Mk VIII	W5661 W5671 W5676

The derelict control tower at Limavady. This was home to No 7 (Coastal) OTU from 1942 to 1944. (BD Davies)

No.6 (Fighter) Operational Training Unit

Formed on 9 March 1940 from No 11 Group Fighter Pilot Pool this unit was based at Sutton Bridge in Lincolnshire. It was equipped with Hurricanes, Gladiators, Harvards, Masters and Mentors. Hurricane Mk I N2357 was lost when it spun in on approach to Sutton Bridge on 27 September. Shortly afterwards in November 1940 the unit was renamed No 56 OTU.

Bases

9 Mar 40 - Nov 40	Sutton Bridge

Aircraft types used	Examples
Gladiator Mk I	K8015 K8020 K8027 K8052
Harvard Mk I	N7175 N7176 N7177 N7178
Hurricane Mk I	N2329 N2338 N2341 N2343
Master Mk I	N7493 N7720 N7778 N7803
Mentor	

Hurricane Mk II KZ777:A-14 of a Middle East OTU. Hurricanes were used by a large number of fighter OTU's, AFU's and BDT Flights throughout the war. (WD Park)

No.7 (Pilot) Advanced Flying Unit

No 7 (P) AFU was formed at Peterborough on 1 June 1942 and was equipped initially with Miles Masters and a few Ansons. Sibson was used as a satellite from June 1942 and two flights of the unit, operating Oxfords, were permanently based there with a third being formed in 1943.

Due to overcrowding at Peterborough and Sibson, Kings Cliffe was brought into use as a RLG during June and July 1943. 1943 was a very busy year for the unit and its losses were high. Peterborough lost Master Mk I N7434 when its canopy blew off on take off on 26 July and T8659 crashed after the pilot lost control and abandoned the aircraft on 19 August. Sibson lost several aircraft including Master Mk I T8633 which crashed on approach to Sibson on 13 May followed by Master Mk II W9062 which crashed on landing on 28 June.

In March 1944 the unit received some Hurricanes and operated them from Peterborough. On 21 April 1944 the unit lost a Master Mk II when it was shot down by a night fighter near Peterborough. The unit ceased to use Sibson from August 1944 and Sutton Bridge was brought into use for the units Oxfords in June 1944. Shortly afterwards on the 19th August Master Mk II W9061 was hit whilst parked by Oxford RG643 at Peterborough. The AFU continued to operate from Peterborough and Sutton Bridge until 21 December 1944 when it was renamed No 7 SFTS. The unit used numbers codes, eg. Master T8454:61 and DL122:50.

Bases

1 Jun 42 – 21 Dec 44	Peterborough
1 Jun 42 – 8 Aug 44	Sibson (Satellite)
25 Jun 43 – Jul 43	Kings Cliffe (RLG)
21 Jun 44 – 21 Dec 44	Sutton Bridge (Satellite)
Aircraft types used	**Examples**
Anson Mk I	K6260 R3587
Hurricane Mk I	N2620 P2919 T9534 V6957
Hurricane Mk IIa	Z2695
Master Mk I	N7434 N7444 T8280 T8282

Master Mk II	W9030 W9063 AZ106 AZ323
Oxford Mk I	N6294 T1017 X6866 AT651
Oxford Mk II	V3529
Prefect	K5065

Master Mk Is were used by many OTU's and SFTS.
(WD Park)

No.7 (Coastal) Operational Training Unit

This unit formed at Limavady on 1 April 1942 for General reconnaissance and ASV training. It was equipped with Wellingtons and Ansons and the training included bombing and navigation. Mullaghmore was used as a satellite from December 1942. During its stay at Limavady the unit lost Wellington Mk Ic R1021 when the pilot lost his way and crashed near Cork, Eire on 26 September 1942. This was one of several aircraft lost by this unit. In January 1944 the unit moved to Haverfordwest and remained there for another five months before being redesignated No 4 Refresher Flying Unit. This unit used number codes.

Bases

1 Apr 42 - 4 Jan 44	Limavady
29 Dec 42 - 4 Jan 44	Mullaghmore (Satellite)
4 Jan 44 - 16 May 44	Haverfordwest

Aircraft types used	**Examples**
Anson Mk I	N4587 N4953 N5000 N5001
Wellington Mk Ia	N3009 P9233
Wellington Mk Ic	N2750 R1000 R1021 R1277
Wellington Mk III	X3278 X3636

No. 7 (Fighter) Operational Training Unit

This OTU was based at Hawarden from June 1940 and was formed to train fighter pilots for No 10 Group. It was equipped with Spitfires, Hurricanes and Masters. The Hurricanes were soon replaced by more Spitfires, which the unit then standardised on. Battles were also operated as target tugs.

Three of the units Spitfires were kept at armed readiness and one of these shot down a Heinkel He 111 on 14 August 1940. The unit also managed to shoot down a Junkers Ju 88 and a Dornier Do 215 on 7 and 18 September respectively.

For identification aircraft of the unit had coloured spinners in the Flight colours, 'A' Flt were red, 'B' Flt yellow, 'C' Flt blue and the Masters had black. No 7 OTU was renamed No 57 OTU on 28 December 1940.

Bases

15 Jun 40 – 28 Dec 40	Hawarden

Aircraft types used

Aircraft types used	Examples
Battle Trainer	R7372 R7373 R7374 R7375
Hurricane Mk I	N2338 N2467 N2478 N2606
Master Mk I	N7830 N7831 N7832 N7833
Spitfire Mk I	K9790 K9800 K9801 K9821

No.8 (Coastal) Operational Training Unit

This OTU was formed at Fraserburgh on 18 May 1942 to train photo-recce crews. It was formed from the Advanced Training Flight of No 1 PRU and the PR Conversion Flight of No 3 School of General Reconnaissance. The unit was initially equipped with Spitfires, Masters and Mosquitoes. Losses whilst based at Fraserburgh included Master Mk III W8786 which hit the ground whilst low flying near Peterhead on 29 July 1942, Spitfire PR Mk VI P9310 which went missing on a training flight on 1 October 1942 and Spitfire Mk I R6886 which caught fire in the air and was abandoned by the pilot over Newton Moor, Inverness on 5 November 1942. Due to lack of space at Fraserburgh the unit moved to Dyce in March 1943.

During its stay at Dyce the unit was reorganised into two flights, one using the Spitfires and Masters, the other the Mosquitoes and Ansons. Losses through 1943 and 1944 were continuous and included Master Mk I T8691 which hit a haystack low flying near Ellon on 21 March 1943, Spitfire PR Mk V R7198 flew into a mountain on the Isle of Skye on 19 June 1943, Spitfire Mk Va force landed near Fraserburgh on Boxing day 1943. One of the units Mosquitoes was lost when Mk I W4061 crashed on take off on 22 February 1944 and Mk IV W4066 was lost in a crash after an engine fire near Coningsby on 6 November 1944.

The unit moved to Haverfordwest on 12 January 1945 and shortly afterwards 'A' Flt was detached to the satellite at Templeton. Brawdy came into use as a second satellite on 27 February 1945 but the unit did not remain in Wales for long, moving to Mount Farm in June 1945. Another move followed in July 1946, this time to Chalgrove. By this time the unit was mainly equipped with Spitfire PR Mk XIs and Mosquito PR Mk 34s. The unit left Chalgrove in October 1946. Initially the unit used number codes, eg. Mosquito DK319:86. Later letters were used and the unit was allocated the letter BE and LP.

Bases

18 May 42 – 9 Mar 43	Fraserburgh
9 Mar 43 – 12 Jan 45	Dyce

12 Jan 45 – 21 Jun 45	Haverfordwest
Jan 45 – 27 Feb 45	Templeton (Satellite)
27 Feb 45 – 21 Jun 45	Brawdy (Satellite)
21 Jun 45 – 4 Jul 46	Mount Farm
4 Jul 45 - Oct 46	Chalgrove

Aircraft types used	Examples
Anson Mk I	N5146 N5340
Beaufighter Mk IIf	R2384
Maryland Mk I	AR740
Master Mk II	W9058 W9086 AZ548
Master Mk III	W8956 W8786 W8844 W8930
Mosquito Mk I	W4051 W4059 W4061
Mosquito Mk IV	W4066
Mosquito PR Mk 34	
Spitfire Mk I	K9906 N3162 R6886 R6986
Spitfire Mk IIa	P8086
Spitfire PR Mk III	X4383
Spitfire PR Mk IV	N3113 R6900 R7030 R7031
Spitfire PR Mk V	N3270 R7168 X4333 X4487
Spitfire Mk Va	N3059 P7324 P8236 W3412
Spitfire Mk Vc	AB169
Spitfire PR Mk VI	P9310 P9385 R6902 R6905
Spitfire PR Mk VII	P9518 R6910 R7059 R7131

A Master Mk II coded CX of an unidentified unit. Master Mk IIs were operated by several OTU's and AFU's. (WD Park)

No.9 (Coastal) Operational Training Unit

Formed at Aldergrove on 7 June 1942, No 9 OTU trained long-range fighter crews. The unit was equipped with Beaufighters and Beauforts. Training continued after a move to Crosby on Eden on 9 September 1942. The unit comprised a Beaufighter Conversion Squadron, a Beaufort Conversion Squadron, an Air Firing Squadron and an Instrument & Night Flying Squadron. Unusually, the unit's aircraft carried Greek code letters in 1944. Prior to this the unit used number/letter codes, eg. Beaufighter EL357:4-L.

Another aircraft type used was the Oxford operated by 'O' Flt. Longtown was used as a satellite between September 1942 and October 1943 and again from January to August 1944. Losses from the unit included Beaufighter Mk Ic T3292 which dived into the ground on overshoot at Crosby on 15 May 1943, Beaufighter Mk VIf which hit some HT cable after losing power and force landed at Harby Brow, Cumberland on 11 July 1943, Beaufort Mk I N1161 crashed on landing at Longtown on 30 July 1943 and Beaufighter Mk VI T5013 crashed into the sea off Silloth Pier on 13 April 1944.

Bases

7 Jun 42 – 9 Sep 42	Aldergrove
9 Sep 42 – 11 Aug 44	Crosby on Eden
Nov 42	Thornaby (Detachment)
Sep 42 – Oct 43	Longtown (Satellite)
Jan 44 – 11 Aug 44	Longtown (Satellite)

Aircraft types used	**Examples**
Beaufighter Mk Ic	T3234 T3292 T3321 T3329
Beaufighter Mk VI	T5103 T5104 T5108 T5130
Beaufighter Mk VIf	X8036 X8062 X8072 X8084
Beaufort Mk I	N1014 N1038 N1096 N1161
Oxford	R6347 V3505 W6548 W6618

No.10 (Bomber) Operational Training Unit

No 10 OTU formed at Abingdon from No 97 and No 166 Sqns on 2 April 1940. 'A' Flt was equipped with Whitley's and 'B' Flt with Whitley's and Ansons. By July 1940 the unit had expanded and was organised into 'A', 'C' and 'D' Flts with Whitley's and 'B' Flt with Ansons. 'C' Flt began to use Stanton Harcourt in September 1940 but was disbanded in February 1941 its place being taken by 'A' Flt. Mount Farm was also used as a satellite from July 1941 to February 1942. Target towing Lysanders were introduced in August 1941 and replaced by Martinets in April 1943.

In April 1942 a Whitley detachment was formed at St Eval in Cornwall and remained there carrying out operational sorties until July 1943. During this time the detachment sank one U-boat and damaged three others. Losses were high with thirty-three aircraft failing to return from these sorties. The main body of the OTU also flew operationally from time to time on leaflet raids, bombing sorties and took part in the 'Thousand Bomber' raids on Cologne, Essen and Bremen.

By February 1943 the unit was flying Whitley Mk Vs and Mk VIIs, Ansons and Lysanders. It also had a single Defiant. During 1943 the unit was reorganised with 'A' and 'B' Flts at Stanton Harcourt and 'C', 'D' and 'G' Flts at Abingdon. In March 1944 the whole unit moved into Stanton Harcourt while runways were laid at Abingdon, returning to Abingdon in November 1944.

In June 1944 Hurricanes replaced the Martinets and in July Wellington Mk Xs began to replace the Whitley's. By March 1945 the unit also had some Masters and continued to operate until 10 September 1946 when it was disbanded. The unit reformed as a Mosquito OTU and continued post war.

Losses from the unit included Whitley Mk III K8597 which crashed at Northcote near Stratford on Avon on 8 April 1940. Whitley Mk III K8981 which crash landed at Stanton Harcourt on 5 November 1941 and Whitley Mk V N1316 which caught fire on the ground at Abingdon on 3 July 1942. Anson Mk I N5004 force landed at Pitstone, Bucks on 18 November 1942 and Whitley Mk V Z6464 collided with a Liberator on take off from St Eval causing the depth charges to explode on 12 January 1943. Whitley Mk V Z6753 was damaged by a Junkers Ju 88 and crashed in bad weather at Cleave on 22 January 1943.

Codes used by the unit included JL for aircraft of the St Eval detachment, eg. Whitley BD282:JL-L. Aircraft based at Stanton Harcourt used RK, eg. Whitley Mk V T4175:RK-H, Wellington Mk X NC601:RK-L. UY was also used on Whitley's, Wellingtons, Lysanders, Ansons, Masters, Martinets and Spitfires, eg. Whitley Mk V LA817:UY-S, Lysander Mk II P9088:UY-V, Master Mk II EM270:UY, Martinet Mk I JN283:UY-X, Anson Mk I AX297:UY-J, Spitfire Mk IX TB344:UY-U, Wellington Mk X LP348:UY-R. No 10 OTU also used ZG, eg. Whitley Mk IV K9013:ZG-X, Whitley Mk V T4131:ZG-K and Wellington Mk X LN451:ZG-A. The unit was also allocated EL and JY but no use is known.

Bases

2 Sep 40 –20 Mar 44	Abingdon
20 Mar 44 – 16 Nov 44	Stanton Harcourt
16 Nov 44 – 10 Sep 46	Abingdon
10 Sep 40 – 15 Jan 46	Stanton Harcourt (Satellite)
23 Jul 41 – 12 Feb 42	Mount Farm (Satellite)
Aug 42 – 23 Jul 43	St Eval (Detachment)

Aircraft types used	Examples
Anson Mk I	N5004 N5005 N5006 N5007
Defiant Mk I	AA327
Defiant Mk II	N1687
Hurricane	
Lysander Mk I	R2586 R2630
Lysander Mk II	P1668
Lysander Mk III	T1745
Lysander Mk IIIa	V9542
Lysander TT Mk III	T1684
Martinet	JN283
Master Mk II	AZ723 EM270

Wellington Mk III	X3948
Wellington Mk X	LN451 LP438 NC601
Whitley Mk II	K7219 K7221 K7222 K7227
Whitley Mk III	K8936 K8940 K8941 K8942
Whitley Mk IV	K9017 K9019 K9021 K9023
Whitley Mk V	N1346 N1349 N1350 N1354
Whitley Mk VII	Z6969 Z9368

*The badge of No 10 OTU. The
torch is indicative of learning
and the bomb refers to the
duties the crews were being
trained for. The motto reads
'Strength through knowledge.'*

N⁰·11 (Bomber) Operational Training Unit

Formed from No 215 Sqn in April 1940 and based at Bassingbourn, No 11 OTU was equipped with Wellingtons. Ansons were introduced in June 1940 and on 10 April 1941 the unit lost Wellington Mk I L4253 to a night fighter. The Wellington crashed at Ashwell. Two weeks later on the 24th Wellington Mk Ic N2912 was attacked and shot down over Bassingbourn. The Wellington crashed onto Wellington R1404 which was parked in a dispersal and Sgts Alstram and Wilson were killed, Sgt Nicholls, one of the pilots, was injured. A further Wellington, R3227 was lost to a night fighter on 7 May, crash landing on fire at Wendy Village. The crew escaped with injuries. On 18 July Wellington Mk Ic X3619 was attacked and damaged by a night fighter but managed to land at Steeple Morden. Four days later Wellington Mk Ic R1334 collided in mid air with a Ju 88 and crashed at Ashwell. Wellington Mk Ic N2747 crashed at Whaddon on approach to Bassingbourn on 24 July 1941 and on 20 August Wellington Mk Ia N3005 was shot down near Barrington, all of the crew were killed. In December 1941 the unit moved to its satellite at Steeple Morden to enable runways to be laid at Bassingbourn. The OTU was using Lysanders as target tugs during this period.

In April 1942 the unit returned to Bassingbourn and training continued. Aircraft of the OTU took part in the 'Thousand Bomber' raids and raids against Dusseldorf and Bremen before moving to Westcott in October 1942.

The Wellington Mk Ic's were supplemented by Mk Xs in September 1943 and the gunnery training flights were based at Oakley. Wellington Mk Ic N2761 was lost when it was abandoned after engine failure near Market Harborough on 7 February 1943. By February 1944 the Wellington Mk Ic had been phased out and the unit standardised on Mks III and X. In the spring of 1944 the output from the unit was mainly for overseas squadrons and in March 1944 Hurricanes and Martinets were brought in for gunnery training. Training continued until the unit disbanded on 3 August 1945.

Codes used by the unit included KH, KJ OP and TX, eg. Hurricane LF772:KH-B, Wellington Mk I L4381:KJ-A, Wellington Mk Ic R3212:KJ-L, Wellington Mk X LP430 KJ-H, master Mk II AZ382:KJ-E, Martinet

JN587:KJ-B and Defiant L7011:KJ-A, Wellington Mk I L4227:OP-R, Wellington Mk Ic N2750:OP-J and Wellington Mk X LP978:OP-K, Anson Mk I N5173:TX-F, Wellington Mk Ic R1661:TX-E and Wellington Mk X LP707:TX-V.

Bases

Apr 40 – Dec 41	Bassingbourn
Apr 40 –Dec 41	Steeple Morden (Satellite)
Dec 41 – 24 Apr 42	Steeple Morden
Dec 41 – 24 Apr 42	Tempsford (Satellite)
24 Apr 42 – 2 Oct 42	Bassingbourn
24 Apr 42 – 2 Oct 42	Steeple Morden (Satellite)
2 Oct 42 – 3 Oct 45	Westcott
2 Oct 42 – 3 Oct 45	Oakley (Satellite)

Aircraft types used	Examples
Anson Mk I	K6184 K6190 K6193 K6194
Defiant	L7011
Hurricane	LF772
Lysander TT Mk III	T1743
Lysander TT Mk IIIa	V9724
Martinet	JN587
Master Mk II	AZ382
Tutor	K3277
Wellington Mk I	L4381
Wellington Mk Ia	N2866 N2875 N2876 N2887
Wellington Mk Ic	N2747 N2761 N2801 P9280
Wellington Mk III	X3277 X3350 X3363 X3474
Wellington Mk X	LP430 LP707 LP978

No. 12 Air Gunnery School

No 12 AGS formed on 1 August 1943 at Bishops Court, County Down, equipped with Ansons and Martinets. The Martinets had a low serviceability rate and an engineer from Bristol's was sent to investigate the engine problems. During its existence the AGS trained forty-seven courses before disbanding on 26 May 1945. The unit used letter and number/letter code combinations, eg. Anson Mk I LT336:J4 and Martinet MS618:NS

Bases

1 Aug 43 – 26 May 45	Bishops Court

Aircraft types used	Examples
Anson Mk I	N4587 N9780 LT336
Tutor	K6100
Martinet	MS618
Spitfire Mk VII	
Wellington Mk X	LN836

No.13 (Bomber) Operational Training Unit

Formed from Nos 104 and 108 Sqns at Bicester on 8 April 1940, No 13 OTU trained Blenheim crews. Satellite airfields at Weston on the Green and Hinton in the Hedges were in use at this time. The unit trained crews for both home and overseas squadrons but concentrated mainly on crews for overseas from October 1941.

Hinton in the Hedges was used by the unit from November 1940 till March 1941 and again from May 1941 when the Ansons of 'D' Flt were based there. 'A' Flt used Hinton for its Blenheim Mk IVs from October 1941. Early losses from the OTU were Anson Mk I N5114 which crashed at Launton near Bicester and Blenheim Mk IV N3563 which force landed near Brackley on 26 November 1940 and 14 January 1941 respectively. Another casualty was Blenheim Mk I K7109 which crashed on landing at Hinton on 24 February 1942.

Finmere became the unit's satellite in July 1942 replacing Hinton in the Hedges. Turweston was also brought into use from October to November 1942 and again in 1943. By mid 1943 the unit was training crews for Blenheim Mk Vs and was absorbed into No 70 Group in June 1943. At this time the unit was still flying Blenheims but was also producing crews for Boston and Mitchell units. A few Spitfires were held on the strength for fighter affiliation. The Mitchell's and Boston's were based at Finmere. By February 1944 the Blenheims had been phased out and from January 1944 Mosquitoes began to be flown.

Turweston was used by the Mitchell's from April to August 1943 and in October 1944 the unit moved from Bicester to Harwell. On 22/23 May 1944 one of the unit's Ansons, LT476 was attacked and damaged by a night fighter but managed to land safely at Little Staughton. The pilot, FG Off Davidson was killed and FS Blyth the navigator was injured. The Mosquitoes from Finmere also moved to Harwell. Mitchell's and Boston's remained at Finmere and in March 1945 No 60 OTU arrived with its Mosquitoes and was absorbed into No 13 OTU. Boston flying ceased in March 1945 and by April 1945 the unit strength was forty-seven Mosquito, eight Anson, one Proctor, one Dominie and a Tiger Moth based at Finmere and sixty Mitchell, seven Spitfires and an Anson at Harwell. Mosquito Mk II W4096 was lost in a crash landing at Finmere on 5 April 1945.

Mitchell flying ended at Harwell in late May 1945 and Finmere became the main base. In June 1945 six Tempest Mk IIs arrived and the unit moved to Middleton St George in July 1945. The unit remained Middleton St George until May 1947 when it moved to Leeming and combined with No 54 OTU to form No 228 OCU.

Codes used by the unit were AT, FV, KQ, OY, SL, XD and XJ, eg. Blenheim Mk V AZ897:AT-18, Blenheim Mk IV V5688 FV-B, Mitchell FW114:FV-D, Mosquito Mk IV TA538:FV-K, Blenheim Mk IV V6083:KQ-S, Mosquito Mk III HJ973:KQ-A, Mosquito Mk VI HJ741:OY-G, Anson Mk I AX498:SL-N, Tempest Mk II MW759:SL-X Mosquito Mk VI TA476:SL-A, Boston Mk III BZ346:XD-P, Blenheim Mk I L6620:XJ-D, Mosquito Mk III HJ776:XJ-M and Mosquito Mk IV PZ475:XJ-V.

Bases

8 Apr 40 – 12 Oct 44	Bicester
12 Oct 44 – Jul 45	Harwell
Jul 45 –May 47	Middleton St George
Apr 40 –Nov 42	Weston on the Green (Satellite)
Nov 40 – Jul 42	Hinton in the Hedges (Satellite)
41 – 41	Finmere (Satellite)
31 Jul 42 – Jul 45	Finmere (Satellite)
1 Oct 42 – 28 Nov 42	Turweston (Satellite)
30 Apr 43 – 43	Turweston (Satellite)
15 Mar 45 – Jul 45	Hampstead Norris (Satellite)
45 – 46	Croft (Satellite)

Aircraft types used	Examples
Anson Mk I	N5114 N5116 N5117 N5152
Blenheim Mk I	K7063 K7109 K7176
Blenheim Mk IV	AZ884 AZ889 AZ904 AZ930
Blenheim Mk V	AH435 AH447
Boston Mk III	W8299 Z2185 Z2262 AL479
Defiant Mk I	T4055
Dominie	R5930

Lysander TT Mk IIIa	V9901
Martinet	
Mitchell	FW114
Mosquito Mk II	W4096
Mosquito Mk III	HJ776 HJ973
Mosquito Mk IV	PZ475 TA538
Mosquito Mk VI	HJ741 TA476
Oxford Mk II	V3819 V3833
Proctor	
Spitfire Mk IIa	P7527 P8396
Tempest Mk II	MW759
Tiger Moth	N6965

Type C hangar at Middleton St George in October 1988. No 13 OTU used this airfield from 1945 to 1947. (Authors collection)

No.14 (Bomber) Operational Training Unit

This OTU was formed at Cottesmore from No 185 Sqn on 5 April 1940. It was equipped with Hampdens, Herefords and Ansons. Between July and December 1940 the unit's aircraft carried out several leaflet raids over France. Woolfox Lodge was used as a satellite from December 1940 till August 1941 and Saltby was used from August 1941 to August 1943. Losses in 1940 and 1941 included Anson Mk I N5037, which crashed on approach to Cottesmore on 8 June 1940, Hampden P2092 which was shot down by a night fighter and crashed at Little Blytham killing Sgt RJ Holborow and two others and Hampden P1155 which stalled and dived into the ground near Buckminster on 27 November 1941.

No 14 OTU took part in all three 'Thousand Bomber' raids losing four aircraft out of the ninety-five OTU aircraft despatched. In September twelve aircraft were despatched to Essen in the units last operational sorties and the unit moved to Market Harborough on 1 August 1943.

By the time it moved to Market Harborough the OTU was flying Wellingtons, Ansons and Oxfords and a satellite was established at Husbands Bosworth. One of the aircraft lost in 1942 was Wellington Mk Ic R1401 which crashed on landing at Cottesmore on 1 October 1942. Husbands Bosworth was used until 15 June 1944 when the part of the unit based there was renumbered No 85 OTU. No 14 OTU remained at Market Harborough as a ¾ strength OTU until disbanded on 24 June 1945.

The unit used the code AM, GL and VB on its aircraft, eg. Wellington Mk Ic Z8963:AM-G, Wellington Mk X LN862:AM-Q, Hurricane Mk IIc MW341:AM-A and Martinet HP522:AM-B, Hampden P1276:GL-M1, Hereford L6070:GL-A2, Wellington Mk Ic AD594:GL-U, Anson Mk I R9607:VB-O2 and Wellington Mk I L7850:VB-Y.

The badge of No 14 OTU.

Bases

5 Apr 40 – 1 Aug 43	Cottesmore
13 Dec 40 – Aug 41	Woolfox Lodge (Satellite)
Aug 41 – 1 Aug 43	Saltby (Satellite)
1 Aug 43 – 24 Jun 45	Market Harborough
1 Aug 43 – 15 Jun 44	Husbands Bosworth (Satellite)

Aircraft types used	Examples
Anson Mk I	K6186 K8824 N4911 N5037
Defiant	
Hampden	N9062 P1155 P1157 P1158
Hereford	L6070
Hurricane Mk IIc	MW341
Lysander TT Mk III	R9013 T1504 V9845
Martinet	HP522
Oxford Mk II	V3993 V3994 V3996 V4020
Wellington Mk I	L7850
Wellington Mk Ic	N2819 R1019 R1039 R1048
Wellington Mk II	W5352
Wellington Mk III	
Wellington Mk X	LN862

No.15 (Pilot) Advanced Flying Unit

This unit formed at Leconfield on 1 March 1942 and used Acaster Malbis and Kirmington as satellites. The unit was equipped with Oxfords and 'W' and 'X' Flts used Acaster Malbis from 7 March 1942 till 25 January 1943. Kirmington was used from March till October 1942 and Caistor was used as a Relief Landing Ground (RLG) from may till November 1942. Losses at the AFU were heavy in 1942 and included several mid-air collisions. Oxford Mk I V3912 collided on landing with another Mk I V3957 on 9 Mar 1942. V3322 was hit by V3952 taking off at Kirmington on 2 Apr 1942. Mk I R6378 collided with Oxford R6154 over Weston on the Green on 27 May. Oxford Mk I V4214 crashed on landing on the Q-site at Great Timber, Lincs. On 14 August and V3882 hit a balloon cable at night and crashed near Hull on 13 October.

The AFU moved to Andover on 15 December 1942 and used Tatenhill as a satellite from 7 November 1942 until this detachment moved to Grove in May 1943. Goxhill had also been used as a satellite from 15 May 1942 till 4 June 43. The AFU remained at Andover until November 1943 when it moved to Babdown Farm. There were several losses in 1943 including Oxford Mk I P9034, which ran away unmanned and hit N3572 at Ramsbury on 19 February. Mk I V3949 collided with ED136 and crashed at Ramsbury on 27 May and R6388 a Mk I dived into the ground near Ramsbury on 7 June. Oxford Mk I V3955 collided with LX168 and crashed at Bishopstone, Wilts on 24 June.

While at Andover, Ramsbury was used as a satellite and in July 1943 'K', 'L' and 'M' Flts, which had been based at Grove, moved in. The Ramsbury detachment moved out in October 1943. Another detachment was based at Greenham Common from December 1942 till September 1943. When the AFU moved to Babdown Farm the maintenance squadron was left at Andover until January 1944.

The unit remained at Babdown Farm until 20 June 1945 when it disbanded. Castle Combe was used as a satellite from November 1943 until June 1945 and Long Newnton was used by the detached flights, which had moved in from Greenham Common in September 1943. Conditions a Long Newnton were not always suitable for flying and during October and November of 1944 Charmy Down was used due to waterlogging at Castle Combe. Down farm was also used for circuit training and night flying from October 1944 until April 1945.

As well as mid air collisions hitting trees on approach or take off was a fairly common occurrence at the AFU in 1944 and 1945. Oxford Mk I N6322 hit a tree on approach to Babdown Farm and crashed on 28 August 1944 and R6280 did the same at Horton Court, Chipping Sodbury on 27 July. In 1945 V4080 hit LX142 taking off from Babdown Farm on the night of 8 August. The unit was allocated two letter codes, eg. Oxford R6277:DT.

Bases

1 Mar 42 – 15 Dec 42	Leconfield
Mar 42 – Oct 42	Kirmington (RLG)
7 Apr 42 – 25 Jan 43	Acaster Malbis (RLG)
May 42 – Nov 42	Caistor (RLG)
15 May 42 – 4 Jun 42	Goxhill (Satellite)
7 Nov 42 – May 43	Tatenhill (Satellite)
15 Dec 42 – Oct 43	Andover
Dec 42 –Sep 43	Greenham Common (Detachment)
Dec 42 – Oct 43	Ramsbury (Detachment)
Oct 43 – 20 Jun 45	Babdown Farm
Nov 43 – Jun 45	Castle Combe (RLG)
Sep 43 – Apr 45	Long Newnton (RLG)
May 43 – 3 Jul 43	Grove (Detachment)
Oct 44 – Nov 44	Charmy Down (RLG)
Oct 44 – Apr 45	Down Farm (RLG)

Aircraft types used	Examples
Anson Mk I	K6153 N4193 N5014 AX638
Oxford Mk I	N4560 N4567 N4577 AT794
Oxford Mk II	P1077 T1059 V3501 AP389

No. 16 (Bomber) Operational Training Unit

.No 16 OTU was formed from No 5 Group Pool at Upper Heyford on 22 April 1940. The unit was equipped with Hampdens and Ansons and began to receive Herefords in May 1940. From July till October 1940 the unit flew operations over France. Brackley came in to use as a RLG in July 1940.

The Herefords were phased out of service by April 1941 and the unit carried on training with Hampdens, Ansons and Oxfords until April 1942 when the first Wellington Mk Ic's began to arrive. The night of 12 June 1941 was a bad one for the unit with attacks on three aircraft by night fighters. Hampden Mk I P1341 was attacked and overshot landing at Akeman Street. Ansons N5014 and R9691 escaped with damage, both landing at Brackley. On the night of 31 August Anson Mk I N5074 was attacked and damaged by a night fighter. Plt Off Bosch was killed and three others were injured. On 20 September 1941 the unit was attacked again when Hampden P5314 was shot down near Croughton with the loss of Sgt Van der Merwe and his crew.

Hinton in the Hedges replaced Brackley as the satellite in July 1942 and the Wellingtons of 'A' Flt were based there until April 1943 when they moved to Barford St John which had come into use as Upper Heyford's satellite on 15 December 1942.

During 1942 Wellingtons of the unit carried out sorties including some on the 'Thousand Bomber' raids. By March 1943 the unit was flying Wellington Mk Ic, Ansons, Defiants and Lysanders. Wellington Mk IIIs began to arrive in September 1942 and were based mainly at Barford St John. The unit continued to fly 'Nickel' sorties over France and began to receive Wellington Mk Xs in 1943. The unit was disbanded on 12 December 1944 but reformed on 1 January 1945 when No 1655 Mosquito Training Unit, which had arrived at Upper Heyford on 30 December 1944 was renamed. The OTU was equipped with Mosquito Mks III, IV, VI, XX and XXV and also operated some Oxfords. No 16 OTU left Upper Heyford and Barford St John for Cottesmore in March 1946.

The unit used the codes GA, JS and XG, eg. Anson Mk I 767:GA-A, Oxford AS146:GA-V, Lysander T1435:GA-Y, Master Mk II AZ574:GA-A,

Mosquito Mk III RR289:GA-L, Mosquito KB501:GA-C, Mosquito Mk XVI PF488:GA-T, Hampden P1246:JS-W, Wellington Mk Ic R1236:JS-K, Wellington Mk III DF263:JS-T, Mosquito Mk XVI PF482:JS-B, Hampden X2980:XG-A, Wellington Mk Ic DV509:XG-I2, Wellington Mk III BJ190:XG-F and Wellington Mk X NC808:XG-R. XG was used up to December 1944 and whilst at Cottesmore post-war the unit used the code FMO.

Bases

4 Apr 40 – 12 Dec 44	Upper Heyford
Jul 40 – Jul 42	Brackley (RLG)
Jul 42 – Apr 43	Hinton in the Hedges (Satellite)
15 Dec 42 – 12 Dec 44	Barford St John (Satellite)
1 Jan 45 – Mar 46	Upper Heyford
1 Jan 45 – Mar 46	Barford St John (Satellite)
Mar 46 – Mar 47	Cottesmore

Aircraft types used	Examples
Anson Mk I	N4988 N4989 N4995 N4998
Defiant Mk I	AA282 AA325
Hampden	N9065 N9106 P1145 P1146
Hereford	
Hurricane	
Lysander Mk III	T1507 T1694
Lysander TT Mk III	T1693
Martinet	
Master Mk II	AZ574
Mosquito Mk III	RR289
Mosquito Mk IV	
Mosquito Mk VI	
Mosquito Mk XVI	PF482 PF488
Mosquito Mk XX	
Mosquito Mk XXV	
Oxford Mk I	P1284 T1019 V3191 V3874
Oxford Mk II	P1094 T1053 T1076 V3851

Wellington Mk Ia	N2875 N2877 P9217
Wellington Mk Ic	N2761 N2819 R1025 R1039
Wellington Mk III	X3397 X3404 X3447 X3450
Wellington Mk X	NC808

Pilot Robert Wishart (left) and crew member Don Lindsay pose before a No 16 OTU Hampden at Upper Heyford in early 1942. Wishart was killed in July 1942 serving with No 408 Sqn. Lindsay and the rest of the crew were killed on 3 March 1942 when Hampden P1221 crashed. Wishart had missed the flight due to a bout of flu. (Robert W Mackenzie)

No. 18 (Polish) Operational Training Unit

No 18 OTU was formed at Hucknall on 14 March 1940 to train Polish crews and was equipped with Fairey Battles. It did not remain at Hucknall for long and moved to Bramcote on 15 June 1940. At Bramcote the unit operated Wellington Mks Ic and III and Bitteswell was used as a satellite from February 1942 till June 1943. Thurleigh was also used as a satellite from March 1942 till 3 June 1942.

The unit took part in the 'Thousand Bomber' raids in 1942 and from 26 January 1942 till January 1943 the Navigation Flt was based at Finningley. On 18 March 1943 the whole unit moved to Finningley. Nuneaton was brought into use as a satellite in February 1943 but was only used until the unit moved to Finningley.

Losses in 1941 and 1942 included Wellington Mk Ia P9221 which undershot and hit a crane at Bramcote on 3 February 1941, Wellington Mk Ic N2848 flew into a hill whilst in cloud at Buckden Pike on 31 January 1942 and Wellington Mk Ic N2806 crashed on 17 May. Wellington Mk Ic N2813 was abandoned by the crew in icing conditions near Radnor and crashed on 20 May 1942. Wellington Mk IV Z1325 stalled at low altitude and crashed at Hinckley on 8 November 1942.

Another satellite used by the unit from June 1943 was Doncaster. Training on Wellingtons continued at Finningley and Defiants, Lysanders and Martinets were used as target tugs. The OTU took part in further operational sorties throughout the year and began to use Bircotes (Bawtry) as a satellite from October 1943. Bircotes remained in use until August 1944 and Worksop was also used from 11 November 1943 until 1945.

The unit moved to Worksop on 15 November 1943 while runways were laid at Finningley and returned to Finningley on 23 May 1944. 'B' Flt remained at Worksop. Training continued until the beginning of 1945 when the unit was disbanded.

Bases

14 Mar 40 – 15 Jun 40	Hucknall
15 Jun 40 – 18 Mar 43	Bramcote

Feb 42 – Jun 43	Bitteswell (Satellite)
26 Jan 42 – Jan 43	Finningley (Detachment)
Feb 43 – Mar 43	Nuneaton (Satellite)
18 Mar 43 – 15 Nov 43	Finningley
Jun 43	Doncaster (Satellite)
Oct 43 – Aug 44	Bircotes (Satellite)
11 Nov 43 – 15 Nov 43	Worksop (Satellite)
15 Nov 43 – 23 May 44	Worksop
23 May 44 – 45	Finningley
23 May 44 – 45	Worksop (Detachment)

Aircraft types used	Examples
Anson Mk I	N5022 N5029
Battle	K9181 K9272 K9474 K9476
Defiant TT Mk III	V1112
Lysander TT Mk III	T1525 Y1586 T1737
Lysander TT Mk IIIa	V9900
Martinet	
Oxford Mk I	V4086 V4087 V4088 V4089
Tomahawk	
Wellington Mk Ia	P9221
Wellington Mk Ic	N2750 N2806 N2813 N2848
Wellington Mk III	X3335 X3343 X3357 X3401
Wellington Mk IV	Z1220 Z1253 Z1268 Z1280

No.20 (Bomber) Operational Training Unit

No 20 OTU was formed at Lossiemouth on 27 May 1940 with Wellingtons and Ansons. Elgin was brought into use as a satellite at the end of June 1940. Training continued at Lossiemouth until November 1941 when some of the unit's aircraft were detached to Lakenheath due to the unservicability of Lossiemouth's grass surface.

A sodium flarepath was laid out at Elgin during June 1941 for simulated night flying training. Losses in 1941 included Wellington Mk Ic N2820 which hit a hangar in bad visibility at Lossiemouth on 18 April and such accidents were to continue throughout the units existence. Wellington Mk Ia N2873 was lost when it caught fire on start up at Elgin on 15 March 1942. P2516, another Mk Ia, was lost when it swung on take off and hit an excavator at Lossiemouth on 18 May and Wellington Mk Ic N2758 flew into a cliff in low cloud east of Macduff in Aberdeenshire on 29 September 1942.

In September 1942 Wellingtons of the unit were detached to Elsham Wolds to take part in a raid on Dusseldorf. January 1943 saw the loss of Wellington Mk Ic N2769 which is presumed to have ditched in the sea. Several other OTU aircraft were lost in this manner. On 15 March 1943 the OTU lost another Wellington Mk Ic, N2823 which hit trees taking off from Elgin.

Milltown came into use as a satellite in June 1943 and remained in use until September 1944. 1944 saw more aircraft losses including Wellington X3225 which crashed into the sea off Jura in the Hebrides in April. By the end of 1944 the grass surface at Elgin was

The badge of No 20 OTU. The key is the symbol of learning, the sword is symbolic of fighting and the thistle represents the Scottish location of the unit.

deteriorating under the heavy use and in January 1945 the detachment returned to Lossiemouth. Elgin was repaired using bar and rod tracking and reopened for use in March 1945 remaining in use with No 20 OTU until June 1945. The unit was disbanded in July 1945.

Aircraft of No 20 OTU carried the codes JM, MK, XL, YR and ZT, eg. Wellington Mk Ic's N2859:JM-W, Z8977:XL-C, R1089:YR-B and R3232:ZT-H. Wellington Mk III HE490:XL-A. Wellington Mk X LP752:JM-L and Anson Mk I LT959:MK-F.

Bases

27 May 40 – Jul 45	Lossiemouth
30 Jun 40 – Jan 45	Elgin (Satellite)
24 Nov 41 – 12 Jan 42	Lakenheath (Detachment)
14 Jun 43 – 1 Sep 44	Milltown (Satellite)
20 Mar 45 – 24 Jun 45	Elgin (Satellite)

Aircraft types used	Examples
Anson Mk I	N4860 N4948 N5017 N5083
Defiant Mk I	T3930
Hurricane Mk II	
Lysander TT Mk III	P9128 R9025 R9115
Master Mk II	
Wellington Mk Ia	N2873 N2883 N2884 N2885
Wellington Mk Ic	N2578 N2769 N2819 N2820
Wellington Mk III	X3223 X3225 X3275 X3277
Wellington Mk X	LP752

No.21 Heavy Glider Conversion Unit

When The Heavy Glider Conversion Unit (HGCU) returned to Brize Norton from North Luffenham on 15 October 1944 plans were being made for another Rhine crossing and an expansion of this unit was required. Therefore other similar units were formed and the HGCU became No 21 HGCU. The unit was equipped with Whitley's and Horsa's. In January 1945 the unit began to re-equip with Albemarles and new glider types, Hadrians and Hamilcars were introduced.

The Albemarles were not well suited to glider towing and several were lost in 1945. V1993 crashed in a forced landing near Brize Norton on 14 February and three days later V1983 crashed on the approach. On 19 February V1862 was lost when it dived into the ground after releasing its glider near Brize Norton and another Albemarle, V1994 crashed in a forced landing on 4 June. The Albemarles began to be replaced by Halifaxes just before the unit moved to Elsham Wolds in December 1945.

The unit renamed at Elsham Wolds until November 1946 when it moved to North Luffenham. By now the unit had added Dakotas to its strength and operated these alongside the Halifax, Horsa and Hamilcar until December 1947 when it disbanded. Post-war the unit used the codes FEP, e.g. Halifax FE: PB, FEQ, FER, eg, Horsa FE: RV, FES and FET.

Bases

Nov 44 – Dec 45	Brize Norton
Dec 45 – Nov 46	Elsham Wolds
Nov 46 – 3 Dec 47	North Luffenham

Aircraft types used	Examples
Albemarle	P1380 V1821 V1852 V1863
Dakota	
Hadrian	
Halifax Mk A3	
Halifax Mk A7	
Horsa	
Stirling Mk III	BF532 LJ837
Whitley	

No.25 (Bomber) Operational Training Unit

No 25 OTU was formed from 'C' Flt of No 106 Sqn at Finningley on 1 March 1941 and was equipped with Hampdens and a few Ansons. On the day of its formation German aircraft attacked the unit and two landmines were dropped. In April the unit lost Hampden P1248 which hit a balloon cable and crashed at Concord Park, Sheffield on the 19th.

In May the airfield was attacked again and some damage was caused to aircraft and buildings. Losses to other reasons continued and on the 19th Hampden P1233 went missing on a training flight and on the 30th P1220 hit a gun post on landing. A few Avro Manchester's arrived for the OTU in May but they did not remain for long. The Hampdens were also on the way out by the end of the year being replaced by Wellingtons.

In June 1941 the OTU took over Balderton as a satellite and lost Hampden P2111 on a training flight on the 12th followed by Wellington R1708 which was shot down by and enemy aircraft in the circuit at Finningley and crashed at Misson, Yorkshire on the 13th. Sgt Collyer and his crew were all killed. Balderton continued to be used until November 1941 when Bircotes was taken on as a satellite. Training continued and so did the losses. Wellington Mk Ic R1767 dived into the ground near Chatteris, Cambs. On 10 September 1941. This was followed by a spate of Hampden crashes. P4302 and P1194 crashing at Balderton on the 16th and 27th respectively. Yet again a balloon cable was the downfall of a Hampden when P1234 crashed at Weybridge on 25 October. The Ansons were not immune to accidents either. AW939 was abandoned at night when the crew got lost and it crashed near Lofthouse on 22 November.

During 1942 the OTU took part in all three 'Thousand Bomber' raids and the satellite at Bircotes was improved with several new buildings and additional training aids. Even with the new aids accidents were frequent and in June 1942 Wellington R1454 crashed at Finningley on the 12th and R1375 crashed at Bircotes the next day. In September one of the Wellington Mk III's, X3940 caught fire in the air and crashed near Tadcaster.

By the end of 1942 Finningley airfield was in a poor state and was reduced to care and maintenance for repairs. No 25 OTU disbanded in January 1943. The codes carried by the unit are not known though the Manchester's are thought to have been coded PP.

Bases

1 Mar 41 – Jan 43	Finningley
Jun 41 – Nov 41	Balderton (Satellite)
Nov 41 – 7 Jan 43	Bircotes (Satellite)

Aircraft types used	Examples
Anson Mk I	N4913 N5014 N5023 N5077
Hampden Mk I	P1277 P1204 P1221 P1222
Lysander TT Mk IIIa	V9899 V9900
Manchester Mk I	R5769 R5770 R5771 R5772
Martinet	
Wellington Mk Ic	N2801 N2805 N3013 P9238
Wellington Mk III	X3332 X3353 X3564 X3813

No.26 Elementary Flying Training School

No 26 EFTS was formed at Sheffield Farm on 21 July 1941 with an establishment of 24 Tiger Moths. The unit provided six-week ab initio courses for up to sixty pupils and all maintenance was run by civilians. Sheffield farm was renamed Theale on 15 August 1941. The first course commenced on August 21st and ab initio training continued until 1943 when the EFTS became a grading school.

As well as the Tiger Moths the unit also operated a few Hinds, Mentors and Puss Moths. By May 1944 grading had given way to assessment courses for potential flying instructors. Flying at the EFTS ceased on 30 June 1945 and the unit disbanded on July 7th.

Bases

21 Jul 41 – 7 Jul 45	Theale (Sheffield Farm)

Aircraft types used	**Examples**
Hind	
Mentor	
Puss Moth	
Tiger Moth	N5471 N5481 N6522 N6535

No. 30 Elementary Flying Training School

This unit was formed at Burnaston just south west of Derby in September 1939 by renaming the combined No 30 ERFTS and No 27 ERFTS which had arrived from Tollerton. The unit was run and administered by a civilian organisation, Air Schools Ltd, and was equipped with Tiger Moths, Magisters, Harts and Battles. The unit came under the control of No 51 Group and during the invasion scare of 1940 bomb racks were fitted to the aircraft. During this period it was decided to standardise on the Magister and the other types were passed on to other units. The Germans attacked the airfield in 1940 but little damage was caused. The heavy wear and tear of operating 54 Magisters in three Wings and the congested circuit caused the unit to look for satellites and Battlestead Hill was brought into use. The EFTS was renumbered No 16 EFTS on 10 May 1940.

Bases

Sep 39 – 10 May 40	Burnaston
10 May 40 –	Battlestead Hill (Satellite)

Aircraft types used	Examples
Battle	
Hart	
Magister	N3775 N3778 N3785 N3787
Tiger Moth	

No. 41 Operational Training Unit

This unit formed from part of No 1 School of Army Co-operation at Old Sarum on 20 September 1941. It had an establishment of twenty-eight Tomahawks plus Harvards and Magisters. Oatlands Hill was used as a satellite until November 1942 and Chilbolton was also used whilst the airfield was under repair.

Due to the nature of the tactical reconnaissance training carried out and the small size of Oatlands Hill accidents, particularly mid-air collisions were common. Tomahawk Mk IIa spun into the ground on 12 December 1941. The unit had a mix of Tomahawks Mustangs, Harvards and Hurricanes by April 1942 and Mustang Mk I AG350 collided with Tomahawk Mk I AH776 on landing at Oatlands Hill on 30 May 1942. Another collision occurred when Tomahawk Mk IIa AK159 was hit by Mustang Mk I AG396 on 27 June 1942. A week later Tomahawk Mk I AH809 flew into the ground in cloud near Wells and in August Mustang Mk I AG381 was hit by AL691 at Oatlands Hill.

No 41 OTU left for Hawarden in November 1942 and began to use Poulton as a satellite from March 1943 basing its Day Fighter Wing there. 1943 saw no let up in the accident rate and Mustang Mk I AP199 collided with AG515 near Whitchurch on 14 January. The Harvards were not immune either and Mk I N7178 crashed on 4 April. April was not a good month with the loss of another Mustang, AG363 which crashed after the engine failed on the 6th and AM183 dived into the ground at Gwernaffield in Flint on 6 May.

A Mustang of No 41 OTU at Old Sarum. (D Annand)

One of the last losses before the unit re-equipped with Spitfires on 25 July 1944 was Hurricane Mk I Z4631 which crashed on approach to Cranage on 31 March. In September and October 1944 the Seafires of No 808 and No 885 Sqns of the Fleet Air Arm were temporarily attached to No 41 OTU for tactical recce training. In March 1945 the Fighter recce Wing moved from Hawarden to Chilbolton retaining the designation No 41 OTU whilst the Day Fighter Wing moved into Hawarden from Poulton and became No 58 OTU on 12 March 1945. The unit arrived at Chilbolton equipped with Spitfires, Hurricanes, Masters and Martinets for target towing and finally disbanded on 26 June 1945. The unit used the code IO on its aircraft and the code 6R was allocated to the unit but its use is not confirmed.

Bases

20 Sep 41 – Nov 41	Old Sarum
Sep 41 – 14 Nov 42	Oatlands Hill (Satellite)
- 14 Nov 42	Chilbolton (Satellite)
Nov 41 – 23 Mar 45	Hawarden
1 Mar 43 – 23 Mar 45	Poulton (Satellite)
23 Mar 45 – 26 Jun 45	Chilbolton

Aircraft types used	Examples
Harvard Mk I	N7015 N7021 P5182 P5860
Hurricane Mk I	N2329 P2570 V6557 W9314
Hurricane Mk X	P5209 AF975 AF986 AG199
Magister Mk I	T9704 T9977
Martinet	
Master Mk I	N7486 N7692 T8405 T8753
Master Mk II	W9025 AZ312 AZ588 AZ619
Master Mk III	W8633 W8634
Mustang Mk I	AG346 AG367 AL986 AM117
Spitfire Mk IIa	P8753
Spitfire Mk Vb	W3322 W3377 W3405 W3445
Tomahawk Mk I	AH752 AH800
Tomahawk Mk IIa	AH894 AH900 AH901 AH910
Tomahawk Mk IIb	AK116 AK121 AK135 AK162

No.42 Operational Training Unit

This unit was formed at Andover in July 1941 from half of No 2 School of Army Co-operation the other half moving to Thornaby to form No 6 (Coastal) OTU. The unit's role was to convert Lysander crews to the Blenheim and Thruxton was used as a satellite. One of the first losses was Blenheim Mk IV T2123 which went missing on an exercise on 12 July. October 1941 was a bad month for the unit and it lost three Blenheim Mk IV aircraft in four days; V5762 crashed after hitting a tree in fog at Flag Fen House, Peterborough on the 7th, V5383 crashed taking off at night from Andover on the 8th and on the 10th T2333 undershot and crashed landing at night at Andover.

No 42 OTU moved to Ashbourne on 26 October 1942 and was now equipped with Blenheims, Whitleys, Oxfords and Ansons. The unit came under the control of No 70 Group and taught army support. The first Albemarles arrived in September 1943 and the unit was the main training establishment for this type. The move to Ashbourne saw no decrease in aircraft losses and two weeks after arriving Blenheim Mk IV N3567 was lost when it hit trees after take off and crashed to the west of Ashbourne. Whitley Mk V Z9134 was lost on 19 November when it collided with an Oxford near Grantham and in January Blenheim Mk IV V5752 stalled in cloud and dived into the ground south of Ashbourne on the 15th.

The unit had four flights and initial training was on Blenheims before progressing to Whitleys then Albemarles. By June 1943 control had transferred to Fighter Command and by July the Blenheims had been phased out and the main type was the Whitley. Whitley accidents were regular and Z6742 crashed on approach to Thruxton on 4 March 1943. N1202 is presumed to have crashed into the sea on 4 August and T4339 dived into the Severn on the 23rd.

'A' Sqn was detached to Darley Moor with Ansons and Oxfords. September also saw command of the unit transferred to No 38 Group and training now concentrated on airborne forces techniques including glider towing. 'A' Sqn trained Air Gunners and WOps and in addition to the Ansons and Oxfords had Martinets and Lysanders for target towing. One of the Oxfords, R6271, was lost when it hit HT cables near Holbourne, Derbyshire on 21 May 1943.

Four Albemarles were detached to Hampstead Norris for operations on D-Day and one, P1442, failed to return. The Albemarle was somewhat underpowered and prone to accidents and the unit lost several throughout 1944 including V1604, which crashed at Bradley Lodge, Ashbourne on 12 March. V1609, V1610 and P1592 were all lost in April, V1610 being attacked and shot down by a night fighter near Lowestoft, three of the crew were killed but Sgts Davis and Thorogood baled out safely. P1472 crashed on landing at Ashbourne on 11 June. V1618 crashed at Hollington on 14 June and several others followed. The last loss of the year was P1554, which hit a house on the approach to Ashbourne on 18 December. Whitley losses continued and in 1945 Whitley Mk V Z7643 crashed at Ashbourne on 6 February and Z6665 hit LA820 taxiing on the 22nd.

The unit used the codes GO on its Whitleys, eg; Z9487:GO-H. No 42 OTU disbanded on 20 March 1945.

Bases

Jul 41 – 26 Oct 42	Andover
Jul 42 – 26 Oct 42	Thruxton (Satellite)
26 Oct 42 – 20 Mar 45	Ashbourne
12 Jun 43 – Feb 45	Darley Moor (Satellite)

Aircraft types used	Examples
Anson Mk I	N5017 N9608 N9609 AX144
Albemarle	P1363 P1373 V1622 V1625
Blenheim Mk I	K7124 K7175
Blenheim Mk IV	N3523 P4829 R3871 V5378
Lysander Mk II	N1222 N1250
Lysander Mk III	P9122 T1613
Lysander TT Mk IIIa	V9848
Martinet	
Oxford Mk I	N6265 N6238 R6093 T1021
Oxford Mk II	W6582 AP399
Whitley Mk V	N1202 P4941 T4200 Z6636

No.51 (Night Fighter) Operational Training Unit

Formed on 25 August 1941 its role was night fighter training. The unit was based at Cranfield equipped with Blenheims and used Twinwood Farm as a satellite from April 1942. In October 1941 Blenheim Mk IV R3617 was shot down by an enemy aircraft at Sherington, Bucks on the 13th. On 5 December Blenheim Mk IV N6172 crashed forced landing at Beckering Park in Bedfordshire and Blenheim losses continued into 1942. One of the last Blenheims lost by the unit was V5743 when its undercarriage jammed and it crashed on landing at Grantham on 18 May 1943. No 3 Sqn of the unit flew Blenheims and Beauforts used for initial conversion from Twinwood Farm. The first Beaufighters arrived in August 1942 and dual control Beauforts were used for twin engine conversion training. The Beauforts also had

Many units operated Lysanders as target tugs. V9281, a Mk IIIa was operated by No 1 SAC and No 41 OTU before being converted for target towing and shipped to Canada. (GKN Westland)

their fair share of losses and X8918 was lost in a belly landing after an engine cut near Stoney Stratford on 6 march 1944. The aircraft was damaged by fire and written off. On 7 may 1944 AW195 had its undercarriage collapse on landing at Cranfield and on 31 October W6482 crashed forced landing at Uthington, Cheshire. The Blenheims were retained until 1943 and the unit also used Martinets and Lysanders for target towing.

During March and April 1943 Wellington Mk XIs were used to train night fighter Mosquito crews for No 100 group and in May and June American crews were trained by the unit on Beaufighters. By July 1944 the unit was operating Beaufighters, Beauforts and Mosquito Mk IIs, the first of which had arrived in June. Beaufighter losses were frequent throughout the OTUs existence and Mk If R2097 was lost in a forced landing at Milton Keynes on 30 November 1942. 1943 saw the loss of R2098, which spun into the ground at Putnoe Wood, Bedford on 15 April and V2833, which crashed on landing at Twinwood Farm on 20 August. Mk If R2126 crashed on approach to Cranfield on 17 March 1944 and in the same month R2069 was lost when the pilot lost control during a dummy attack on a B-17 and crashed at Easton Maudit, Northants. On 18 July R2080 hit a balloon and crashed near Kingsdown, Kent. The Mosquitoes were used by No 4 Sqn and crews were posted to No 100 Group. Mosquito losses included W4088, which flew into Mynydd Mawr in North Wales on 1 November 1944, W4079 which crashed on overshoot at Cranfield at the end of the same month and W4097 which was struck off charge on 27 December 1944 having lost part of its skinning on 1 November.

By February 1945 the Beaufighters had been withdrawn and the unit disbanded on 14 June 1945. The unit was allocated the codes BD and PF, eg. Blenheim Mk V BA138:PF-B. The Blenheims of No 3 Sqn at Twinwood Farm used the code BD, eg; Blenheim Mk I BD-V.

Bases

25 Aug 41 – 14 Jun 45	Cranfield
9 Apr 42 – Jun 45	Twinwood Farm (Satellite)

Aircraft types used	**Examples**
Beaufighter Mk I	R2059 R2060

Beaufighter Mk If	R2077 T4624 T4630 V8288
Beaufighter Mk IIf	R2321 T3415 V3189 V8184
Beaufighter Mk VIf	V8433 V8552 V8555 V8556
Beaufort Mk I	N1019 W6467 AW191 AW198
Blenheim Mk I	K7159
Blenheim Mk IV	N3554 N3565 T1870 V5563
Blenheim Mk V	BA138
Dominie Mk I	X7373 X7368
Lysander TT Mk IIIa	V9779 V9795
Magister Mk I	N3939 N3944 P2465 R1978
Mosquito Mk II	W4079 W4081 W4088 W4097

When No 56 OTU reformed in December 1944 it operated Hawker Tempests. (Authors collection)

No. 56 Operational Training Unit

No 56 OTU was formed at Sutton Bridge by renaming No 6 OTU in November 1940. The unit's main equipment was the Hurricane but it also used Gladiators, Harvards, Masters and Mentors. The operational training of fighter pilots was intensive and accidents were common. Several aircraft were lost in crashes including Hurricane Mk I N2460 which dived into the ground south of Wiggenhall, Norfolk on 25 February 1941. The units losses did not all come from crashes however and Harvard Mk I N7171 was lost in an air raid on Sutton Bridge on 11 May 1941. On 25 July 1941 Master Mk I N7510 lost a wing and crashed into the Wash.

The unit moved from Sutton Bridge to Tealing, near Dundee in March 1942. By now the unit was equipped with Hurricanes, Masters and target towing Lysanders. A satellite at Kinnell was brought into use on 29 March and the OTU located two flights there alongside the target towing Lysanders. One of which, TT Mk III R9129 was hit by Hurricane W9171 whilst parked on 12 October 1942. Due to the unsuitability of Tealing for night flying all of the night flying training was carried out at Kinnell. Kinnell was used by courses during the last three weeks of training for realistic exercises that copied the types of operation the pilots would carry out on posting to operational squadrons. These exercises included simulated convoy escorts and practice attacks on airfields. Much of the flying was done at low level and several aircraft were lost. Hurricane Mk I P2754 collided with V6913 and crashed near Montrose on 27 April 1943. In October 1943 No 56 OTU was renamed No 1 Combat Training Wing and later No 1 Tactical Exercise Unit.

No 56 OTU was reformed on 14 December 1944 at Milfield in Northumberland equipped with Typhoons and Tempests and a few Hurricanes, Spitfires and Masters. From January 1945 a satellite at Brunton was used, mainly for the last phase of the training course. The Typhoon could be a handful for an inexperienced pilot and several were lost. Typhoon Mk Ib EJ965 crashed attempting a forced landing north of Wooler on 15

January 1945 and a month later EK348 was abandoned in bad weather in the same area. On 27 March MN532 flew into Stoney Hill and on 13 July RB210 flew into the ground in low cloud at North Chalton. Training courses continued after the war had ended but at a much slower pace and the unit was closed down on 14 February 1946.

During its existence No 56 OTU used the codes FE, GF, HQ and OD. FE was used by 'C' and 'D' Flights, eg. Hurricane Mk I Z4669:FE-U, Typhoon Mk Ib's MN956:FE-P, RB372:FE-G, RB439:FE-N, JR149:FE-V. GF was used on Hurricanes, Typhoons and Tempests of 'A' and 'B' Flts, eg. Tempest Mk Vs EJ493:GF-S andEJ861:GF-M. 'X' Sqn of the OTU used HQ on its Typhoons and Tempests, eg. Typhoon Mk IBC's EK173: HQ-I, MN240: HQ-J, JP746: HQ-P and SW474: HQ-K and Tempest Mk V EJ804: HQ-M. The unit also used OD on Typhoon Mk IBC's EK290: OD-B, JP790: OD-F and PD533: OD-H and Tempest Mk V NV825:OD-12.

A mixed course of RAF and RAAF pilots trained on Hurricanes at No 56 OTU in February 1941. Barton Campbell is 4th from right, centre row. (Mrs VM Campbell)

Bases

1 Nov 40 – 27 Mar 42	Sutton Bridge
27 Mar 42 – 5 Oct 43	Tealing
29 Mar 43 – 5 Oct 43 (Satellite)	Kinnell
14 Dec 44 – 14 Feb 46	Milfield
Jan 45 – 21 May 45	Brunton (Satellite)

Aircraft types used	Examples
Gladiator	
Harvard Mk I	N7175 N7177 N7178 N7179
Hurricane Mk I	N2328 P2688 Z4306 AF958
Hurricane Mk IIb	
Hurricane Mk IIc	
Hurricane Mk X	P5188 P5190 P5196 P5202
Lysander TT Mk II	P9061

Lysander TT Mk III	R9068 R9129 T1427 T1564
Master Mk I	N7416 T8286 T8341 T8342
Master Mk II	W9022 W9077 AZ309 AZ362
Master Mk III	W8523 W8526 W8591 W8633
Mentor	
Spitfire Mk IIa	P7683
Spitfire Mk Vb	AB174 AB178 AB382 AD425
Spitfire Mk Vc	AR552
Tempest Mk V	EJ493 EJ804 EJ861 NV825
Typhoon Mk Ia	R7615
Typhoon Mk Ib	DN256 EJ903 EK154 JP380

A mixed course of RAF and RAAF pilots trained on Hurricanes at No 56 OTU in February 1941. Barton Campbell is fourth from right, centre row. (Mrs V.M. Campbell)

No.84 (Bomber) Operational Training Unit

This bomber OTU was formed at Desborough on 1 September 1943. The unit was controlled by No 92 Group and was equipped with various marks of Wellington and a small number of other types. The average course length at the unit was ten weeks and new courses started eevry fortnight. Like all of the OTU's, No 84 had its fair share of crashed and lost Wellington LN238 in a crash at Geddington Chase Wood on 21 January 1944. On the 27th Mk III X3392 caught fire in the air and crashed near Molesworth and on the same day HZ484 was lost, crashing at Arthingworth.

A satellite at Harrington came into use on 1 April 1944 but was handed over to the Americans in April 1944. The units establishment was reduced to ¾ strength and training continued until 14 June 1945 when the unit disbanded.

No 84 OTU used the codes CZ and IF, eg. Martinet HP354:CZ-P, Anson EG375:IF-P and Wellington Mk X,s LN233:IF-Q and LN247:IF-G.

Bases

1 Sep 43 – 14 Jun 45	Desborough
26 Dec 43 – Apr 44	Harrington (Satellite)

Aircraft types used	Examples
Anson	EG375
Hurricane Mk X	
Martinet	HP354
Master Mk II	
Wellington Mk Ic	N2751
Wellington Mk III	X3392 X3645 X3995
Wellington Mk X	LN233 LN238 LN247

No.85 Operational Training Unit

No 85 OTU was formed from part of No 14 OTU at the former units satellite airfield of Husbands Bosworth on 15 June 1944. The unit was equipped with Wellingtons and a few Hurricanes, Martinets and Masters. The units role was the training of transport crews and the station and its 1,900 personnel were controlled by No 92 Group. Training continued at Husbands Bosworth after the end of the war in Europe and the unit finally disbanded in July 1945. The unit used the code 9Pand 2X , eg. Wellington Mk X HE813:9P-O, Martinet Mk I JN596:2X-V and Master Mk II DK297:2X-Y.

Bases

15 June 44 – Jul 45	Husbands Bosworth

Aircraft types used	Examples
Hurricane	
Martinet Mk I	JN596
Master Mk II	DK927
Wellington Mk Ic	T2468
Wellington Mk X	HE813

The badge of No 85 OTU awarded in May 1945.

No.101 (Glider) Operational Training Unit

No 1 (Glider) OTU was formed at Kidlington near Oxford on 1 January 1942 under the control of No 70 Group but was renamed No 101 (Glider) OTU in February 1942. Initially the unit used Hotspurs and the towing aircraft were obsolete Hectors. Later the unit also received a few Audax and Tiger Moths. Using a syllabus prepared by the Central Landing Establishment at Ringway the unit gave glider pilots tactical training and night flying experience.

In common with all of the training units No 101 OTU had its accidents and Tiger Moth Mk II N6611 was lost when it hit HT cables low flying near Tockley on 25 March. A week later T7190 hit the ground in a turn whilst low flying and crashed at Islip. Just over a week later Hector Mk I K9738 went out of control while towing two Hotspurs and hit the ground at Kelmscott. In June Tiger Moth Mk II R5029 was lost when it dived into the ground at Innsworth on the 14th and on the 22nd Hector Mk I crashed on landing at Kidlington. Eventually Glider Training School and Glider OTU courses were combined and No 101 OTU was absorbed into No 4 GTS in July 1942. The unit used single leter codes on its Hotspurs, eg. Hotspur BT505:B

Bases

Feb 42 – Jul 42	Kidlington

Aircraft types used	Examples
Audax	K2006
Hector Mk I	K8093 K8099 K8134 K8150
Hotspur	BT505
Tiger Moth Mk I	K4254
Tiger Moth Mk II	N6611 R4764 T5379 T7121

No. 104 (Transport) OTU

Formed at Nutts Corner in Co Antrim on 12 March 1943 this unit's role was training of transport crews. The unit was equipped with Wellingtons, mainly Mk IVs and had a high accident rate. On 10 July 1943 a detachment of eight Wellingtons moved into Toome on the shores of Lough Neagh and a week later the unit suffered the loss of Mk IV Z1460 which crashed on take off at Nutts Corner. Three days later on the 20th Z1315 crashed force landing near Ballyronan.

On 7 September 1943 the detachment at Toome returned to Nutts Corner and 'A' Flt moved to Maghaberry. The unit lost Wellington Z1416 when it flew into high ground descending out of cloud in Glenarm on 1 October. 'A' Flt moved from Maghaberry to Mullaghmore on 3 October 1943. Meanwhile at Nutts Corner the unit lost Z1469 when it ran off the runway during an emergency landing on 10 October and two aircraft on 18 November when Z1395 ran off the end of the runway and Z1403 crashed on landing. Less than a week later Z1313 flew into Mount Divis above Belfast. December was a bad month for the unit and Z1253 was lost on the 18th when it crashed on landing. Two more were lost two days later, R1515 crashed on take off at Mullaghmore and Z1378 crashed on landing at Nutts Corner. On the last day of the year R1520 crashed into a hill south of Dundrod.

The final month of the units existence saw more incidents the last of which were the loss of Z1490 which crashed into the sea thirty miles west of Iona on 26 January and Z1206 which crashed on the beach at Uigg on Lewis the same day.

Bases

12 Mar 43 – Jan 44	Nutts Corner
10 Jul 43 – 7 Sep 43	Toome (Detachment)
7 Sep 43 – 4 Oct 43	Maghaberry (Detachment)
4 Oct 43 – Jan 44	Mullaghmore (Detachment)

Aircraft types used	**Examples**
Wellington Mk Ic	R1077
Wellington Mk IV	R1490 R1525 Z1220 Z1268

No. 131 (Coastal) Operational Training Unit

No 131 OTU formed at Killadeas in Co Fermanagh on 20 July 1942 to train Catalina flying boat crews. Initially due to a lack of accommodation the unit used St Angelo for its headquarters and later based it target towing and communications flights there. The flare path at Castle Archdale was used for night flying and Catalina W8414 crashed on landing there on 26 May 1943.

Since February 1943 the unit had been using Bowmore, a satellite for Oban, on the West Coast of Scotland for alighting practice. Another Catalina was lost on 16 October 1943 when AH551 spun into the ground at Ballinamallard and the following month W8408 hit the water after take off at Killadeas and had to be beached. The new year saw Z2147 crash on landing on the 9th and on 17 April 1944 AH541 crashed using the night flare path on Lough Erne.

By 1944 the unit was also operating Sunderland and a satellite was being used at Boa Island from 31 May 1944. The unit continued to train Coastal Command flying boat crews until 1 July 1945 when it disbanded.

Bases

20 Jul 42 – 1 Jul 45	Killadeas
Jul 42 – Jul 45	St Angelo (Target towing & comms flts)
Feb 43 – Jul 45	Bowmore (RLG)
31 May 44 – Mar 45	Boa Island (Satellite)

Aircraft types used	Examples
Catalina Mk I	W8410 Z2143 AH538 AJ159
Catalina Mk II	AM266 AM270
Sunderland Mk II	W6056
Sunderland Mk III	W6007 W6011 W6032 W6066

No. 301 Ferry Training Unit

No 301 FTU was formed at Lyneham by combining the Ferry Training Unit, No 1444 Flt and No 1445 Flt on 3 November 1942. The unit trained crews to deliver multi-engined aircraft to overseas units. 'A' Flt operated Beaufighters, Beauforts, Blenheims and Wellingtons while 'B' Flt had Hudsons and 'C' Flt operated Halifaxes and Liberators.

On 14 March 1943 Beaufighter Mk VIf of 'A' Flt was lost when it bellylanded at Lyneham and on 28 June another Beaufighter, V8897 was lost when it crashed force landing near St Ives in Cornwall. The training included long-range flights to train the crews in fuel endurance flying and on 16 September Hudson Mk V AM885 crashed at Ballyellame in Eire. 'A' Flt lost another Beaufighter, T4710 a Mk Ic when it crashed on landing at Lyneham on 22 September and on 7 October Mk VIf V8470 hit the ground while low flying at Dunkerton near Bath.

On 16 March 1944 No 301 FTU left Lyneham for Pershore and remained there until absorbed into No 1 Ferry Unit in April 1945.

Bases

20 Mar 42 – 16 Mar 44	Lyneham
16 Mar 44 – Apr 45	Pershore

Aircraft types used

Aircraft types used	Examples
Albemarle	P1407 P1449 P1473
Beaufighter Mk Ic	T3325 T4642 T4710 T4895
Beaufighter Mk If	V8246 V8247 X7802 X7815
Beaufighter Mk IIf	R2477
Beaufighter Mk VIf	T5346 V4808 V8443 X7884
Beaufort Mk I	N1039 AW198 AW313 AW374
Blenheim Mk I	K7125
Blenheim Mk IV	N3544 R2775 T2431 Z6341
Blenheim Mk V	AZ877 AZ924 AZ986 AZ987
Halifax Mk II	V9990 W7487

Hudson Mk I	P5125
Hudson Mk III	V9166 AE513
Hudson Mk IV	AE634 AE636
Hudson Mk V	AE639 AE643 AM527 AM555
Liberator Mk II	AL520 AL541 AL571 AL625
Oxford Mk I	R5948 W3721 V3727 V3745
Wellington Mk II	Z8375 Z8535
Wellington Mk X	R3221

Fighter dispersal at St Angelo photographed in May 1994. The HQ Comms Flight and TT Flight of No.131 OTU used this airfield at various times. (Author).

No. 303 Ferry Training Unit

No 303 FTU formed at Stornoway on 15 December 1942 equipped with Wellingtons. The unit trained crews in the techniques required for long range ferrying to overseas units. In March 1943 the unit moved to Talbenny in Dyfed and became responsible for the training of Ventura and Warwick crews. Talbenny was temporarily out of use in mid-1944 to have a *Drem* lighting system installed and No 303 FTU moved to Dale near Milford Haven. No 303 FTU was disbanded in late 1945.

Bases

15 Dec 42 – Mar 43	Stornoway
Mar 43 – 44	Talbenny
44 - 44	Dale
44 – 45	Talbenny

Aircraft types used	**Examples**
Oxford Mk I	V3727
Ventura Mk II	AJ216
Warwick	
Wellington Mk Ia	N2871 N2877 P2519 P9231
Wellington Mk Ic	N2856 P8289 X9827
Wellington Mk XVI	R1409 R1531 R1659 R3217

No. 305 Ferry Training Unit

No 305 FTU was formed at Errol, situated between Dundee and Perth, on 1 January 1944. This unit's role was unusual in that it was formed to train Russian crews on the Armstrong Whitworth Albemarle. The Albemarle was somewhat underpowered and not an easy aircraft to fly. An early loss was P1455, which was lost with its crew en-route to Russia on 10 March 1943. Another Albemarle was lost on 29 May when P1503 crashed into a hill near Kenmore. In 1944 the unit also began to give the Russian crews training on Mosquitoes but the unit was to be short lived and disbanded on 18 April 1944.

Bases

1 Jan 43 – 18 Apr 44	Errol

Aircraft types used	Examples
Albemarle	P1371 P1379 P1476 V1598
Mosquito Mk IV	DK296

No 1332 HCU operated the Avro York.
This particular York served with No 242 Sqn. (BD Davies)

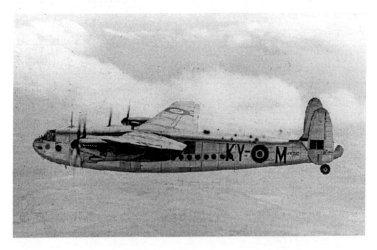

No. 1332 Heavy Conversion Unit/ Transport Conversion Unit

No 1332 HCU formed at Longtown on 11 August 1944 to convert crews onto the transport versions of the Stirling and Liberator. The unit also operated Yorks and a single C-87. No 9 OTU also used Longtown and due to difficulties with overcrowding and inadequate facilities the HCU moved to Nutts Corner in Northern Ireland on 6 October 1944. The first course commenced on 17 October 1944 and comprised fifteen crews. The course syllabus was three weeks ab initio training followed by three weeks on the Liberator and York conversion course.

Nutts Corner was not a lucky station for the HCU and several aircraft were lost. The Stirling with its very tall undercarriage was particularly prone to swinging on take off and landing and three weeks after the unit arrived at Nutts Corner Stirling Mk I EF405 swung on take off and the undercarriage collapsed on 24 October. Four Stirlings were damaged in a gale on 16 November 1944 and two weeks later Stirling LJ470 piloted by Flt/Lt FES Gardner went missing on a cross-country exercise. The unit's aircraft searched for LJ470 until 1 December without success. Stirling Mk IV LK497, built by Shorts at Belfast, overshot on landing and the undercarriage collapsed when it struck a ditch on 4 January 1945. Another Mk IV, LJ443 piloted by Sqn Ldr FJ Austin was lost whilst on an acceptance test. The aircraft wheels sank into soft ground after a swing on take off and the Stirling tipped onto its nose on 13 January. By February 1945 the unit was operating Stirlings in 'A' Flt whilst 'B' Flt operated Yorks and 'C' Flt operated Liberators and C-87s. The pilot of Stirling Mk IV LK621 swung off the runway to prevent overshooting the end on 26 March resulting in an undercarriage collapse and breaking the aircraft back. The previous day Liberator Mk III FK221 piloted by Flt/Lt LG Healy (RAAF) had crash-landed at Prestwick due to undercarriage failure. April 1945 was no better with two Stirlings lost. Mk III EE948 overshot and tipped on to its nose on the 12th and the next day Mk III EH923 swung onto soft ground after a heavy landing and the undercarriage collapsed.

On 25 April 1945 No 1332 HCU left Nutts Corner for Riccall in Yorkshire. Just prior to the move three interpreters were posted in to the unit to assist in training a French crew to fly General De Gaulle. The unit remained at Riccall until 7 November 1945 and then moved to Dishforth. During 1945 the unit was redesignated No 1332 Transport Conversion Unit and remained at Dishforth with its Yorks and Liberators until it was redesignated No 241 OCU on 5 May 1948.

The unit carried the codes YY on its Stirlings, Liberators and Yorks, eg. Liberator Mk VI KK222:YY-X and York Mk I MW264:YY-C.

Bases

11 Aug 44 –7 Oct 44	Longtown
7 Oct 44 – 25 Apr 45	Nutts Corner
25 Apr 45 – 7 Nov 45	Riccall
7 Nov 45 – 5 Jan 48	Dishforth

Aircraft types used	Examples
C-87 (Liberator)	LW628
Halifax	
Liberator Mk III	FK221 FK238 FL298
Liberator MK VI	KK222
Oxford Mk II	V3507
Stirling Mk I	EF405
Stirling Mk III	EE941 EF258 EF507 LJ446
Stirling Mk IV	LK491 LK619 LK622 LK623
York Mk I	MW264

No. 1429 (Czech) Operational Training Flight

The Czech Training Unit based at East Wretham was renamed No 1429 (Czech) OTF in January 1942 and was equipped with Wellingtons and Oxfords. One of the units Wellingtons, Mk Ic P9299 was lost in a crash on 6 April 1942 and on the night of 30/31 May 1942 the unit took part in the first 'Thousand Bomber Raid' against Cologne sending six Wellingtons. This was followed by six aircraft taking part in the second raid on Essen on the night of 1st/2nd June and two more Wellingtons were sent to Bremen on 25 June. The unit left East Wretham for Woolfox Lodge on 1 July 1942. The stay at Woolfox Lodge was brief and the unit moved again on 31 August to Church Broughton where it was absorbed by No 27 OTU.

Bases

Jan 42 – 1 Jul 42	East Wretham
1 Jul 42 – 31 Aug 42	Woolfox Lodge
31 Aug 42 – Aug 42	Church Broughton

Aircraft types used	Examples
Oxford	
Wellington Mk Ic	N2775 R1771 T2468 X9806

No. 1443 Ferry Training Flight

No 1443 Ferry Training Flight operated various marks of Wellington and Ansons from Harwell in Oxfordshire from January 1942. The unit's role was to train crews in long range ferry techniques prior to despatch overseas. The unit also used Hampstead Norris and despatched hundred of Wellingtons overseas during its existence. A record number for one month was established when 81 Wellingtons were despatched in April 1942. The training of crews and the delivery of the aircraft was not without loss and Wellington Mk II Z8575 collided with BB512 at Luqa on Malta and was damaged beyond repair on 4 April. In August Mk II W5565 went missing on a ferry flight from Portreath to Bathurst on the 12th and Wellington Mk Ic R1232 was lost when it hit trees on overshoot at Moreton in Marsh on 31 August 1942. The unit was absorbed into No 310 FTU on 30 April 1943.

Bases

Jan 42 – 30 Apr 43	Harwell
Jan 43 – Apr 43	Hampstead Norris (Satellite)

Aircraft types used	Examples
Anson Mk I	N9944
Wellington Mk Ic	R1774 T2545 X9985 AD639
Wellington Mk II	W5353 W5359 W5366 Z8418
Wellington Mk VIII	Z8712 Z8715

No. 1446 Ferry Training Flight

No 1446 FTF was formed at Bassingbourn with Wellingtons, Ansons and Oxfords but soon moved to Moreton in Marsh in Gloucestershire in May 1942. The unit controlled the training of ferry flight training for crews being despatched overseas. The ferry route was via Portreath in Cornwall and the unit despatched upwards of thirty Wellingtons per month. In December 1942 the unit establishment was twelve Wellingtons and a few Ansons and Oxfords. One of the Wellingtons, Mk II W5494 was lost when it hit a hill whilst low flying east of Bethesda in Caernarfon on 22 December. On 1 May 1943 the unit became No 311 FTU.

Bases

42 – May 42	Bassingbourn
May 42 – 1 May 43	Moreton in Marsh

Aircraft types used	**Examples**
Anson Mk I	N9747
Oxford	
Wellington Mk Ia	N2994
Wellington Mk Ic	Z1174 Z1179 AD638
Wellington Mk II	W5353 W5368 Z8402 Z8405
Wellington Mk VIII	

No.1501 Beam Approach Training Flight

In December 1941 No 1 BAT Flt equipped with Oxfords and Ansons was renumbered No 1501 BAT Flt at Abingdon. The unit gave training in the use of the Lorenz Beam approach aid. The flight moved to Stanton Harcourt on 18 April 1943 and operated from this Oxfordshire base until 31 December 1943 when it disbanded.

Bases

Dec 41 – 18 Apr 43	Abingdon
18 Apr 43 – 31 Dec 43	Stanton Harcourt

Aircraft types used	Examples
Anson	
Oxford Mk I	X6748

The AML Bombing Teacher building on the technical site at Stanton Harcourt photographed in April 1993. (Authors collection)

No. 1509 Beam Approach Training Flight

No 9 BAT Flt at Thornaby near Middlesborough was renumbered No 1509 BAT Flt in November 1941. The unit was equipped with Oxfords. The unit trained crews in beam approach techniques here until 6 April 1942 when it moved to Church Lawford. The stay at Church Lawford was brief with the unit moving again in May to Dyce near Aberdeen. No 1509 BAT Flt remained at Dyce until it disbanded on 14 August 1944.

Bases

Nov 41 – 6 April 42	Thornaby
6 Apr 42 – May 42	Church Lawford
May 42 – 14 Aug 44	Dyce

Aircraft types used	**Examples**
Oxford Mk I	V4045 AT666

No.1512 Beam Approach Training Flight

This unit was formed by renumbering No 12 BAT Flt at Dishforth in November 1941. No 1512 BAT Flt was equipped with Airspeed Oxfords and remained at Dishforth until 25 May 1943 when it moved north to Banff on the Moray Coast. During its stay at Banff the unit also used Dallachy and Fraserburgh as satellites. No 1512 BAT Flt was disbanded on 31 August 1943.

Bases

Nov 41 – 25 May 43	Dishforth
25 may 43 – 31 Aug 43	Banff
May 43 – Aug 43	Dallachy (Satellite)
May 43 – Aug 43	Fraserburgh (Satellite)

Aircraft types used	Examples
Oxford Mk I	V4079 V4080 V4131 V4132

No.1651 Conversion Unit/Heavy Conversion Unit

No 1651 CU formed at Waterbeach from No 26 Conversion Flight on 2 Jan 42 equipped with Short Stirling Mks I and III. The unit would operate Stirlings until January 1945 and the loss rate. Particularly from singing on take off and landing was high. The tall Stirling undercarriage was prone to collapse when sideways stress was applied and the unit lost at least nineteen due to swings.

Of the forty-eight aircraft lost by Bomber Command in the 'Thousand Bomber raid' on Bremen on the night of 25/26 June 1942, No 1651 CU lost one. Stirling Mk I W7442 was shot down and crashed in the Waddenzee in Holland. At this period of the war it was

The badge of No 1651 CU. The motto is 'Thus trusty and strong' and the figure of Hercules alludes to the large and heavy Hercules engined Stirlings the unit flew.

common for OTU and HCU crews to be sent on operations either to bolster the Bomber Command force or to act as diversionary raids. On the night of 28/29 July 1942 256 aircraft bombed Hamburg. Seventy-one were Stirlings and of the nine Stirlings lost three, N6069, N6102 and W7509, were from No 1651 CU. During August 1942 the unit absorbed the Stirlings of No 214 Conversion Flight.

On 14 September 1942 another of the units Stirlings was lost when N3684, a Mk I, crashed at Feltwell on return from Bremen. This was the only Stirling despatched and lost on that raid. During the early part of 1943 the unit had the famous Stirling Mk I N6086 'MacRoberts Reply' on strength but whilst night flying on 14 March it suffered an engine failure and crashed in Oakington village.

On 21 November 1943 No 1651 CU moved to Wratting Common. The unit had begun to receive Stirling Mk IIIs in July and by November these had mostly replaced the Mk Is. The unit would remain at Wratting Common for a year during which Stirling Mk III losses included EF490, which collided with EF189 during a bombing exercise and attempted a landing at Wratting Common running onto soft ground, which tore off the undercarriage on 6 July 1944. Just over a week later LK565 was lost when the pilot lost control in a turn at 3,000 feet on a cross-country exercise. The aircraft went into a steep spiral dive and crashed at Short Grove Park, Saffron Walden on the 15th. Two aircraft were lost on 18 August when the pilot of LK519 lost control while trying to lower the undercarriage and the port outer engine failed. During landing at Wratting Common the aircraft crashed into EF514. On 19 October 1944 the crew of LK488 became lost and flew into Mickle Fell in Yorkshire in bad visibility. They were on a low-level cross-country exercise and were thirty-five miles west of track when they crashed.

After a year the unit took its Stirlings to Woolfox Lodge on 10 November 1944. By now it was also equipped with Lancaster Mk Is and IIIs. The unit also had a collection of Spitfires, Hurricanes, Oxfords and Beaufighters on strength used for fighter affiliation, target towing and communications duties. Although not so prone to accident as the Stirlings, which were phased out in January 1945, the Lancasters of the unit suffered losses too. Two months after moving to Woolfox Lodge two aircraft were lost. On 7 December Lancaster Mk I PB749 exploded in mid-air and crashed at Langtoft. This was followed by Mk I NG270 which crashed near Ailsworth in bad weather on 11 December. On 3/4 March 1945 German intruders were active over the UK in one of the last attempts by the Luftwaffe to seriously disrupt night bomber activity and two of the HCU's aircraft were lost. JB699:F crashed near Cottesmore killing the crew and ND387:K fell near Woolfox Lodge the only survivor being Sgt Thompson, the rear gunner, who was injured. The unit's last loss was Lancaster Mk I PB871 which crashed on take off at Woolfox Lodge on 24 March 1945. No 1651 HCU was disbanded on 13 July 1945.

During its existence the unit used individual aircraft letters until early 1943 then the codes BS, GG, QQ and YZ, eg. Stirling Mk Is

W7442:B, N6048:BS-P and R9197:YZ-U, Stirling Mk IIIs EF389:YZ-T and LJ570:QQ-K. Lancaster Mk I HK655:BS-F and Lancaster MK IIIs ME325/G:BS-P and RF302:BS-G.

Bases

2 Jan 42 – 21 Nov 43	Waterbeach
21 Nov 43 – 10 Nov 44	Wratting Common
10 Nov 44 – 13 Jul 45	Woolfox Lodge

Aircraft types used	Examples
Beaufighter Mk VI	
Hurricane	
Lancaster Mk I	L7544 R5503 W4231 DV340
Lancaster Mk III	ED413 JB185 LM594 ME319
Oxford	
Spitfire Mk Vb	AR423 AR452
Stirling Mk I	N3652 R9147 W7427 BF373
Stirling Mk III	BF311 EE898 EF133 EH879

No. 1652 Conversion Unit/Heavy Conversion Unit

No 1652 CU was formed at Marston Moor from Nos 28 and 107 Conversion Flights on 3 January 1942. The unit was equipped with various marks of Halifax and unusually operated a single Stirling MK II LJ464. The unit also operated Spitfires and Hurricanes in the fighter affiliation role.

One of the unit's first losses was Halifax Mk II R9431 that caught fire and crash-landed at Marston Moor on 16 April. On the night of 1st/2nd June 1942 Bomber Command carried out its second 'Thousand Bomber Raid'. The target was Essen and Halifax Mk II of No 1652 CU

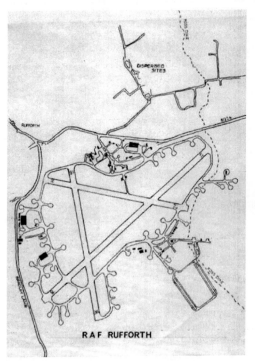

Map of Rufforth. (Ian Foster/57Rescue)

The badge of No 1652 CU. The motto reads 'making greater efforts'.

failed to return. Three weeks later Mk II R9377 was lost when it swung on landing at Marston Moor and on the night of 25/26 June aircraft from the unit took part in the third 'Thousand' operation against Bremen, Mk II V9993 failing to return.

In July 1942 the unit moved to Rufforth and a few weeks later moved again to Dalton before returning to Marston Moor in August. On 7 October 1942 the unit was redesignated No 1652 Heavy Conversion Unit and absorbed the Halifaxes of No 35 Conversion Flight on the same day. From April to September 1943 Gp Capt Leonard Cheshire who then went on to command No 617 Sqn commanded the unit. During 1943 the unit was operating Halifax Mks II and V and in 1944 began to receive Mk IIIs.

Halifax losses continued right up till the unit was disbanded and one of the last was Halifax Mk II LW573 which swung on take off and crashed on 13 June 1945. One month previously on 2 May the unit lost one of its fighter affiliation Spitfires when AB198 crashed on take off at Marston Moor. The unit finally disbanded on 25 June 1945.

The HCU used the codes GV and JA, eg. Halifax Mk II DT721:GV-G, DT786:JA-A and HR748:JA-J. Halifax Mk IIIs LK748:GV-A and MZ557:GV-J and Halifax Mk V LL237:JA-W.

Bases

3 Jan 42 – Jul 42	Marston Moor
Jul 42 – 13 Jul 42	Rufforth
13 Jul 42 – Aug 42	Dalton
Aug 42 – 25 Jun 45	Marston Moor

Aircraft types used	**Examples**
Halifax Mk I	
Halifax Mk II	R9367 R9434 W1004 W1006
Halifax Mk III	LK748 LW753 MZ557
Halifax Mk V	LL237
Hurricane Mk IV	
Spitfire Mk Vb	AB198

No.1655 Mosquito Conversion Unit/ Mosquito Training Unit

This unit was formed at Horsham St Faith as the Mosquito Conversion Unit on 30 August 1942. Soon afterward it moved to Marham equipped with Blenheim Mk Vs and various marks of Mosquito and was renamed No 1655 MCU and on 18 October 1942 the unit was renamed No 1655 MTU. One of the Blenheims, Mk V AZ961 crashed in a forced landing at Parke, Suffolk on 26 January 1943. The unit disbanded at Marham on 1 May 1943 but reformed at

AML Bombing Teacher building at Warboys in 1997. (Authors collection)

Finmere as No 1655 MTU on 1 June 1943 to train Mosquito crews for Bomber Command.

One month later on 1 July 1943 the unit was back at Marham and remained there until 7 March 1944 when it moved to Warboys. By 1944 the unit was equipped with Mosquito Mks III, IV and XX and a few Oxfords. The unit's final move was to Upper Heyford and its satellite Barford St John on 30 December 1944. The unit was now mainly equipped with Mosquito Mks III, XX and XXV. The Mk IIIs and Oxfords being based at Barford St John. Two days later the unit was redesignated No 16 OTU. The unit used the code GA from December 1944, eg. Mosquito MK IIIs RR289:GA-L, RR292:GA-F and Mk XXV KB501:GA-C.

Bases

30 Aug 42 – 29 Sep 42	Horsham St Faith
29 Sep 42 – 1 May 43	Marham
1 Jun 43 – 1 Jul 43	Finmere
1Jul 43 – 7 Mar 44	Marham
7 Mar 44 – 30 Dec 44	Warboys
30 Dec 44 – 1 Jan 45	Upper Heyford
30 Dec 44 – 1 Jan 45	Barford St John (Satellite)

Aircraft types used	Examples
Blenheim Mk V	AZ947 AZ950 AZ955 AZ969
Mosquito Mk III	W4075 RR289 RR292
Mosquito Mk IV	W4071 W4072
Mosquito Mk XX	
Mosquito Mk XXV	KB501
Oxford Mk II	P1094 T1347 V3851 AS732

No. 1657 Conversion Unit/Heavy Conversion Unit

No 1657 CU was formed from the conversion flights based at Oakington in October 1942 and immediately moved to Stradishall. . The unit was equipped with Stirlings, Oxfords and radial engined Lancaster Mk IIs. One of the units first losses was Stirling Mk I W7470 which crashed at Catley Hill, Motty attempting a forced landing in a field after all of the engines had cut on 27 October 1942. The unit lost Lancaster MK II DS603 when it crashed on overshoot at East Wretham on 16 April 1943.

On 7 September 1943 Stirling Mk I W7455 was attacked by an enemy aircraft and crashed in a cornfield at Great Thurlow. The instructor, Plt Off LF Smith was killed and the student crewmembers were all injured. Stirling Mk I R9192 was struck off charge on 6 November after colliding in mid air over Suffolk with Wellington X3637 of No 27 OTU. Stirling Mk I W7571 crashed at Stradishall on 20 January 1944 with potentially disastrous consequences for the station. The starboard outer engine failed and the Stirling crashed into the ammo dump and caught fire.

In April 1944 the unit was redesignated a Heavy Conversion Unit. On the 18th of April Stirling Mk III EJ108 struck a cyclist on take off and shortly afterwards a loud bang was heard. The aircraft climbed steeply and was abandoned by the crew. The Stirling crashed at Little Glenham in Suffolk. During 1944 the unit used Sheperds Grove as a satellite. At this airfield Stirling Mk III BK689 swung on take off and collided with EK454 on 28 May. Meanwhile at Stradishall on 29 May Stirling Mk I R9298 was shot down by an enemy aircraft on approach to the airfield. The Stirling crashed into LK506 and R9283 and all of the crew, captained by Fg Off WAC Yates were killed. Another serious crash occurred on 26 July 1944 at Sheperds Grove when Stirling Mk III EF252 crashed into the Watch Office after its starboard outer failed. The Stirlings were phased out in December 1944 leaving the Lancaster's. The unit disbanded on 24 February 1945.

The unit used the codes AK and XT on its aircraft, eg. Stirling Mk Is N3758:XT-K and R9192:AK-B and MK III EE881:XT-T.

Bases

Oct 42 – Oct 42	Oakington
Oct 42 – 24 Feb 45	Stradishall
44 – 44	Sheperds Grove (Satellite)

Aircraft types used	Examples
Lancaster Mk I	R5485
Lancaster Mk II	DS 601 DS605 DS608 DS610
Oxford	
Stirling Mk I	N3682 R9144 BK598 EF332
Stirling Mk III	BF323 BK772 EE881 EF183

A student crew at No 1658 HCU at Riccall with a Halifax Mk II. Left to right:
Sgt Burn RCAF, navigator; Sgt Brown, rear gunner; RD Davies, pilot; Sgt
Scarth RAAF, flight engineer; Sgt Hayward, mid-upper gunner; Fg Off Corbett
RCAF, bomb aimer and Sgt Tilker, WOp.

No. 1659 Heavy Conversion Unit

No 1659 CU formed at Leeming from Nos 405 and 408 Conversion Flights on 6 October 1942.to train Canadian crews for Bomber Command. On formation the unit was equipped with Halifaxes. One of the first Halifaxes lost by the unit was Mk II W1052 which crashed on take off at Leeming on 3 December 1942. Another Halifax was lost when W1146 flew into hills in cloud north west of Thwaite on 28 January 1943.

On 14 March 1943 the unit moved to Topcliffe. Four days later Halifax R9448 dived into the ground near Selby. The unit also received Lancasters in March 1943. Further Halifax losses followed including R9423 which spun into the ground near Millbridge, Surrey on 24 July and W1251 was lost when it broke up in the air over Stradishall Rusken on the Isle of Man on 6 November 1943. Training continued at Topcliffe until the unit disbanded on 10 September 1945.

The unit used the codes FD and RV on its Halifaxes and Lancaster's, eg. Halifax HX268:FD-V, Mk III MZ505:RV-J, Lancaster Mk Is HK565:RV-A, HK742:RV-D, HK745:RV-F, PB810:RV-P, PP676:RV-M and Lancaster MK IIIs DV310:RV-L, EE136:RV-G (this aircraft had been named *Spirit of Russia* whilst serving with No 189 Sqn and completed 109 operations.), LM692:FD-A, LM753:FD-B, PB146:RV-K, PB259:FD-G and RF148:FD-M.

Bases

6 Oct 42 – 14 Mar 43	Leeming
14 Mar 43 – 10 Sep 45	Topcliffe

Aircraft types used	Examples
Halifax Mk II	R9363 R9437 R9483 W1150
Halifax Mk III	HX268 MZ505
Lancaster Mk I	HK693 LL843 ME455 NG178
Lancaster Mk III	ED971 JB745 LM391 ND442
Oxford Mk II	AS741
Spitfire Mk Vb	W3412 AB403

No.1667 Heavy Conversion Unit

This heavy Conversion unit was formed with Lancaster's and Halifaxes at Lindholme on 1 June 1943. The first Lancaster lost was Mk I R5667 which crashed on landing at Lindholme on 19 August. The next aircraft lost was Lancaster Mk I W4904 which dived into the ground near Marston Moor on 28 September followed two days later by R5685 which crashed on approach to Faldingworth. The following month on 8 October the unit moved to Faldingworth. The unit moved again in February 1944 to Sandtoft. This unit had a reputation for crashed and there were six in the first week of operation from the station. Among the crews the station was known as 'Prangtoft'.

Part of the WAAF domestic site at East Moor. (J Seed via Ian Foster/57 rescue)

Among the first Halifaxes lost was Mk V EB194, which collided with Halifax Mk II HR657 of 1662 HCU during a bombing practice and crashed near Gainsborough on 7 March. Another of the losses that month was Mk II JD293 which collided with Mk V EB144 whilst trying to avoid hitting a hangar after undershooting its landing with a failed port engine on the 25th. On 1 June 1944 the HCU lost Mk V LL414 which dived into the ground in Glenisla after the pilot lost control. A week later Mk V LL459 was lost in similar circumstances south of Howden Dyke Island. On 15 October 1944 Mk V DK116 crashed at Caplestone Fell after the crew abandoned her when the port inner engine caught fire.

The Lancaster's fared little better at this unit and several were lost including Mk I W4890 which crashed at Thorney Island on 10 February 1945. Just over a week later W4154 was lost at Sandtoft on landing. The crashes at Sandtoft continued throughout the unit's existence and the last Lancaster lost was Mk III JB316, which crashed on 25 August 1945. The unit was disbanded on 10 November 1945.

No 1667 HCU used the codes GG, KR and LR on its Halifaxes and Lancaster's, eg. Halifax Mk Vs EB190:GG-H and LL535:GG-N and Lancaster Mk Is HK751:GG-G, ME682:GG-H, R5542:GG-J, HK734:GG-K, PB869:LR-C, ME682:LR-H, PD444:LR-J and HK740:LR-K. The Lancaster Mk IIIs were coded JB306:GG-E later LR-E, JB734:LR-D and ND477:LR-G.

Bases	
2 June 43 – 8 Oct 43	Lindholme
8 Oct 43 – 14 Feb 44	Faldingworth
14 Feb 44 – 10 Nov 45	Sandtoft

Aircraft types used	Examples
Halifax Mk II	JD998
Halifax Mk V	DG 293 EB149 LL414 LK642
Lancaster Mk I	L7541 R5500 W4132 HK734
Lancaster Mk III	DV161 ED473 EE201 JA693
Spitfire Mk Vb	AR390

No. 1679 Conversion Unit/Heavy Conversion Unit

No 1679 HCU was formed at East Moor in Yorkshire on 20 May 1943. The unit was equipped with Lancaster Mk IIs and tasked with training crews for the Canadian squadrons of No 6 Group equipped with this mark of Lancaster. The unit's first loss was DS635, which crashed on landing on 3 September. Just under three weeks later DS648 was lost in a crash on the 21st. November saw another crash when DS649 hit trees on a farm near Torrington on the 6th. On 11 December DS615 ran into Halifax DT548 on landing at Topcliffe. Two days later the HCU moved to Wombleton.

The units stay at Wombleton was brief but they still managed to lose two aircraft, DS624 which was destroyed on the ground on 24 December and DS839 which crashed at Ridgemont in Bedfordshire on 23 January, before disbanding on 27 January 1944.

Bases

20 may 43 – 13 Dec 43	East Moor
13 Dec 43 – 27 Jan 44	Wombleton

Aircraft types used

	Examples
Lancaster Mk II	DS650 DS651 DS657 DS688

No.1681 Bomber Defence Training Flight

No 1681 BDT Flt was formed at Pershore on 5 June 1943 equipped with various marks of Curtiss Tomahawk. Although the BDT Flights were not in themselves crew-training units they played a vital part in the training of bomber crews. Their role was to provide realistic fighter affiliation exercises, simulating enemy fighter attacks, for the trainee bomber crews at OTU's.

The Tomahawks used by the unit had come from Army Co-operation Command squadrons and were well worn. Tomahawk Mk I AH746 was lost in a forced landing near Worcester on 31 July 1943 and two weeks later on 15 August AH776 swung on landing at Pershore causing the undercarriage to collapse.

The Flt moved to Long Marston on 8 March 1944 and began to replace the Tomahawks with Hurricanes. One of the Tomahawk Mk IIa's, AH885, was lost on 4 April 1944, just before the unit phased out the type, when it crashed on landing at Long Marston. During June 1944 the unit also operated from Honeybourne and was disbanded at Long Marston on 1 August 1944.

Bases

5 Jun 43 – 8 Mar 44	Pershore
8 Mar 44 – 1 Aug 44	Long Marston
Jun 44 – Jun 44	Honeybourne

Aircraft types used	Examples
Hurricane Mk IIc	LF118
Tomahawk Mk I	AH797 AH822 AH833 AH852
Tomahawk Mk IIa	AH881 AH885 AH920 AH939
Tomahawk Mk IIb	AK141 AK156 AK163

No. 1686 Bomber Defence Training Flight

This BDF Flt was formed at Hixon on 6 June 1943 and provided fighter affiliation training for the co-located No 30 OTU. The unit was equipped with Tomahawk Mk Is and IIs. The Flt was equipped with only a small number of aircraft but still managed to lose a few.

Tomahawk Mk IIb Ak128 was taxied into a fuel bowser at Hixon on 23 December 1943 and MK I AH832 was lost when it crashed on take off at Hixon on 11 March 1944. The unit also lost Tomahawk Mk IIa AH926 when its undercarriage collapsed on landing at Peplow on 14 April 1944. Hurricanes began to replace the Tomahawks but the unit was disbanded in July 1944. The unit used the codes FI, eg. Hurricane Mk IIc LF380:FI-D.

Bases

6 Jun 43 – 12 Jul 44	Hixon

Aircraft types used	Examples
Hurricane Mk IIc	LF380
Tomahawk Mk I	AH769 AH783 AH850 AH852
Tomahawk Mk IIa	AH898 AH908 AH926
Tomahawk Mk IIb	AK122 AK128

The control tower at Hixon is still in use in the 1990s albeit as a domestic residence. (Authors collection)

No.1696 Bomber Defence Training Flight

This BDT Flt was formed at Bourn on 15 Feb 44 equipped with Martinets, Hurricanes, Spitfires, Oxfords and Tomahawks. In March 1944 the unit sent a detachment to Ipswich which remained there until 24 April 1945. The Flt moved to Gransden Lodge in April 1944 returning to Bourn on 30 October 1944. Another detachment operated from Warboys from 24 April to 28 June 1945 with the whole unit moving to Warboys on that day and remaining until l disbanded on 28 September 1945.

Bases

15 Feb 44 – Apr 44	Bourn
Mar 44 – 24 Apr 45	Ipswich (Detachment)
Apr 44 – 30 Oct 44	Gransden Lodge
30 Oct 44 – 28 Jun 45	Bourn
24 Apr 45 – 28 Jun 45	Warboys (Detachment)
28 Jun 45 – 28 Sep 45	Warboys

Aircraft types used	Examples
Hurricane Mk IIc	LF532
Martinet	HP528
Oxford Mk II	N4739
Spitfire Mk IIa	P7775 P8035
Spitfire Mk Vb	W3128 AA728 AB183
Tomahawk Mk IIa	AH986

A T2 hangar at Warboys in 1997. No 1696 BDT Flt were based here from April to September 1945. (Authors collection)

Heavy Glider Conversion Unit

The HGCU was formed at Shrewton on 29 June 1942. The unit equipment was to be Horsa's and Whitley's but as Shrewton was found to be unsuitable for those types the unit moved to Brize Norton on 15 July where it was given its aircraft, thirty four Whitley Mk Vs and fifty six Horsa's. The unit later received Albemarles to supplement the Whitley's. When Brize Norton was having its runways re-surfaced the HGCU was moved to Grove from 10 February to 20 April 1943.

Training of glider pilots continued until the unit moved to North Luffenham in March 1944. The unit remained at North Luffenham until 15 October 1944 when it returned to Brize Norton. The following month the unit was redesignated No 21 HGCU.

Bases

29 Jun 42 – 15 Jul 42	Shrewton
15 Jul 42 – 10 Feb 43	Brize Norton
10 Feb 43 – 20 Apr 43	Grove
20 Apr 43 – Mar 44	Brize Norton
Mar 44 – 15 Oct 44	North Luffenham
15 October 44 – Nov 44	Brize Norton

Aircraft types used	**Examples**
Albemarle	P1367 P1553 V1642 V1842
Horsa	
Oxford Mk I	V3194
Oxford Mk II	W6579
Tiger Moth Mk II	T6900
Whitley Mk V	N1435

Operational & Refresher Training Unit

The ORTU was formed by renaming the Glider Pilot Exercise Unit at Shrewton in March 1944. The unit was equipped with Whitley's, Horsa's and Tiger Moths. ORTU moved to Hampstead Norris the same month but left a flight of Tiger Moths at Shrewton until 11 November 1944. One of the Shrewton detachments Tiger Moths, T6363 was damaged beyond repair in a heavy landing on 10 May 1944. . During 1943 the unit also used Thruxton and from 1943 to 1944 operated from Netheravon where Tiger Moth R4858 stalled while low flying and crashed south of the airfield on 18 July 1944.

July 1944 was not a good month for the Albemarles of the unit. V1745 went missing on the 2nd and on 10 July P1593 spun into the ground near Peterhead. P1605 crashed on approach to Cottesmore on the 28th and on 6 September P1643 crashed on landing at Harwell.

At Hampstead Norris the unit was equipped with nine Whitley's, twenty Albemarles, thirty-three Tiger Moths and a large number of Horsa's. On 27 February 1945 ORTU moved to Matching. By now the Whitley's had been replaced by Stirlings and these in turn began to be replaced by Halifaxes in April 1945. The preceding month Stirling Mk IV PW391 was lost when it collided with Master DM336 of No 7 SFTS while on a cross-country flight. The Stirling crashed at Thorney Toll, Northants. The next move for the unit was to Wethersfield on 15 October 1945 where it remained until it was redesignated No 1385 HTSCU on 1 April 1946. The ORTU used the codes OX on its aircraft

Bases

Mar 44 – Mar 44	Shrewton
Mar 44 – 11 Nov 44	Shrewton (Detachment)
Mar 44 – 27 Feb 45	Hampstead Norris
43 –43	Thruxton (Satellite)
43 –44	Netheravon (Satellite)
27 Feb 45 – 15 Oct 45	Matching
15 Oct 45 – 1 Apr 46	Wethersfield

Aircraft types used	Examples
Albemarle	P1392 P1403 V1603 V1768
Halifax Mk III	
Halifax Mk A5	
Halifax Mk A7	
Horsa	
Oxford Mk II	AS870
Stirling Mk IV	PK229 PK230 PW387 PW392
Stirling Mk IV (SD)	LK334 LK357 LK358 LK361
Tiger Moth Mk II	T6034 T6683 T6823 T6920
Whitley Mk V	

A Spitfire Mk V coded C of a Middle East OTU. Several marks of Spitfire were operated by fighter OTU's throughout the war. (WD Park)

Pathfinder Force Navigation Training Unit

The PFF NTU was formed at Gransden Lodge on 10 April 1943 equipped with Halifax Mk IIs and Stirlings. The unit remained at Gransden until 11 June 1943 when it moved to Upwood where it used Halifaxes, Lancaster's and a few Stirlings. The unit moved again on 5 Mar 44 to Warboys. While at Warboys the unit lost several of its Lancasters including EE120 which crashed on take off on 9 march 1944. The following month JB471 crashed near Brecon on the 10th and on 21 July ED908 was lost. ED592 was lost in a taxiing accident at Florennes in Belgium on 5 October. The next Lancaster loss was on 11 march 1945 when PB669 crashed near Polebrook and the following month two aircraft were lost on the 28th when JB155 and ND928 both crashed on overshoot at Warboys.

From September 1944 the unit also operated Mosquitoes and was responsible for training crews in the navigational techniques unique to the Pathfinder Force, including the use of 'Oboe' and 'H2S'. The PFF NTU used the codes QF on its Lancasters, Mosquitoes and Oxfords, eg. Lancasters W4957:QF-P, ED317:QF-T, ED368:QF-T, ED842:QF-Z, EE120:QF-P, EE128;QF-Z, EE201:QF-T, EE371:QF-T,JB183:QF-M,QF-R and QF-W, JB306:QF-W, JB316:QF-Y, JB384:QF-L, JB404:QF-X, JB484:QF-S, NE142:QF-H and PB405:QF-A, Mosquito Mk XX KB351:QF-A2 and Oxford Mk I P6798:QF;C3.

Bases

10 Apr 43 – 11 Jun 43	Gransden Lodge
11 Jun 43 – 5 Mar 44	Upwood
5 Mar 44 – 45	Warboys

Aircraft types used	Examples
Halifax Mk I	
Halifax Mk II	
Lancaster Mk I	R5565 W4315 ED368 SW248
Lancaster Mk III	ED474 EE128 JA677 JB183
Mosquito Mk XX	KB351
Oxford Mk II	N4739 N6435 P6798

School of Air Navigation

Pre-war the School of Air Navigation was based at Manston but with war imminent the unit moved to St Athan in Wales on 1 September 1939. The unit was equipped with Anson Mk Is and during its stay at St Athan several were lost. Six weeks after arriving Anson N5055 was ditched off Bude in Cornwall on 19 October. The next day K8790 ran out of fuel and ditched off Selsey Bill.

The New Year saw the losses continue and 15 January was a particularly bad day with three aircraft being lost. K6271 crashed in a forced landing near Barnstaple, K8712 ditched, out of fuel, south of Eddystone Lighthouse and K8819 was abandoned by the crew when they got lost and crashed at Castle Cary in Somerset. Another Anson was lost when N5056 was ditched in Aberdaron bay on 26 March and three months later K6272 dived into the ground and blew up at Monkton, Ayrshire.

The unit's last loss at St Athan was K6262, which crashed into the sea fifty miles west of Lundy Island on 12 September. Shortly afterwards the SAN was moved overseas to Canada.

Bases

1 Sep 39 – Sep 40	
	St Athan

Aircraft types used

Aircraft types used	Examples
Anson Mk I	K6155 K6157 N4928 N4966

The badge of the School of Air Navigation depicts a star, which is closely linked with navigation.

School of Flying Control

The School of Flying Control was formed from the Bomber Command Regional Control School at Watchfield on 15 December 1941. The unit was equipped with Ansons to act as aircraft to be controlled by the trainee flying control officers. In February 1942 the SFC received some Dominies to give the students air experience.

The school trained airfield controllers and the first course commenced on 18 July 1942. Courses lasted two weeks. From 14 June 1943 Wanborough was used as a RLG and many of the airfield controllers were trained there. The airfield controller training was moved to Watchfield and Kelmscott by 18 December 1943.

For a short period from November 1942 Ansons of SFC were detached to Halfpenny Green but soon returned to Watchfield. One of the Ansons, N9645 was lost in a crash on 15 November 1944 and training continued until April 1946 when the school was renamed the School of Air Traffic Control.

Bases

15 Dec 41 – Apr 46	Watchfield
14 Jun 43 – 18 Dec 43	Wanborough (RLG)
Nov 42 -	Halfpenny Green (Detachment)
Dec 43 – Apr 46	Kelmscott (Satellite)

Aircraft types used	Examples
Anson Mk I	N5098 R3325 AX625 AX638
Dominie	X7492 X7493

School of General Reconnaissance

The School of General Reconnaissance formed at Thorney Island in March 1938 equipped with Nimrods, Ospreys and Sharks but these were soon replaced by Avro Ansons. Due to an influx of operational units the S of GR moved to the Channel Island of Guernsey on 22 April 1940.

The unit operated from Guernsey until the threat of invasion forced another move, this time to Hooton Park. The unit moved out on 16 June 1940. Hooton Park was only a temporary stay and the unit moved on to Squires Gate in July. Whilst at Hooton park the unit was renamed No 1 School of General Reconnaissance.

Bases

Mar 38 – 22 April 40	Thorney Island
22 Apr 40 – 16 Jun 40	Guernsey
16 Jun 40 – Jul 40	Hooton Park

Aircraft types used	**Examples**
Anson Mk I	K6154 K6201 R3407 R3441

The badge of the School of General Reconnaissance shows a petrel on a eight pointed star indicating the long range flying and navigation skills required of this unit.

ABBREVIATIONS

AAS	Air Armament School
ACSC	Aviation Candidate Selection Centre
AG	Air Gunner
AGS	Air Gunner School
ANS	Air Navigation School
AONS	Air Observer and Navigation School
AOS	Air Observer School
ARC	Aircrew Reception Centre
ATC	Armament Training Camp
BAS	Beam Approach/Blind Approach School
BATF	Beam Approach Training Flight
BDTF	Bomber Defence Training Flight
B & GS	Bombing and Gunnery School
CGS	Central Gunnery School
CU	Conversion Unit
EANS	Empire Air Navigation School
EATS	Empire Air Training Scheme
ECFS	Empire Central Flying School
EFTS	Elementary Flying Training School
FIS	Flying Instructors School
FTF	Ferry Training Flight
FTS	Flying Training School
FTU	Ferry Training Unit
GRS	General Reconnaissance School
GTS	Glider Training School
HCU	Heavy Conversion Unit
HGCU	Heavy Glider Conversion Unit
HTCU	Heavy Transport Conversion Unit
ITS	Initial Training School
ITW	Initial Training Wing

LFS	Lancaster Finishing School
MCU	Mosquito Conversion Unit
MTU	Mosquito Training Unit
(O) AFU	(Observer) Advanced Flying Unit
OCU	Operational Conversion Unit
OTF	Operational Training Flight
OTU	Operational Training Unit
O & RTU	Operational and Refresher Training Unit
(P) AFU	(Pilot) Advanced Flying Unit
PFF NTU	Pathfinder Force Navigation Training Unit
RLG	Relief Landing Ground
RS	Radio School
SAC	School of Army Co-operation
SFC	School of Flying Control
SFTS	Service Flying Training School
S of AN	School of Air Navigation
S of GR	School of General Reconnaissance
SS	Signal School
TCU	Transport Conversion Unit
TEU	Tactical Exercise Unit
TSCU	Transport Support Conversion Unit
TTU	Torpedo Training Unit
WOp/AG	Wireless Operator/Air Gunner
WS	Wireless School

No. 1 OPERATIONAL TRAINING UNIT
ROYAL AIR FORCE

TRAIN TO TRIUMPH

Also published by Woodfield...

The following titles are all available in our unique high-quality softback format

RAF HUMOUR

Bawdy Ballads & Dirty Ditties of the RAF – A huge collection of the bawdy songs and rude recitations beloved by RAF personnel in WW2. Certain to amuse any RAF veteran. Uncensored – so strictly adults only! *"Not for the frail, the fraightfully posh or proper gels – but great fun for everyone else!"* **£9.95**

Upside Down Nothing on the Clock – Dozens of jokes and anecdotes contributed by RAF personnel from AC2s to the top brass... still one of our best sellers. *"Highly enjoyable."* **£6.00**

Upside Down Again! – Our second great collection of RAF jokes, funny stories and anecdotes – a great gift for those with a high-flying sense of humour! *"Very funny indeed."* **£6.00**

Was It Like This For You? – A feast of humorous reminiscences & cartoons depicting the more comical aspects of life in the RAF. *"Will bring back many happy memories. Highly recommended."* **£6.00**

MILITARY MEMOIRS & HISTORIES – THE POST-WAR PERIOD

I Have Control... Former RAF Parachute instructor **Edward Cartner** humorously recalls the many mishaps, blunders and faux-pas of his military career. *Superb writing; very amusing indeed.* **£9.95**

Korea: We Lived They Died Former soldier with Duke of Wellington's Regt **Alan Carter** reveals the appalling truth of front-line life for British troops in this now forgotten war. *Very funny in places too.* **£9.95**

Meteor Eject! Former 257 Sqn pilot [1950s] **Nick Carter** recalls the early days of RAF jets and his many adventures flying Meteors, including one very lucky escape via a Mk.2 Martin-Baker ejector seat... **£9.95**

Pluck Under Fire Eventful Korean War experiences of **John Pluck** with the Middlesex Regiment. **£9.95**

Return to Gan • Michael Butler's light-hearted account of life at RAF Gan in 1960 and the founding of 'Radio Gan'. *Will delight those who also served at this remote RAF outpost in the Indian Ocean.* **£12.00**

Tread Lightly into Danger • Bomb-disposal expert **Anthony Charlwood**'s experiences in some of the world's most dangerous hotspots (Kuwait, Iraq, Lebanon, Somalia, etc) over the last 30 years. **£9.95**

The Spice of Flight • Former RAF pilot **Richard Pike** delivers a fascinating account of flying Lightnings, Phantoms and later helicopters with 56, 43(F) & 19 Sqns in the RAF of the 1960s & 70s. **£9.95**

Flying the Waves • **Richard Pike** describes his eventful second career as a commercial helicpter pilot, which involved him in many Coastguard Air/Sea Rescue operations in the Shetlands and North Sea. **£9.95**

MILITARY MEMOIRS & HISTORIES – WORLD WAR 1 & 2

2297: A POW's Story • Taken prisoner at Dunkirk, **John Lawrence** spent 5 years as a POW at Lamsdorf, Jagendorf, Posen and elsewhere. *"A very interesting & delightfully illustrated account of his experiences."* **£6.00**

A Bird Over Berlin Former Lancaster pilot with 61 Sqn, **Tony Bird DFC** tells a remarkable tale of survival against the odds during raids on the German capital & as a POW. *"An incredible-but-true sequence of events."* **£9.95**

A Journey from Blandford The wartime exploits of motorcycle dispatch rider **B.A. Jones** began at Blandford Camp in Dorset but took him to Dunkirk, the Middle East, D-Day and beyond... **£9.95**

A Lighter Shade of Blue A former Radar Operator **Reg O'Neil** recalls his WW2 service in Malta and Italy with 16004 AMES – a front-line mobile radar unit. *'Interesting, informative and amusing.'* **£9.95**

A Shillingsworth of Promises Delightfully funny and ribald memoirs of **Fred Hitchcock** recalling his years as an RAF airman during the war and later amusing escapades in the UK and Egypt. *A very entertaining read.* **£9.95**

Beaufighters BOAC & Me – WW2 Beaufighter navigator **Sam Wright** served a full tour with 254 Sqn and was later seconded to BOAC on early postwar overseas routes. *'Captures the spirit of the Beaufighter'* **£9.95**

Coastal Command Pilot Former Hudson pilot **Ted Rayner**'s outstanding account of his unusual WW2 Coastal Command experiences, flying in the Arctic from bases in Iceland and Greenland. **£9.95**

Cyril Wild: The Tall Man Who Never Slept – **James Bradley**'s biography of a remarkable Japanese-speaking British Army officer who helped many POWs survive on the infamous Burma railway. **£9.95**

Desert War Diary by **John Walton** Diary and photos recording the activities of the Hurricanes and personnel of 213 Squadron during WW2 in Cyprus and Egypt. *"Informative and entertaining."* **£9.95**

From Fiji to Balkan Skies Spitfire/Mustang pilot **Dennis McCaig** recalls eventful WW2 operations over the Adriatic/Balkans with 249 Sqn in 43/44. *'A rip-roaring real-life adventure, splendidly written.'* **£9.95**

From Horses to Chieftains – Long-serving Army veteran **Richard Napier** recalls an eventful Army career that began with a cavalry regiment in 1935; took in El Alamein & D-Day and ended in the 1960s. **£9.95**

Get Some In! The many wartime adventures of **Mervyn Base**, a WW2 RAF Bomb Disposal expert **£9.95**

Just a Survivor Former Lancaster navigator **Phil Potts** tells his remarkable tale of survival against the odds in the air with 103 Sqn and later as a POW. *'An enlightening and well written account.'* **£9.95**

Memoirs of a 'Goldfish' • The eventful wartime memoirs of former 115 Sqn Wellington pilot **Jim Burtt-Smith**, now president of the Goldfish Club - exclusively for aviators who have force-landed into water. **£9.95**

No Brylcreem, No Medals – RAF MT driver **Jack Hambleton** 's splendid account of his wartime escapades in England, Shetlands & Middle East blends comic/tragic aspects of war in uniquely entertaining way. **£8.00**

Nobody's Hero • Former RAF Policeman **Bernard Hart-Hallam**'s extraordinary adventures with 2TAF Security Section on D-Day and beyond in France, Belgium & Germany. *"Unique and frequently surprising."* **£9.95**

Once a Cameron Highlander • This biog of Robert Burns, who, at 104 was the oldest survivor of the Battle of the Somme; takes in his WW1 experiences, later life in showbusiness and celebrity status as a centenarian. **£9.95**

Operation Pharos • **Ken Rosam** tells the story of the RAF's secret bomber base/staging post on the Cocos Keeling islands during WW2 and of many operations from there. *'A fascinating slice of RAF history.'* **£9.95**

Over Hell & High Water • WW2 navigator **Les Parsons** survived 31 ops on Lancasters with 622 Sqn, then went on to fly Liberators in Far East with 99 Sqn. *'An exceptional tale of 'double jeopardy'.* **£9.95**

Pacifist to Glider Pilot • The son of Plymouth Brethren parents, **Alec Waldron** renounced their pacifism and went on to pilot gliders with the Glider Pilot Regiment at both Sicily & Arnhem. *Excellent photos.* **£9.95**

Pathfinder Force Balkans • Pathfinder F/Engineer **Geoff Curtis** saw action over Germany & Italy before baling out over Hungary. He was a POW in Komarno, Stalags 17a & 17b. *'An amazing catalogue of adventures.'* **£9.95**

Per Ardua Pro Patria • Humour and tragedy are interwoven in these unassuming autobiographical observations of **Dennis Wiltshire**, a former Lancaster Flight Engineer who later worked for NASA. **£9.95**

Ploughs, Planes & Palliasses • Entertaining recollections of RAF pilot **Percy Carruthers**, who flew Baltimores in Egypt with 223 Squadron and was later a POW at Stalag Luft 1 & 6. **£9.95**

RAF/UXB The Story of RAF Bomb Disposal • Stories contributed by wartime RAF BD veterans that will surprise and educate the uninitiated. *"Amazing stories of very brave men."* **£9.95**

Railway to Runway • Wartime diary & letters of Halifax Observer **Leslie Harris** – killed in action with 76 Sqn in 1943 – poignantly capture the spirit of the wartime RAF in the words of a 20-year-old airman. **£9.95**

Seletar Crowning Glory • The history of the RAF base in Singapore from its earliest beginnings, through the golden era of the flying-boats, its capture in WW2 and on to its closure in the 1970s. **£15.00**

The RAF & Me • Former Stirling navigator **Gordon Frost** recalls ops with 570 Sqn from RAF Harwell, including 'Market-Garden' 'Varsity' and others. *'A salute to the mighty Stirling and its valiant crews.'* **£9.95**

Training for Triumph • **Tom Docherty**'s very thorough account of the amazing achievement of RAF Training Command, who trained over 90,000 aircrew during World War 2. *'An impressively detailed book.'* **£12.00**

Un Grand Bordel • Geoffrey French relates air-gunner **Norman Lee**'s amazing real-life adventures with the French Maquis (Secret Army) after being shot down over Europe. *"Frequently funny and highly eventful."* **£9.95**

UXB Vol 2 More unusual and gripping tales of bomb disposal in WW2 and after. **£9.95**

Wot! No Engines? • Alan Cooper tells the story of military gliders in general and the RAF glider pilots who served on Operation Varsity in 1945 in particular. A very large and impressive book with many photos. **£18.00**

While Others Slept • Former Hampden navigator **Eric Woods** tells the story of Bomber Command's early years and how he completed a tour of duty with 144 Squadron. *'Full of valuable historical detail.'* **£9.95**

WOMEN & WORLD WAR TWO

A WAAF at War • Former MT driver **Diana Lindo**'s charming evocation of life in the WAAF will bring back happy memories to all those who also served in World War 2. *"Nostalgic and good-natured."* **£9.95**

Corduroy Days • Warm-hearted and amusing recollections of **Josephine Duggan-Rees**'s wartime years spent as a Land Girl on farms in the New Forest area. *"Funny, nostalgic and very well written."* **£9.95**

Ernie • **Celia Savage**'s quest to discover the truth about the death of her father, an RAF Halifax navigator with 149 Sqn, who died in WW2 when she was just 6 years old. *"A real-life detective story."* **£9.95**

In My Father's Footsteps • **Pat Bienkowski**'s moving account of her trip to Singapore & Thailand to visit the places where her father and uncle were both POW's during WW2. **£9.95**

Lambs in Blue • **Rebecca Barnett's** revealing account of the wartime lives and loves of a group of WAAFs posted to the tropical paradise of Ceylon. *"A highly congenial WW2 chronicle."* **£9.95**

Radar Days • Delightful evocation of life in the wartime WAAF by former Radar Operator **Gwen Arnold**, who served at Bawdsey Manor RDF Station, Suffolk. *"Amusing, charming and affectionate."* **£9.95**

Searching in the Dark The amusing wartime diary of **Peggy Butler** a WAAF radar operator 1942-1946 – written when she was just 19 yrs old and serving at Bawdsey RDF station in Suffolk **£9.95**

20th CenturyFarmers Boy • Sussex farmer **Nick Adames** looks back on a century of rural change and what it has meant to his own family and the county they have farmed in for 400 years.   **£9.95**

Call an Ambulance! • former ambulance driver **Alan Crosskill** recalls a number of light-hearted episodes from his eventful career in the 1960s/70s. *'Very amusing and entertaining'.*   **£9.95**

Harry – An Evacuee's Story • The misadventures of **Harry Collins** – a young lad evacuated from his home in Stockport UK to Manitoba, Canada in WW2. *'An educational description of the life of an evacuee'*   **£9.95**

Just Visiting... • Charming and funny book by former Health Visitor **Molly Corbally**, who brilliantly depicts colourful characters and entertaining incidents from her long career.   **£9.95**

Occupation Nurse • **Peter & Mary Birchenall** pay tribute to the achievement of the group of untrained nurses who provided healthcare at Guernsey's only hospital during the German occupation of 1940-45.   **£9.95**

FICTION

A Trace of Calcium by **David Barnett** – A commuter comes to the aid of a young woman in trouble, becomes implicated in murder and must use all his resources to clear his name.   **£9.95**

Double Time by **David Barnett** – A light-hearted time-travel fantasy in which a bookmaker tries to use a time machine to make his fortune and improve his love-life with hilarious consequences.   **£9.95**

Last Sunset by **AA Painter** A nautical thriller set in the world of international yachting. A middle aged yachtsman becomes accidentally embroiled with smugglers, pirates and a very sexy young lady...   **£9.95**

Retribution by **Mike Jupp** A very funny comedy/fantasy novel for adults and older children, featuring bizarre goings-on in a quiet English seaside town. Brilliantly illustrated.   **£9.95**

The Cherkassy Incident by **Hunter Carlyle** A tense international thriller featuring a terrorist plot to steal nuclear missiles from a sunken Russian nuclear submarine.   **£9.95**

MISCELLANEOUS SUBJECTS

Just a Butcher's Boy by **Christopher Bolton** Charming account of small town life in the 1950s in the rural Leiston, Suffolk and idyllic summers spent with grandparents who owned the local butcher's shop.   **£5.95**

Impress of Eternity by **Paul McNamee** A personal investigation into the authenticity of the Turin Shroud. A former shcoolmaster examines the evidence and comes to a startling conclusion.   **£5.95**

Making a Successful Best Man's Speech An indispensable aid to anyone who feels nervous about making a wedding speech. Tells you what to say and how to remember it.   **£5.95**

Near & Yet So Far by **Audrey Truswell** The founder of an animal rescue charity tells charming and heart-warming tales of the rescue and rehabilitation of many four-legged friends in need.   **£9.95**

Reputedly Haunted Inns of the Chilterns & Thames Valley by **Roger Long** – A light hearted look at pubs & the paranormal in the Heart of England   **£5.95**

A Selection of London's Most Interesting Pubs by **David Gammell** – A personal selection of London's most unusual and historic hostelries with instructions how to find them.   **£5.95**

Unknown to History and Fame by **Brenda Dixon** – Charming portrait of Victorian life in the West Sussex village of Walberton via the writings of Charles Ayling, a resident of the village, whose reports on local events were a popular feature in *The West Sussex Gazette* over many years during the Victorian era.   **£9.95**

Woodfield Publishing

BABSHAM LANE ~ BOGNOR REGIS
WEST SUSSEX ~ ENGLAND
PO21 5EL

www.woodfieldpublishing.com